Rogue Captain:

How Far Would a Father Go to Save His Daughter's Life?

by

Roger C. Dunham

Chapter 1

Pearl Harbor, Hawaii 0246 Hours

It was second-class Petty Officer Kevin Yadley who first spotted the disappearing lights across the black waters of Pearl Harbor.

Perched at the top of the Control Tower, as everybody called the four-story structure rising above the harbor's ships and submarines, the young sailor saw the first tiny white light blink out and, ten seconds later, blink back on again. He leaned over the edge of the balcony encircling the observation deck and tried to focus his night-vision binoculars on the streetlights at Ford Island in the center of the bay. Slowly, he swept his scope across the lights near the Arizona Memorial and further toward the channel leading to the Pacific. At that instant, a second light on Ford Island blinked off, and not more than five seconds later, blinked back on again.

"What the hell..." Yadley whispered, as two more lights blinked out and back on again. He turned toward the glass-enclosed room behind him where he could see the burly shape of Senior Chief Michael Nichols, coffee cup clenched in his right hand, pacing back and forth with his usual nervous energy.

"Hey, chief! Check this out!" Yadley hollered and an instant later, Nichols stood next to his watchstander, binoculars at his eyes.

"Whatyagot, Yadley?" Nichols' deep voice rumbled as the two men studied the darkness.

The night was quiet and warm with the typical Hawaiian humidity, and at that hour, there was near-silence across the dark bay in front of them.

"There, right there!" Yadley hollered, pointing at a cluster of lights going out across the water. "And, whatever is blocking those lights is also creating a heat signature from a diesel exhaust!"

"Something is definitely moving in the water," Nichols agreed, "across the harbor, without running lights."

"What do you think it is, chief?"

"Hell, I don't know, I'll check the radar repeater scope," Nichols answered as he turned and rushed back into the room behind them to a dark-green radar screen.

A moment later, he hollered to Yadley, "The Doppler sweep shows the shape of a submarine. But, no submarine movements are scheduled, not since the *Monterey* came into port at twenty-one hundred hours last night."

Yadley poked his head through the door.

"The *Monterey* sure as hell ain't going back out again, not after its two month patrol. Maybe we should give the OOD a quick call? Who's on-call tonight, chief?"

Nichols hesitated a second and finally barked, "Lt. Commander Cooper."

Yadley winced. "Oh, Christ, that would be Martin, 'don't call me Marty,' Cooper, right?"

"One and the same, Yadley. I'll call after we figure this thing out."

The last time the chief had called this particular Officer of the Deck, Cooper had made his policy *abundantly* clear to the chief with a blasting message, "Don't call me unless it's *really, really* important, do you understand, chief?" Examples of really, really important, the OOD had sarcastically advised, would include a PT boat with jihad markings flying the ISIS flag and filled with explosives, or perhaps an incoming squadron of Japanese Zeros. "Otherwise, *Chief Nichols,*" the officer had said condescendingly as if he was talking to a child, "just note down what you're supposed to note down, confirm any ships' movements with the computer list of scheduled ships' movements, and we'll talk about it all at the change of watch, which means when there's absolutely nothing better to do."

The chief glanced again at the schedule for ships' movements for that night and took another sip of Yadley's acid caffeine-loaded brew. According to the schedule, the Arleigh Burke class guided missile cruiser, the USS *Stout* (DDG-55), was scheduled to sail toward the open sea in another hour or so, and the tour boat operators would begin their little sightseeing operations with civilians at daybreak. Nothing about submarines.

He looked back up, narrowed his eyes, and stared out the window into the dark. Something on the surface was definitely moving across Pearl Harbor in the direction of the Pacific Ocean and, whatever it was, it sure as hell displayed no running lights and it had made no announcements to the Control Tower. He looked at the computerized ship's schedule a final time, reassuring himself there were no vessels scheduled for arrival or departure. Finally, he stared at the ghostly radar echo, studied the screen and adjusted the resolution to the highest possible level.

A minute later, Yadley popped back into the building.

"Gotta better look, chief," he said, "it's definitely a sub, Los Angeles class, Battle Effectiveness E on her sail but can't make out her numbers. And, sure as hell, she's not displaying any running lights."

"*What the fuck is going on out there*?" Nichols asked as he poured the remnants of his coffee down the drain of a nearby sink. "There's nobody scheduled to come or go. You are certain it had the Battle E?"

"It did, chief," Yadley answered. "Any subs besides the *Monterey* with that?"

"Not this year," Nichols said. "But the *Monterey* already passed by a few hours ago—it's all recorded here on the log. Any sign of its escort boat, any word about scramble missions from the Submarine Base?"

"No escort and no scramble missions that I know of, chief," Yadley said. "Maybe one of us should really call the OOD or do something. It's heading for the channel."

"Right, I suspect the sub is probably just doing a night-ops kind of thing off Barber's Point. And, I really don't want to bug the OOD. Another couple of minutes and they'll probably radio what they're up to."

The two men moved back outside as more lights across the waters transiently disappeared and then became visible. The moving shape finally crossed in front of the *USS Arizona* memorial and moved in front of more Ford Island street lights. Finally, the chief petty officer focused his goggles on the outline of the hull, turned the night vision system to full intensity, and stared intently at the shape. There was nobody at the top of the submarine sail in the cockpit. That was weird as hell—subs *always* have a pair of lookouts and the Officer of the Watch standing in the cockpit, often with the sub's captain, all with binoculars searching the surrounding waters for traffic or various objects. Nichols focused on the shape as crisply as possible and listened intently. The faint glow of its exhaust pipe confirmed the distant grumble of diesel operations.

"Fuck!" Nichols muttered as he finally spun around and walked back into the harbormaster's office, grabbing the telephone receiver.

"Chief?" Yadley called. "You going to call the OOD?"

"Yup," Nichols answered. "Why don't you finish making a fresh pot of coffee so we can stay awake the rest of the night, then get out the log book and start writing about our night phantom out there?"

"Sir?" Nichols barked into the telephone. "Hello, Mr. Cooper? Chief Nichols here at the harbormaster tower. I'm sorry to bother you, sir, but...." He listened for a moment then finally blurted. "Yes, sir, I know that." He listened again. "Yes, sir, I know you said that before, but there is an unscheduled nuclear submarine with a Battle E moving across Pearl Harbor." He hesitated again. "There appear to be no lookouts at the top of the sail, and there are no escort boats." He held the receiver away from his ear and winced. "Yes, sir, but something is very unusual, it is running on its diesel. And, for the life of me, sir, I do not know why a nuke boat has his diesel running... no, sir, I haven't tried to raise it yet, no, sir, we haven't put any boats after it, sir, yes, sir, no, sir. Uh...no, sir, I hadn't thought about that. It *could* be that it might be testing its diesel while running on its nuclear plant. Yes, sir, we'll do that right away, sir."

He hung up the telephone and glared at Yadley.

"Are you done with the Goddamn coffee yet, Yadley?" he hollered.

Nichols reached over to his radio and dialed in the common harbor traffic frequency. He grabbed the radio transmitter microphone at the corner of his desk and his sweating hand squeezed the transmit button.

"This is the harbormaster receiving on 119.7 megahertz," he hollered into the device. "Submarine moving across Pearl Harbor, identify yourself."

After fifteen seconds of silence, Chief Nichols turned to Yadley. "Goddamn it," he fumed. "Send a patrol boat after that son-of-a-bitch, and let's bring some proper attention and respect for the rules and regs of Pearl Harbor."

It was three fifteen in the morning when the telephone next to Rear Admiral Samuel Sullivan's bed began to ring. It was a distant ring, a faraway sound intruding on his deep sleep, previously set to a barely audible level long ago to minimize the disruption of his wife's sleep from the random night calls. He quietly swung his feet off the bed and sat up straight, reaching out for the receiver. There had been only two rings and a quick glance behind him confirmed that Martha was still soundly asleep.

"Admiral Sullivan," he spoke quietly into the receiver.

"Admiral," a crisp voice responded, "I'm sorry to wake you, sir, this is Lieutenant Martin Cooper, OOD at Pearl, and we seem to have an unauthorized submarine moving across the harbor."

Sullivan sat up straighter and pressed the receiver tightly against his ear. "What the hell are you talking about, Cooper? An unauthorized *American* submarine? Does it have its escort? Have you raised it on the Sierra One Charlie receiver?"

"Negative for an escort, sir. The chief-of-the-watch, fellow named Nichols, in the harbormaster tower has tried to raise the sub without an answer. Sir, from its markings, we believe the submarine is the USS *Monterey* SSN 749, a Los Angeles class nuke boat. It came in earlier last night as scheduled…."

"It came in at exactly 2100 hours last night, Cooper; I was there at the pier when she tied up. This doesn't make any sense. When I left, the *Monterey* was still at the pier and the topside watch was set. Have you tried to contact the watch?"

"We called the land line to the boat, three times, sir, and the line is disconnected. We sent out an intercept patrol boat to divert the sub, and then two more. We're following it now, but there's no response from the sub. The patrol boats have done everything they can to get the sub to stop, damn near got rammed by it twice. And, there's nobody on the bridge at the top of the sail. It's almost out of the channel, approaching the open sea. Another half hour and she's gone, sir. Also, it is without running lights, and it seems to be making headway on its diesel engine. At least, it's running its diesel engine. They have their onboard surface search radar going and the periscopes are both fully raised and rotating, but it is moving like it is on autopilot."

Sullivan struggled to keep from hollering.

"Jesus Christ, Cooper, the *Monterey* isn't a Goddamn airplane! Nuclear submarines don't use autopilots when crossing harbors! Has anybody gone out to the sub base, to the pier, *where I just left the submarine*, to talk with anybody there, to find out what exactly in holy hell is going on? Has anybody talked to the topside watch?"

Sullivan heard his wife stirring.

"We sent a couple of cars there five minutes ago," the OOD said rapidly, "and the first has already reported that there is no sign of the topside watch. Furthermore, sir, they just reported there is no sign of the submarine. "

Sullivan felt a sudden chill run through his entire body. From behind him, a soft and sleepy female voice asked, "Is everything okay, honey?"

Ten minutes later, Admiral Sullivan's black military car squealed around three steel dumpsters, past a harbor police car with flashing blue lights, and screeched to a halt next to two dark Navy sedans at the empty pier. Sullivan jumped out of the car, noted two civilian harbor police officers standing in front of a dark red Corvette and two other cars, writing tickets. Two lieutenant commanders walked up to the admiral, snapped a salute, and the taller of the two said, "I'm Commander Jordan, and this is Lieutenant Cooper with the Pearl Harbor OOD office. There's nobody here to even ask about the *Monterey*, admiral." He pointed at the empty pier and added, "She's just gone."

"I can see that," Sullivan said. He turned toward the Harbor Police. "Has anybody asked *them* if they've seen anything?"

"Yes, sir," Jordan responded, "we did ask them. They've been driving around giving tickets on the base all night, and neither one of them saw anything relating to boats or ships. They told us it's not their job to watch ships. However, sir, from talking with them, I doubt if they *would* have noticed much of anything, anywhere, no matter what."

"Let's talk with them, again" Sullivan said, walking over to the police officers.

"Hello, gentlemen," Sullivan said, "Do you have the names of the owners of these cars?"

"These *illegally* parked cars, admiral?" the chunkier of the two answered. "Yes, sir, they belong to a Petty Officer second-class Brian Robinson, a Commander Gary Moore, and some Navy SEAL named Jack Olsen.

"Pardon me, admiral," the other policeman asked, "do you know how we can reach these men? They're going to have to move their cars or we're going to tow them."

"Jesus Christ!" Sullivan shouted, ignoring the question and turning to the two naval officers. "Get some patrol boats in front of that submarine if it hasn't reached the open ocean. They only got the captain, a nuke, and a SEAL aboard! The *Monterey's* normal crew is 118 men! I want an ASW[1] mustering of every aircraft and ship available in Pearl Harbor. I don't know what the hell is going on here but the rest of the crew should be on liberty after months at sea. They will be either in Waikiki or at home. It will be hard as hell to find anybody or to even get them to answer their telephones. I want the tapes of the pier CCTV[2] recordings, starting at 2100 hours last night. There should have been a total of three men on that submarine if it was alongside the pier, an armed topside watch and two enlisted men on watch down inside. Start your search at O'Malley's on Hotel Street. In the off chance that he's *not* on the boat, try to call the commanding officer, Commander Moore, top priority, call his home, and call the home of every crewmember with dependents. Call Moore's relatives, call *anybody* you can find! Whoever took the boat sure as hell doesn't know how to run a nuclear reactor by himself or they wouldn't have kept the diesel going. If the diesel is their only source of power, they can't go far…they can't even dive below snorkel depth or the battery will load up and exhaust in short order. We'll find them, I assure you, we'll find out who has decided to go on this little joy ride tonight. They will be held accountable. Now, get to work!"

"I really don't see how we're going to stop them," Lt. Cdr. Jordan said. "Whoever is running that sub hasn't responded to radio calls or our patrol boats. Do you expect them to dive as soon as they clear Pearl?" He looked at his watch. "Which is in about five minutes."

"I didn't ask you for a Goddamn opinion!" Sullivan said, exasperated. "I gave you some orders, now, move!"

The two Pearl Harbor police officers rushed to their car, turned off their flashing blue lights and roared away from the three parked cars which had tickets on their front windshields.

Sullivan turned away, climbed into his car and accelerated in the direction of the Submarine Base headquarters.

Inside the USS *Monterey*, now gliding four miles west of the sub base pier, Commander Gary Moore rotated his starboard periscope a full 360 degrees, his dark brown eyes peering at the remaining segment of the Pearl Harbor channel ahead as he watched the two remaining patrol boats not more than fifty yards behind their vertical rudder. His short cropped hair was prematurely gray just above his ears, the skin across his face demonstrated the *submarine pale* from the absence of sunlight for months beneath the sea. He was not a tall man, a blessing considering the confined spaces of his submarine, and he appeared remarkably physically fit, the reward for a regular exercise program started more than twenty years before after graduating from the U.S. Naval Academy.

Standing beside his captain and clenching the handles of the port periscope, the stocky and intense figure of Chief of the Boat Roy Berry rotated his 'scope while calling out occasional bearing orders to his helmsman. The absence of lighted markers leading to the ocean, other than the red and green navigation lights on both sides of the channel, made visual sightings nearly impossible, even with the 'scopes' LES[3] turned to high power.

"Two patrol boats still behind us, sir," Berry said in his characteristically raspy voice as he peered into his 'scope. "Annoying little bastards. At least they're not trying to block us anymore."

"I don't think they'll try that again," Moore said from behind the starboard 'scope. Five feet away from the men, in the submarine's control center, flaming red-haired Billy Bodine sat at the controls of the helm as the large muscular frame of one of the three Navy SEALs, Thor "Chainsaw" Ostrobothnia, closely watched the radar display on the repeater next to the navigation board. With each order, Bodine would turn the control wheel left or right to keep the *Monterey* in the center of the channel.

Above their heads, a loudspeaker blared, "Attention, submarine *Monterey*! This is the Harbormaster! I repeat, this is the Harbormaster! You are hereby ordered to turn around…."

Chief Berry's face looked pained as he reached up into the electronic systems near the periscopes and shut off the communications radio, bringing the submarine's control center to silence.

"Goddamn skimmer puke..." the chief muttered, followed by a new bearing order to his helmsman. "Billy, three degrees left and prepare to dive, soon as we clear the channel."

"Three degrees left, now steady at 267 degrees, the SEALs are lining up the valves, standing by to dive," Bodine answered. "And, thank you, chief, for shutting off that skimmer in his tower—he was getting a little too intense...."

From the corner of the control center, Chainsaw hunched over, scrutinizing the radar display. "You're exactly in the center of the channel, captain," he said. "Another quarter-mile to open ocean."

"Got it," Moore said crisply. "Half-mile to Mamala Bay, we're doing great. Keep a close eye on our position; the channel is only about five hundred feet wide for the next few minutes. He pulled his head back from the periscope eyepieces. "Bodine, we need to get a report from the engine room about the reactor. We're making only six knots on the diesel. How far up are the control rods and what is the ETA for the nuclear propulsion system to become operational?"

Bodine grabbed the 7 MC microphone and hollered the request into the engine room.

Over the roaring of the diesel engine, the reactor operator's voice shouted. "Control, this is maneuvering. The nuclear reactor is almost operational but the primary coolant is just beginning to generate steam and the steam stops are still closed. Munroe will open the valves for the turbines but the ETA for sustained nuclear power is about three or four minutes and another five minutes to produce steam."

Moore reached up to the microphone connecting the control center with the engine room's maneuvering area. "Robinson. This is the captain speaking. Great work. We need to shut down the diesel and dive below snorkel depth as soon as we clear the Mamala Bay inner waters."

The roar of diesel noise over the loudspeaker filled the control center again. "Aye, aye, sir," Robby's voice carried into the submarine's control center. "Munroe is going *hermantile*,[4] opening steam stops and everything else throughout the engine room. He just went down the ladder to the lower level engine room to cycle a couple more pumps. We'll get the reactor critical[5] as fast as possible."

Captain Moore stepped away from his periscope. "We're going to need some nuke power pretty quick," he said as he walked away from the periscope station and headed aft toward the engine room. He climbed through a watertight door and moved down the central passageway, the silent and empty compartments turning the *Monterey* into a ghost ship, an abandoned submarine, devoid of the usual crowds of men.

He finally reached the large oval watertight door leading into the engine room. Lifting the latch and swinging open the heavy door, Moore stepped into the compartment where the thundering roar of the *Monterey's* diesel engine immediately blasted him with hot air and the steaming oil fumes that filled the compartment. He continued aft, down the starboard passageway, past the shrieking monster of a diesel engine as the burly shape of the sweating machinist mate Manny Munroe paused his work on the equipment to reach out and hand him a pair of silencer ear muffs.

"Protect your ears, captain," Munroe hollered above the noise.

"Thanks, Munroe," Moore hollered back, taking the bulbous ear enclosures and clamping them over his head. "Are we lined up for steam, soon as the nuke plant is operational?"

"Yes, sir, Robbie says we're almost there!" Munroe hollered back. "The plant is still hot from our shutdown when we came in; we're ready here soon as the reactor is on the line!"

"Good work, we'll be diving to snorkel soon, and going deep when the reactor is in the power range!"

"Aye, aye, captain, we'll be ready!"

Moore continued down the passageway to the tightly-confined Maneuvering Room near the back of the engine room, where the towering nuclear and electrical control panels faced two young enlisted men in military dungarees standing in front of their chairs before the wall of meters. They both intently watched the meters on their panels, quickly reaching out to flip various switches and move controls as the array of indicators showed the status of the nuclear reactor and the electrical systems throughout the submarine.

Brian Robinson, the tall and slender reactor operator, stood in the corner of the area, scanning the meters before him as he glanced at the commanding officer now standing at the entry to the maneuvering room.

"Captain, no changes yet. The nuclear startup is almost finished," he said, reaching quickly to his panel and flipping two switches. A veteran of the Navy's three-year nuclear training program followed by nearly three-years on the sub, Robby radiated confidence in his activities with the panel's maze of controls. Just above his head, a ventilation pipe blasted him with cool air like a hurricane of wind whipping his hair back and forth.

"We'll have steam to the turbines in a couple of minutes!" he said confidently.

"Good," Moore said, "we're taking her down soon and will be rigging the boat for deep submergence." He reached up into the overhead and pulled down a microphone that communicated with his chief at the periscope station in the submarine's control center.

"Are we clear of Pearl Harbor channel, chief?" Moore hollered into the microphone.

"Yes, sir, we're into the open sea!" roared back over the loudspeaker and Moore ordered the submarine to dive to periscope depth. For the next thirty seconds, the men felt their submarine world tilt downward into the ocean as the vessel descended below the surface.

Standing next to Robby, Jules Baxter watched his meters with equal intensity. The electrician was a large rotund man in a dark blue khaki uniform, his face sporting an impressive mustache and, as usual, he demonstrated his curious habit of glowering at his gauges as if each one harbored a personal malevolent intent. He briefly turned away from his panel, quickly tugged at his mustache and looked at the captain, hollering over the roar of the diesel, "Sir, the batteries are fully charged, we can shut down the diesel and move below snorkel depth. I got the Battleshort Switch in the full battleshort position. Didn't I hear you order that somewhere?"

"No, actually, I never did order that, Baxter, but I am quite sure I did *want* to order that," Moore said, with a quick flash of a smile.

"Never did *that* before," Baxter muttered as he turned his attention back to his rows of glowering meters.

And with that said, neither man commented on the remarkable and unusual circumstance of rendering the normal automatic safety shutdown circuits non-operational, removing automatic shutdowns and leaving the only means of turning off the reactor in the hands of the skeleton crew. As they both knew, inadvertent reactor shutdown from spurious electrical signals were now eliminated and everybody had speculated about potential "battle" conditions awaiting the submarine.

Moore turned away to return to the boat's control center, when he abruptly stopped and stared down the passageway in shock. Storming in his direction, like a fantasy hallucination filling his mind, was a young and beautiful blonde woman clad only in tight shorts and a loose Hawaiian blouse with images of flowers and surfboards across the front. Her bouncing breasts pushed on the four buttons at the top of her blouse and her eyes flamed with the fire of uncontrolled rage.

She stopped just short of Captain Moore, her blazing eyes daggers of hostility as she began to scream at him.

"Are you the *captain* of this ship? My name is Amanda Peterson and I want off this thing! *I want off, NOW!* Do you hear me, I want off this thing, NOW!"

Moore calmly reached up into the overhead maze of wires and pipes, and while staring continuously at the woman, pulled down a microphone and pushed a button as he began to speak.

"Chief," he said, "make our depth two hundred feet, now. Send Chainsaw to the engine room. He needs to escort an Amanda Peterson to the bow compartment."

She glared at the captain, taking deeper and deeper breaths before finally speaking. "Two hundred feet!" she screamed over the roaring of engine room machinery. "WE ARE TWO HUNDRED FEET BELOW THE SURFACE? And you just ordered somebody…this character "Chainsaw" to come and get me? To take me away? WHAT KIND OF SUBMARINE IS THIS?"

FIVE HOURS EARLIER

South China Sea, Mindoro Strait

She undressed slowly, just beyond the foot of the bed in the luxury yacht, as her husband lay naked beneath the sheets, watching her provocative movements, waiting, his eyes attentively bright and his breath coming more quickly. It was a game, played many times between Caroline and Peter Blackwell, their private game of seduction, a game of holding him back from her warm and soft body as he increasingly anticipated the moments ahead, the moments of arousal awaiting a passionate fulfillment. They said not a word as she smiled and gazed at him from just beyond the bed, *feeling* the intensity of his desire. She smiled again, slowly letting her clothes fall to the floor, feeling a warm surge of pleasure as she began to sense her own hunger before his eyes. While soft music played in the warm darkness of their yacht's palatial stateroom, her beautiful body captured the faint glow through the curtains drawn across the portholes as she moved toward him, now breathing with equal intensity. He lifted the sheet for her to move into his arms as the game merged into the eternal rhythm of love while the yacht *Sweet Caroline* slowly cruised across the calm and glassy surface of the South China Sea.

The pale waters of the surrounding ocean stretched to the west of the boat, all the way to Vietnam, a perfect reflection of the warm blue sky above. The ocean at the Philippine's tranquil Verde Island Passage was unmarred by any disturbance beyond the occasional random darting splashes of sea-going storm petrels as the smooth ripples from the boat's wake created a spear across the water, pointing directly at the stern of the *Sweet Caroline*. The 86-foot motor boat, a magnificent display of ice-blue opulence, the best of the Wally class, cruised nearly silently across the sea, her twin CAT C12 diesels purring as the gyroscopic stabilization system held her from even the slightest rocking from the gentle swell. Her crew of four remained busy at their tasks, on the bridge, at the galley, and in the engine room, all of them sustaining the pristine state of the vessel while remaining discreetly out of sight from the owner and his beautiful young wife, the namesake of the boat.

At the stern quarterdeck of the *Caroline*, Mombo Tyson, the boat's East Indian chef, carefully cleared the Waterford crystal glasses and china plates from atop the white embroidered linen of the elegant table that had held their recent lunch. Taking advantage of the calm seas, Peter Blackwell and his wife had enjoyed the prepared canapés, made to the specifications that had been defined at the start of today's voyage. Since the crew had cast off the *Sweet Caroline's* lines from the pier, three days before in Manila, the weather had been perfect, especially during their time at the pristine scuba-diving waters off Puerto Galera. Mombo gathered the plates and glasses, and glanced at the horizon again, noting the scattered clusters of Filipino fishing vessels in the distance. The calm sea may not last, he knew, and little Nablag Island, south of the sprawling Mindoro Island, was still more than one hundred miles ahead for the yacht.

Finally, as another half-hour passed behind the closed and locked door of the master stateroom, Peter and Caroline Blackwell lay in each other's arms, warm and satisfied beneath the covers of their elegant bed. Peter had gone to sleep almost immediately after their sexual intensity, and Caroline quietly watched him breathing slowly and peacefully, the slumber of a man who had been, once again, fully satisfied by the pleasures with his wife. He was a solid man with a muscular build, just turning forty years of age, his skin deeply tanned, his face adorned with a dark and masculine 2-day growth covering his square jaw and matching exactly the color of his eyes. A trace of white had begun to emerge at each of his temples, projecting an unplanned look of executive authority that matched his persona, another asset as he worked with his father to expand the family's company, Seattle's International Cyber Systems, Inc.

She listened to his slow breathing and thought about the days ahead. During the next week, they would finish the celebration of their third anniversary, enjoying once again doing what Peter liked to call "an extension of our honeymoon." She loved these times at sea, not only because of the exuberant luxury and exciting sexuality that was always the inherent consequence of their time together, but also for the sheer adventure of taking trips to distant exotic destinations in the world. She smiled with pleasure and slowly closed her eyes while listening to the soft strains of the London Philharmonic's Ave Maria floating across the room.

And that was the exact instant, she would remember for the rest of her life, when the first round from the gas-fired AK-47 machine gun crashed through the porthole window on the starboard side of their cabin, and an instant later, exited through the wall directly above the top of their bed.

Peter's eyes flew open, he lifted his head and stared at the shattered porthole. He quickly leaped from their bed as they heard a staccato of splintering sounds from additional rounds hitting the boat.

"Peter!" she screamed.

"Stay here, Caroline!" Blackwell hollered as he pulled on his trousers and raced to the destroyed porthole to look out over the ocean. "Get down on the floor and stay here!" he yelled as he scanned the sea. "There are two motor boats, 'way out there, pirates or terrorists of some kind! They're closing on us and they're still shooting!"

They felt the swaying acceleration of the yacht as the boat sharply turned away from the pursuing vessels as the roar of the yacht's accelerating engines filled the air. Blackwell raced toward the door as Caroline grabbed her clothes and yelled, "What kind of weapons do we have on the boat, Peter? Guns? Rocket-propelled grenades? *Anything*? What are our weapons?"

"Caroline!" he said urgently. "The crew does weapons, that's what the *crew* is for. I pay them lots of money to...."

"This is not a money thing, Peter!" she exclaimed. She pulled up her slacks and quickly looked out the porthole, searching for the skiffs as she pulled her blouse around her shoulders. "This is a *survival* thing. Please tell me, Peter, we're not sailing international waters without weapons, are we?"

Blackwell held up his hands. "Please, honey, I don't want you out there. We have all kinds of weapons but you need to be safe...."

"Safe?" She tossed her head in frustration. "*Jesus*, Peter! They just blew a hole through our cabin! This *Wally* is mostly fiberglass. Nothing here is bullet-proof; nothing is going to stop anything. If we're going into some kind of battle," she looked out the porthole again, "and these boats are closing on us...if we're going to fight, I want to help."

Peter turned away from her and opened the door as Mombo rushed by their stateroom entrance, carrying a large gun and two dark gray metal cases.

"Peter, I want to help..." she called after him. "*You know I can shoot anything, you know I'm an excellent shot*!" she screamed.

"And I want you to be safe, you're staying in the cabin!" Peter hollered back to her as he slammed the door shut behind him. She quickly opened the door but he was gone. She quickly turned back into the stateroom and opened every drawer she could find, trying to remember, searching through clothing and papers until her hands finally closed on the pearl-handled Walther P99 pistol and a fully-loaded 12 round magazine. She clutched the cool steel, feeling some reassurance from the power within...it was her own personal weapon, concealed and tucked away during the early moments of their departure, never discussed, and never even thought about, until now.

With quick movements, she inserted the magazine into the gun, keeping the first round unchambered, and jammed the pistol into her waistband. She opened the door of the suite a couple of inches again and scanned the ocean, searching for the attackers.

Outside the cabin, Peter had barely glanced at Mombo who had set up his tripod under the dark shape of a 50-caliber machine gun. He jumped up the steps to the cockpit where the boat's captain scanned the windows as his right hand clutched the large round steerage wheel. The captain was a large imposing figure of a man, his black skin contrasting with the crisp white of his captain's uniform, his speech that of a highly-educated English professor with a slightly British accent indicating his South African heritage. His name was simply Bo, he had told them the day of departure, a contraction of a much more complicated name with African roots. Not Mr. Bo, not Captain Bo, just Bo, he had said with a big smile showing an impressive array of gleaming white teeth.

"What are we doing?" Peter hollered at the man. "Have you called anybody for help?"

Behind them and on the lower deck, the roaring of the engines were drowned out by Mombo's machine gun opening up with a deafening staccato sound, quick splashes of the rounds hitting the ocean and lifting up into the sky as the yacht rolled.

"We've seen this kind of thing before, Mr. Blackwell," Bo said, turning his high-resolution binoculars in the direction of the two vessels closing the distance behind them. "These boats are holding pirates or some kind of terrorists. They have outboards, easily fifty to a hundred horsepower considering their speed. They had started to move up slow on us in the fishing grounds of the South China Sea, Mr. Blackwell. I had seen them out there nearly a half hour ago. There can be over 6,000 fishermen in these waters at any point in time and that's what I thought, they were just standard Filipino commercial boats. I thought they were fishing boats until they started shooting!"

"That's not reassuring, Bo. Again, have you called for help?" Blackwell repeated.

"Yes, sir, and I'm getting our coordinates again for another call," he said. "I already radioed once but there was no answer. I'm sorry, Boss, this is supposed to be a safe part of the ocean. We studied this before we left Manila. There have been pirates in the Sulu Sea, down to the south. That's one of the reasons we kept our course to the north, through the Mindoro Strait to Nablag."

"Well, that's great, obviously, the pirates don't follow the game plan in the Sulu Sea!"

"No, sir, but usually it is safe out here, unless the Chinese want to stir something up," the tall captain said looking down at their electronic GPS system and grabbing his pen as he noted the fresh coordinates of the *Sweet Caroline* on a sheet of paper.

The Sweet Caroline continued thundering across the sea, her twin screws creating a churning trail of white water behind them. The captain reached over to the radio communications system, quickly looking out the broken aft window at the two boats, now less than a mile away, continuing their pursuit at high speed. There had been a brief moment when it had almost looked like they could escape the attackers. It was time and it was fuel, he knew…let enough time pass as the chase continued, the further the skiffs moved from their source. A mother ship seemed likely to Bo, and if that's where they came from, the more fuel consumed and the more time it would take to *return* to the mother ship.

He grabbed his radio's microphone, pressed on the switch and hollered, "Mayday! Mayday! Mayday! This is, again, the *Sweet Caroline* in the South China Sea off Palawan, 86-foot motor yacht, pursued by two hostile boats firing on us, we are twenty-five miles west of Mindoro, precise coordinates are…"

The glass of the yacht's cockpit around them suddenly shattered as both men ducked to the floor. The air above their heads whistled with the sounds of additional rounds flying through the broken windows as a staccato of bullets slammed into the GPS. Bo reached up to the control console and clutched the microphone in his hand as he punched in channel 16 on one radio and dialed 161.400 on the second one.

At the instant he pressed the microphone to his mouth again, the loudspeakers above their heads boomed out the voice of a radioman on an oil tanker, the *Noguchi Maru*. She was a huge and slow tanker, the voice said in broken English, she was of Japanese registry, and they wanted the coordinates. She was ready to change course if it would be helpful, she was equipped with small arms weapons but no military special defense contractors, and she was willing to help in any way possible. If they were anywhere off Palawan Island, they could be there in a couple of hours.

And, the radioman almost shouted, "What are your *exact* coordinates?"

"The *Noguchi* can't help us," Bo hollered to Blackwell from his crouched position. "There's nobody close enough to help us. At least we're still going full speed ahead. We damn well have to concentrate on defending ourselves."

Suddenly Caroline appeared at the cabin door and hollered, "What the hell are we doing to stop this?"

"Honey, I told you…" Peter started.

"I'm *not* staying below decks!" she screamed at her husband and turned to the captain. "What are we doing besides having Mombo fire his fifty-cals into the ocean?"

Bo cautiously reached up again and pushed against the throttle knobs again, already locked into the Full-Speed Ahead position, as he looked through the cabin's rear window. "He's *not* just 'firing into the ocean,' Mrs. Blackwell, he's letting them know we have powerful weapons. *Nobody* can be here nearly in time," he said, turning to look at Blackwell, his black face becoming intense. "I would suggest, sir, that you join Mombo and the others to ready our weapons, and I would also suggest, sir, that you request Mrs. Blackwell return to your stateroom. She will need to lock the door and stay there until we can come and get her."

"Thank you, Bo, that's a non-starter," Caroline said. "And, don't ignore me again! Where is a shotgun I can use? Honest-to-God, I really know how to shoot!"

With a look of intense exasperation, Bo reached to the back of the cockpit and pulled out a large aluminum shotgun from a concealed rack. "Okay," he said, here you are. This is my personal Remington 870. Do you know…?"

"Where are the shells?" she asked, staring at the captain. "Where are the *fucking* shells?"

"Six boxes in the slot behind the seat, here, already loaded and ready with seven shotgun shells," he hollered at her. "You can reload each shell…"

"I *know* how a pump action shotgun works!"

Peter watched his wife inspect the gun. "How did you know…?"

"My dad, honey, I keep telling you!" she interrupted, looking back at the captain. "I'm ready, Bo, now let's *do* something!"

The captain raised his binoculars again and studied the pursuing boats progressively moving closer to their stern. "Goddammit!" he hollered, "They have ladders with grappling hooks. They're coming right at us, sir, but I think we can put enough distance..."

"Jesus holy mother of God..." Blackwell said as he stared at the two skiffs. He turned back to the cabin and looked at the throttles, black knobs pressed against the forward stops. "What's the maximum we can get, fifteen knots out of this boat?"

"Twelve knots, top speed—we're cranking 1800 RPM out of both engines, anything more than that will blow them out. Those guys are pushing thirty knots in their lightweight boats. They're far enough back that we have time..." He grabbed the microphone connected to the boat's announcement system. "Addison," he called to the lower levels. "Break out the Tasers, the Molotov's, the stun grenades, and get them topside ASAP. Leave the engine room, now!"

He glanced at Caroline and then turned to Blackwell. "If they get close enough, now, we got 'em. We have multiple weapons and the crew knows how to use them. And, with your wife and my Marine Magnum...." He glared at Caroline. "We can hold them off. However, if we can move far enough toward Mindoro and the other northern Philippine islands," he said, "we'll outrun their fuel supply. They'll have to break it off."

Caroline reached into her waistband and pulled out her pistol, quickly sliding a round into the chamber and handing it over to her husband. "As a reminder, the safety is right there, Peter, you have eight shots, 9 millimeter, keep your finger off the trigger until you have released the safety and are ready to shoot. Then, each time you pull the trigger, somebody dies!"

"Jesus..." Peter said, clutching the gun.

"Soon, we'll be making a violent turn," the captain said, "be ready!"

"Captain!" Caroline said, "We are not going to outrun them! Isn't that becoming obvious? We're running out of time!"

There were three men in each of the pursuing boats, and it looked like each of them was holding some kind of automatic rifle, ready for use, the barrels waving threateningly in the general direction of the yacht. Mombo gripped the stock of his 50-caliber machine gun on the starboard side near the edge of the railing and squirted off another burst of shells in their general direction.

"How much longer before they're in range?" Peter called to Mombo over the roaring of the boat's diesel engines as he tried to hold his pistol steady.

"They're *already* in range of us!" Caroline raged. "We have bullet holes…."

"2,000 yards, about a mile, moving into range!" Mombo hollered from his position as Peter clutched Caroline's pistol.

"This may be just a probe," the captain said, "to see what we've got. We'll fire a flare and we'll give them another burst from the 50-cal. That should impress them enough to back off." He stared at the two boats and hollered, "They're coming faster, get ready to fire. In about a minute, we're turning 180 degrees, straight into them, get ready to shoot. I'll be firing some flares in their direction, Mombo will nail them with his 50-cal and you open up with your guns while the rest of our crew fires everything we got."

Caroline and Peter crouched down near the backside of the cockpit, their guns ready, Caroline rapidly pulling extra cartridges from a box and jamming them into the side of her white slacks. She turned to glare at the two boats, her shotgun ready.

"Don't waste any ammunition while they're still so far out there, Peter," she said as Blackwell moved his finger slowly down to the gun's trigger.

Caroline narrowed her eyes, watching the boats pounding the light waves as they closed the distance. The men in the skiffs could clearly be seen now, their dark faces intently studying their yacht-victim while a man in the back of each boat steered them in the direction of the yacht. She felt a sudden chill as she noticed, at the back of the darker skiff, the dark-maroon skiff on the left, another man lifting what appeared to be a tripod-mounted very large machine gun into shooting position. Her mouth opened to sound an alarm in terror at the moment flashes began to appear from the gun in a staccato-like sequence, drowned out immediately by the shrill sounds of incoming rounds slamming into the hull of the *Sweet Caroline* just above the waterline.

"Shoot at the boat on the left," she screamed as Mombo opened fire with his 50-caliber machine gun, a deafening roar immediately filling the air. The bullets splashed into the ocean in front of the skiffs, as arcs of empty casings flew out of the gun to litter the pristine deck of the *Sweet Caroline*. Immediately, the yacht rolled as the captain jammed the rudder to the right for the beginning of a high-speed rotation back into the direction of their attackers. The sudden angling of the turning boat threw off the aim of the machine guns, and the firing suddenly came to a halt.

"The Goddamn gun is jammed!" Mombo hollered as Gus yanked and pulled the ammunition belt feeding into the 50-caliber weapon. "It misfired and jammed."

The crashing sounds of incoming rounds from the skiff's larger gun continued for another ten seconds, shattering the back window of the cockpit as both boats broke off their direct line of attack to begin circling the yacht at high speed, like animals closing in for the kill.

That was the instant when, to the horror of Caroline, an incoming round slammed directly into the cockpit of the *Sweet Caroline*, shattering the remaining fragments of glass into a shower around them and smashing the radio across the panel of the cockpit.

"The radio's gone!" Bo hollered as Mombo pleaded for another weapon.

There was no answer, and suddenly the skiff's gun fired a final set of bullets into the *Sweet Caroline's* stern. Both diesel engines began screaming with the sound of broken and destroyed metal, the smooth roar of diesel power screeching down to silence, abruptly bringing the yacht to a complete halt in the water.

"They hit our engines," the captain yelled. "They're going to try and board, go for the boat on the right," he hollered as he began firing another rifle in the direction of the closer skiff, "Fire everything you got."

As the captain began firing his rifle at one of the skiffs, they came closer into range and Caroline rapidly jerked off the safety on the side of her shotgun. She began squeezing the trigger as fast as she could, firing at the men in the maroon boat that was trying to move closer to the yacht. The rolling of the *Caroline* in the waters pushed her first two shots into the water and then abruptly the third shot flew into the air above the skiff. The three men in the boat continued firing, creating an intense sound of splintering wood and plastic as holes appeared across the upper half of the yacht. She squinted down the barrel of her shotgun and squeezed off the remaining three final rounds in rapid sequence, seeing one of the pirates hit directly in the chest, his gun flying from his hands as he was blown overboard.

On the port side of the boat, Gus squeezed a long sequence of rounds from his semi-automatic rifle, watching the rounds hit the water and finally lift up to directly slam into the body of the pirate standing near the tripod gun as the two skiffs circled their silenced victim. At that very instant the captain of the *Sweet Caroline* suddenly grabbed his stomach in the agony of a direct hit, trying to stop a rush of blood as Gus Addison felt the impact of rounds hitting his right leg and shoulder. Mombo looked down in horror at the man and immediately threw his gun into the ocean and put his hands over his head.

"Don't shoot anymore," Mombo hollered, his voice filled with panic. "We surrender. Don't shoot!"

"Don't surrender!" Caroline hollered. "Jesus Christ! What is wrong with you?" That was when she spotted the grappling hooks of a ladder reaching over the railing of the port side of the yacht, while the second skiff they had been shooting at moved out of range.

"They're coming aboard on the port side," Caroline screamed as Peter turned and they both shot simultaneously into the head of a very skinny dark-skinned man reaching over the railing. He immediately disappeared off the railing, dropping down into the skiff at the side of the yacht.

"Stop shooting," Mombo shouted again, his voice desperate. "They got us. We have to give up."

"No! Don't give up!" Peter yelled at the man as a hand clutching a large dark pistol reached up and over the railing, firing blindly at whoever might be a target. As Caroline and Peter fired back, Mombo yelled, "We're giving up, we're giving up."

From a crouched position, Caroline turned toward Mombo. "You say one more word about giving up, Mombo," she screamed at the man, "and I will shoot you myself!"

Caroline watched the top of the ladder for a return of the hand, as she and her husband dropped to the deck next to the cockpit. She frantically tried to load her shotgun with another seven shells. Next to the boxes of shotgun shells, a cellphone plugged into a charging device blinked a tiny blue light of power. Caroline quickly jammed the device into her slacks as a booming loudspeaker voice in nearly perfect English blasted from the second circling skiff behind them. "Hold your fire and you will not be harmed," the voice said. "Stop shooting and we will bring no harm to you. Your engines are gone, you cannot escape."

Peter looked at his wife, as they crouched near the cockpit door. "We can't get away," he said softly, "and if we keep shooting, they'll kill us all. Mombo is right." He reached out for her hand, seeking to hold her while the second skiff turned in the direction of the yacht. As she pulled away and stepped over the captain's bleeding body into the cockpit, the loudspeaker blared again.

"Throw your guns overboard. Do not shoot at us or we will kill every one of you."

She disappeared through a door on the far side of the cockpit as another pirate reached over the railing from the port side, climbed up to the top step of the ladder, and aimed a huge and very dark pistol directly at Peter Blackwell's head. He stared at Blackwell and said with a heavy African dialect, "Do not move or you will die." He glared at Mombo, standing next to Gus' writhing body and hollered, "Down the ladder, into my boat, NOW!"

Peter Blackwell slowly stood up, aware that he was drenched in sweat and shaking violently. The pirate, an extremely thin dark man with a thick bush of tightly-curled black hair, climbed onto the decking of the yacht, holding his pistol in front of him. With a rock-steady hand, he continued to aim directly at Peter's head as Mombo climbed over the railing and carefully moved down the ladder into the skiff. "Who else is on the boat?" he demanded, his arm outstretched with the pistol held steady.

"There's nobody here now" Peter said, looking down at the writhing bodies and blood around him. "You've managed to shoot most of us and create a hell of a mess,"

"Who else?" the pirate screamed as he turned to the two injured crewmen of the yacht, Bo and Gus, both lying in pools of rapidly expanding blood. With the practiced hand of an executioner, he fired a shot into the head of each of them, bringing all their movement to a permanent and final end.

"Jesus!" Blackwell hollered.

"One last time," he said calmly, almost politely, to Blackwell as he leveled the gun at him again. "Exactly who else is on this boat?"

"Just us," Blackwell finally said. "That's all…don't shoot, please."

"Who is the owner, the master, of this boat?" the pirate asked, waving his gun across the face of Peter.

"I am the owner," Blackwell yelled intensely. "I am the Goddamn owner."

The pirate continued to point the pistol at Blackwell as a second pair of grappling hooks propelled over the rail behind him from the lighter skiff. As another pair of hands reached up to the railing, and another dark body climbed up onto the *Caroline*, the pirate holding the gun stared at Blackwell.

"And now," he said, "we are going to search this boat. If we find anybody else, then you will all die…."

The room in the lower forward spaces of the *Sweet Caroline* was nearly dark, Caroline discovered, a secluded place where the crew rarely ventured, a compartment filled with storage boxes and supplies. A dim light in the overhead gave just enough illumination for her to see the containers filled with large quantities of nonperishables regularly gathered by the crew as the daily requirements demanded. A small amount of light entered through the holes from bullets that had penetrated the hull. Caroline had been there only once, a brief addendum to the initial tour when she had first arrived onboard in Manila, and she had only been given a quick look at the space. For protection, she knew, it was useless. As luxurious as the Wally masterpiece of yachts had been marketed, there had been no word about a safe-room or a citadel in which anyone under siege could find safety until rescued.

There was a single inside lock, she discovered as she rapidly closed the wooden door and bolted it tight, wincing at the audible click. In the distance, she could still hear the muted voices of the attackers, but thankfully no further gunshots. Hiding behind the three larger boxes at the front of the compartment, she pulled out the cellular telephone with the satellite adapter and frantically began dialing the number burned into her mind from so long ago. There was no time, she knew, for a even a single misdialing or a lost connection, and she also knew the chances of reaching him were nearly zero—if he was still at sea and still submerged, there would be no hope.

The sound of her call ringing floated out from the telephone. One ring, a pause, a second ring, a pause, and as the third ring began she took a deep breath of despair as she knew it would be followed by a voice-answering system. There would be his voice, speaking rapidly, leaving a message to leave a message. It would be a recorded voice she needed to hear live now, more than at any time of her entire life. And, at that instant, the live voice came into her ear.

"Commander Moore!"

"Daddy!" her voice gasped into the cell phone. "They're killing everyone on the boat! They're coming to get us, can you…?"

Standing outside O'Malley's Submarine Bar, in the Honolulu alley away from the noise of a celebrating crew within, Captain Gary Moore pressed his cell phone against his ear and bellowed "Who is killing everyone, where are you, Caroline?" His face contorted in the anguish overwhelming as he yelled, "Honey, *tell me where you are! Is Peter with you?"*

Moore could hear the distant sounds of a pounding noise, a fist pounding against a door as he strained to hear every word, the sounds of her breath, struggling to understand the meaning of her presence and her terror. The distant sounds of a demanding voice was replaced with her voice, now whispering and filled with fear.

"We're in our boat somewhere off the Philippines in the Mindoro Strait, on our way to a small island, Daddy. I think it is called Nablag or Nablog or something, a hundred miles away. Two skiffs attacked us, we're dead in the water, they shot up the engines, and they already killed the captain and one of the other men. Peter is being taken captive and almost everybody else is dead."

"Tell me *exactly* where you are," Moore's cried out as the background pounding on the door became louder and punctuating by the sound of splintering wood.

Her voice continued, the loud whisper of a woman struggling to control her panic. "We're far out to sea, we can't see Palawan or any other island—they've been chasing us since Puerto Galera….."

Before she could finish, Moore could hear the crashing sound of breaking wood in the distance and threatening voice of a man, a voice with a strong accent, a voice yelling, "Drop the telephone, NOW! Drop it now, or Blackwell is dead."

And with that final sound, the crackle of static over the telephone intensified. He heard her cell phone crash onto the flooring and the line became silent as the call disappeared into nothingness.

O'Malley's Submarine Bar, Honolulu

They all had drinks in their hands, the celebrating crew of the USS *Monterey*, and the roar of their laughter carried all the way into the alleyway next to the bar. Moore tried to return the call three times, pounding on the keys of the cellphone, each time receiving an infuriating recording that the call could not be completed. The impact of her words and her distress created an internal fury in the captain, a raging that cried out for something to be done, *anything* to protect his daughter, to shield her, to eliminate the threats. His face felt flushed, he found himself breathing faster as his mind struggled to comprehend the incomprehensible.

As he moved back into the bar, feeling almost robotic and disconnected from his body, his eyes focused on Chief Petty Officer Roy Berry, the stocky shape of the mustached man with the raspy voice, the center of the gathering of men, all of them laughing at some ribald joke and all working to make up for lost time with alcohol.

"Chief, now!" Moore said, with a nod of his head to the corner room of O'Malley's, the room for VIP's of the submarine Navy, the room of privacy. The two men briskly moved into the room, the door slammed shut, and Moore began to speak with an intensity never previously seen by the chief. Within two minutes, the entire story was out and before Berry could respond, Captain Moore added, "I'm going to get her."

"Great, captain, you must go, there's gotta be flights to the Philippines…" Berry began.

"I'm taking the *Monterey,*" Moore cut him off. "I'm going to find her, I'm going to get her, and I'm going to kill any man who may have touched her!"

After a moment of shocked silence, Berry exclaimed, "Jesus holy fucking Christ, captain! Do you…"

"There is no other way, chief, I have no choice. They may not even keep her alive, but if they do, they will ransom her, they will ransom her husband, and they will kill them! If I fly there, they will encourage me to go to the consulate and that won't do a damn bit of good!"

Berry looked down at his drink as a moment of silence passed, aware of the hard breathing of his commanding officer.

"Okay," he finally said, "Okay. I'm not even drunk yet, in fact, I'm 'way behind the other guys...." He looked directly at the captain and said with his characteristic raspy voice, "I'm going with you, that's settled!"

"No, chief, there'll be others, I'll find others..."

"Bullshit, captain! You're taking the *Monterey*, you're going to the Philippines, and I'm going too!"

"Your career...."

"Fuck my career! I owe it to you! I'm not going to discuss it further! How many Nukes do you need?"

"You don't owe me..."

"Bullshit! You saved me, do you remember, in the North Pacific? My line broke and I'm over the side at three o'dark in the morning? Do you remember the storm? And the State 6 sea? Not another captain on the planet could have pulled off what you did!"

"Hell, chief, any trained officer..."

"Bullshit again! Goddammit! Damn near burning out the turbines with the sustained backing bell? The fucking control center is flooded and I heard what you said to the engineering officer, 'hold your bell, hold your bell' while he's screaming about oil temperatures! And scouting the 60-foot waves with the fucking periscope until I crested somewhere a mile away? A flash of my light, a bearing recorded? Your team hauled me back aboard, hypothermic, gonna be DEAD in another five minutes? Do you remember *that,* captain? And the Doc, and the booze, and a warm blanket? Goddammit, captain, I'm going with you! Now, how many Nukes do you need?"

"Three, chief! I need three! An electrician, a reactor operator, and a machinist! But..."

"I got three for you, Skipper, they're all at the end of their Navy Nuke careers and like the three SEALs, they'd be non-volunteering from subs if they weren't getting out of the Navy. After what the CIA did to us on this last mission, are you kidding, sir? And, three of our six SEALs are ready to go AWOL, Christ they lost two of their own in that fucking Indonesia debacle! I got you SIX men, and I got leverage on Billy Bodine, currently standing the boat's topside watch—you didn't know about the girl he just let visit the boat, did you, sir? They called me about that! We were going to keep it a fucking secret but his ass is grass now, sir. I promise you, sir, he's coming with us!"

The chief hesitated, studying Moore's anguished eyes. "That is, with your approval, sir?" he said, his raspy voice now a whisper. "And, I think we'd better get going, like, *tonight*, with all due respect, sir?

Chapter 2

Vice Admiral Harris Zehner's Home

In the quiet morning hills above Honolulu, COMSUBPAC[6] Vice Admiral Harris Zehner was ten minutes into his morning treadmill workout when his cell phone began to chime. The admiral was a well-conditioned and slender man, largely the result of his nearly fanatic exercise program, starting at 4 AM sharp with religious regularity and lasting, obsessively compulsively to the second on his stopwatch, precisely forty-five minutes. It was a kind of ritual-fetish for the admiral, an obsessive mandate, regularly drenching him in sweat each morning until he would finally punch the torturing machine to a halt. When he thought about it, which was not that often, the workout was more for his brain than his body, each session seemingly creating a clearer and faster-thinking mind, each morning's efforts an essential asset to blunt the daily pressures dropped on his desk as the commander of all the submarines in the Pacific.

The front of his cell phone displayed Admiral Sullivan from its perch on top of the treadmill. He punched "stop" on the treadmill control panel and picked up the device. A 0420 hours telephone call was never a good thing.

"Admiral Zehner," he said into the cell phone.

"Hello, Harris, this is Sully," crackled into the admiral's right ear. "I know it's early…."

"Get on with it, Sully."

"One of our boats, the *Monterey*, has just been moved from its mooring out into the Pearl Harbor channel, heading for the open ocean. She has no escort, a direct violation of standing orders. We are working…"

"The *Monterey* has just 'been moved out of its mooring?' What the hell does that mean?" Zehner roared into the phone.

"This has just happened, within the past half hour or so," Sullivan's voice said tersely. "Nobody noticed it was leaving until the harbormaster wondered what nuke sub was running around on its diesel engine. The crew is ashore on liberty, we're looking for the skipper, Commander Moore and the XO, and the rest of the crew.

Whoever's on the boat has ignored or was not hearing the OOD's command to stop, they're heading out to sea."

"Jesus fucking Christ!" Zehner shouted. "What happened to the Goddamn topside watch?"

"He's gone sir, and there was not a distress call from him about any hijacking. I've just requested a company of Marines to the Sub Base; to guard the other four submarines tied up at the other piers."

"What weapons are still aboard, Sullivan?"

"All of them, sir, including the two dolphins waiting in the hangar compartment. She moored at 2100 hours last night, finishing a full combat patrol. We don't offload weapons or dolphins at night so she still has her torpedoes and the full complement of Tomahawk missiles—there are at least 12 aboard sir. They were scheduled to be offloaded at 0800 hours this morning."

"Okay, so now you are saying, we have a *fully armed* nuclear sub on its way to sea with no clue who is inside, is that correct?"

"That about sums it up."

"Wonderful, absolutely fucking wonderful. Are there any surface craft available to block the Pearl entrance? Any AEGIS cruisers off the coast, any ASW nuke subs lurking near Oahu?"

"Nothing, Harris, nothing but the guided missile cruiser, the *Stout*. The *Gravely* is still tied up at the pier. Not enough time to move the *Stout* in front of the *Monterey*, but we'll have her underway in pursuit ASAP. She's already outside the channel. The nearest ASW[7] nuke boat is 400 miles to the north—we're diverting it with her next satellite download. If we're going to find them, we gotta deal with the challenges of joining Pearl with Hickam Air Base where they can launch C-17's, Raptors and every other useless piece of crap in-between."

"Great, *Hickam*. Now, I gotta call the Air Force for a *Navy* problem outside Pearl Harbor, wonderful. Do you have any CCTV videos of the pier?"

"Yes, sir, they're working on getting them available," Sullivan said, "By the way there were three cars being ticketed next to the mooring spot…and the OOD has just confirmed that the three cars parked near the mooring spot belonged to Chief Jack Olsen, a SEAL attached to the *Monterey*, and to one of the boat's reactor operators, petty officer first class Brian Robinson. The third car is the captain's

Corvette. None of the men has a wife or local family and right now, we don't know where the hell they are. We need to presume they are aboard and perhaps commandeered the topside watch, we have to presume they hijacked the boat, possibly with a forward watchstander or two onboard."

"Presume nothing, Sullivan, PRESUME NOTHING!" Zehner roared. "You think a SEAL and a nuke took over the boat? And the *captain* took his own boat? That makes no sense. Muster the goddamn crew, get everybody you can find at the pier no later than 0600 hours. We need to notify the FBI, the NSA, and the Goddamn CIA, see if there's any jihadist links to another terrorist agenda. We have to notify Admiral Kent and the CNO. We need an accounting of every man on that boat. I'm going to launch an emergency scramble of whatever surface craft is available at Hickam to stop them and I'm scheduling an emergency COMSUBPAC meeting at 0700 hours. Be there, and be prepared to account for every single sailor on that submarine."

Without waiting for an answer, the admiral punched the phone off and with a sweating index finger, he began punching in the telephone number of the Pearl Harbor OOD. After that, he knew, would be the painful call to the commanding officer of the Pacific Air Forces at Hickam to see if the base has anything that can get into the air and chase submarines. Then there will be a call to COMPACFLT[8] Admiral Stephen Kent, then from him to the Chief of Naval Operations in Washington, and from there everybody would be joined, as they ascended up the *fucking* vortex to oblivion, to the Chairman of the Joint Chiefs of Staff and finally to the President of the United States. Finally, jumping into the black hole with all the rest of the universe would be the entire State Department, the National Security Agency, both houses of Congress, and then every Goddamn reporter in the United States, starting with the communists at CNN.

And, since they didn't stop the submarine before it was outside Pearl, every other major power in the world, starting with China, will become very, very interested in the location of the errant nuclear submarine, USS *Monterey.*

With the treadmill turned off, the room became stunningly silent. A single drop of sweat from his forehead landed directly in the middle of his telephone screen and slowly ran down to the base. He cursed and continued punching in numbers until the connection began to ring.

As the OOD answered the telephone, Vice Admiral Harris Zehner knew this was going to be a very bad morning and one holy hell of a miserable day.

USS *Monterey*, Pacific Ocean

With her thundering diesel powering her out of the waters of the Pearl Harbor channel, the USS *Monterey* moved through Mamala Bay off the western shore of Oahu, submerged and running steady at 200 feet below the surface. Petty Officer Brian Robinson had just completed the fastest nuclear reactor startup in the history of submarine nuclear operations, Manny Munroe had happily shut down the thundering diesel engine after sending the incoming steam to the turbogenerators and propulsion turbines. In the control room at the center of the *Monterey,* Bodine stared at the fathometer attached to the ballast control panel; the boat had now moved beyond the coral reefs of the harbor and the ocean bottom began to rapidly and gratifyingly drop away. Chief Berry had flipped the lever to drop the port periscope as they moved deeper beneath the surface after intense scanning of the lights around the congested waters off Oahu.

"Fathometer reading?" Moore asked the helmsman as he approached the periscope station. Behind him, the hulking figure of Chainsaw led the sulking Amanda in the direction of the bow compartment.

"Three hundred, sixty-four feet and dropping away below us, sir." Bodine immediately answered from the port side of the control center.

"If we can speed up, sir, we'll be moving off the Lanai Shelf in the next ten minutes." Berry reported from the starboard T8 Mod 3 periscope shell. "Infrared display shows the harbor patrol boats are gone."

"Probably retreated back inside Pearl Harbor now," Moore said, smiling. "Kind of difficult for a patrol boat to chase a submerged submarine in the dark."

"Patrol boats don't do well in the open ocean, looking for a submarine in the dark," Chief Berry said, smiling back. "I would guess those boys are quite pissed but not giving up, sir. Do you want us to hold at 200 feet, sir? We're moving well beyond the reef now."

"Make our depth 400 feet, chief, and we'll hold steady there. Passive sonar showing anything?

"Two of the SEALs, Silverback and Jumpin' Jack, are on the sonar headsets, along with the Doc, nothing out there, sir," Berry said.

"Very well," Moore said, turning to move forward and out of the submarine's control room. "Chief, start rotating the watch, get Petty Officer Wilson out of the bow compartment and put him on watch. Maybe get some relief for Bodine here, he's had a long night, rotate with the sonarman and the Doc."

"Aye, aye, sir," Berry said as he watched his captain move down the forward passageway and finally into his stateroom.

Closing the small door behind him, Gary Moore felt the deep aching of advancing fatigue as he realized there was nothing else left for him to do. The three enlisted men in the engine room were rotating their watch stations, allowing them some increments of sleep sandwiched into their long hours ahead on watch. The other men would soon settle into their watch station responsibilities with the routine that always accompanied submarine duty time at sea. For the captain, there never could be complete relaxation and peace. Everything that happened on the submarine, from the turbogenerators in the engine room to Amanda Peterson's angst in the bow compartment, everything came back to the captain who was, *always*, responsible for the consequences.

The *Monterey* was free from her pursuers and the boat was now well on her way into the massive expanses of the Pacific Ocean. There was more search activity to come, he strongly suspected, but for now, they were clear of the initial efforts to stop them. Moore enjoyed his unique privacy in the submarine…the only man on the boat who slept in a cramped bunk not surrounded by other men. The humble compartment was an area of escape for him, the *only* area of escape for the Commanding Officer, an area where the burdens of command could be mentally processed as they often weighed heavily, where he could reflect on the decisions affecting the submarine, the crew, and matters of survival. Now, on this mission, this final mission of his life, he knew, there were eleven people who were counting on his decisions for their success. A small crew, to be sure, with just three nukes in the engine room, three SEALs, a last-minute volunteer Doc, his ever-faithful Chief of the Boat, a topside watch serving penance for allowing Amanda aboard, a trapped torpedoman also serving penance for hosting Amanda, and the feisty and hostile Amanda herself. Ten men and a woman, a crew assembled under remarkable circumstances for only one purpose, with one goal. Unlike the *Monterey's* Indonesia debacle and failure of their recent mission, a debacle that had killed two Americans on foreign soil while putting all their lives at risk, this mission must succeed and could not be diminished by any bureaucratic government agency.

He sat on the thin mattress spanning the length of his small rack; he rubbed his eyes, feeling the weight of fatigue that diminished the clarity of his mind, pushing him down to sleep. With the adrenaline fading and the voyage to the other side of the world now well underway, with the specifics of the mission yet to be clarified and the intelligence yet to be downloaded, he felt the aching exhaustion spreading through his bones, a pleading from his body for some rest.

It had now been more than two days since any meaningful sleep, and Moore knew that his performance would soon be affected if he didn't doze off for an hour or two.

He stood up and washed his face in the small metal sink, watching the water swirl down and out of the steel drain. He dried himself, looking into the small metal mirror at his aging skin, the lines below his eyes--the very timeline for his life that had been passing so quickly and that had changed so suddenly with the loss of sweet Meredith, his loving wife of fifteen years. He raised his eyes and there she was, just above the mirror. It was a small picture, a photograph of his wife sitting with him on the park bench, their little 9-year-old Caroline playing on the grass in front of them. The picture had been taken by Caroline's Aunt Marcy, four years before the pancreatic cancer had developed and Moore had immediately put a copy into a golden frame. They were happy in the picture, all three of them, his wife, Meredith, smiling at their daughter whose face was animated by the rabbit she had just seen.

It was a time for them before the next patrol when there seemed to be not a single worry in the world. It was a *perfection time*, Meredith had said, using her favorite phrase to describe a time without problems. It was a time that contrasted so profoundly with the circumstances of the current mission, the chase to the other side of the world to accomplish something nearly impossible. Moore felt a painful and distant aching in his mind to return to the time forever vanished, *if only for a day,* to enjoy the *perfection time* with his departed wife that was never so great as it had become…when it was gone.

She had died almost exactly twelve years before, when their daughter Caroline was an eager teenager of only thirteen years. Meredith's symptoms had started as an aching in her abdomen, unusual for somebody of such excellent health, and they had made efforts with antacids and changing diets to make it go away. Nothing had worked and she finally made an appearance at the dependents' clinic. The doctor had pressed on her slender abdomen, mumbled something to himself, and checked some blood studies. Two days later on one blustery afternoon, he called to ask her to come back to the clinic "for just one quick look again." Moore had been out to sea that day, as the executive officer aboard the USS *Los Angeles*, and had come back to their home in the late evening to find her crying quietly by herself in the kitchen. The echo was "suspicious," the doctor had said, the chemistry of the blood was "worrisome," but the examination was "inconclusive," leading to more tests.

The CAT scan followed two days later, the biopsy then followed immediately, and the diagnosis of pancreatic cancer became certain. Radiation was followed by a cursing grinding unrelenting pain, a deepening jaundice, and a vicious weight loss from the rapid spread of her metastatic disease, the carcinoma ravaging her thin body with spider-like tentacles that spread through her abdomen. She finally moved down the short and tortuous path to the ending of her life, a path that took her from Tripler Army Hospital finally to the Moanalua Mortuary.

And then, in the worst day of grief Moore had ever known, the body of Meredith had been carried in the Cadillac hearse during a remarkably powerful rainstorm, down the hill to the final resting place at the Nuuanu Memorial Park in Honolulu.

He had tried to shield his daughter from much of the suffering, but her mother's lifespan of only three months after the diagnosis left the need for Caroline's regular and continuous presence at her bedside in the precious little time that was left. Her mother was a woman with vibrant beauty and warm love, a strong woman, trying to survive as she had watched herself rapidly progress down her painful mortality pathway. And during all this time, Caroline had understood that, as her mother suffered so did her father, as he took humanitarian leave from the Navy to be with her as much as possible.

Each day had continued to unravel Meredith's life, like an unrelenting nightmare for both Moore and Caroline, until that final day when her life had ended with a whimper as she clutched their hands. And just three days later they both stood at the gravesite staring in silence at the *larger* tombstone, the one next to the small tombstone placed in the ground four years before, the tombstones with the engravings of their love. To Moore's surprise, it was his daughter who was the stronger through most of those days, and yet when Caroline became overwhelmed with the tragedy of her mother's demise, it was Moore who helped keep her from completely dissolving.

Caroline had taken her father's hand as they stood in front of the gravesites on that terrible and final day, watching the flowers bend in the gusting winds of Oahu, the overwhelming loss magnifying the bond between father and daughter with an intensity beyond understanding. The thirteen year-old-girl seemed to immediately grow into a young woman, right then and at that very moment, with a maturity far beyond anybody in her school. This maturity in the arms of the tragedy threw her into a sudden new life without her mother, her mind advancing to that of a grown woman long before her body caught up.

Continuing in school while living with her doting Aunt Marcy, on the other side of San Diego, Caroline had moved on with her life in the home of the only relative who could fill in for the loss of her mother. Her father visited her when he could as the demands of the submarine scheduling so often required him to disappear at sea for so many days, weeks, and months. The Daddy-dates she had loved to take with him since elementary school continued on increasingly rare occasions during those years, but she was no longer embarrassed to be seen by her friends going to a local movie or restaurant with her father. They had talked about everything from boys to sex, from God to pregnancy, from drugs to life itself, and as she further matured and began to date high school boys, his guidance about standards became her template for life and human relationships.

Kind Marcy stepped in when she was needed, the kind woman who told Caroline she could help the father who had to turn away from the tragedies that filled his own life, the father who increasingly took refuge over the horizon and beneath the sea. She recognized and understood that Captain Gary Moore had become, by the death of his wife, a patriot submariner excelling far beyond just being a father in his daughter's life. He became a man who would never relinquish his responsibilities to his country, no matter the compelling issues of the heart, a driven man of extraordinary competence who broke every record for outstanding command performance in the submarine navy.

The increasingly independent Caroline then also excelled, with the straight A's of high school continuing during her four years at Princeton. And, it was at Princeton that she met thirty-four year-old Peter Blackwell at the corporate headquarters of his company. She had been on a simple post-grad assignment, a quick trip to Seattle for a term paper about a computer project. On the corporate tour, she was able to interview the company's upper level management, and Blackwell was the man, she soon learned, with the interesting background. He had attended Princeton as well, but for reasons of excessive youthful exuberance, he had been kicked out a decade before, frustrating his father's efforts to elevate him with the company. And yet with hard work and determination in the years that had followed, he finally completed his degree in business finance and moved back into his father's good graces.

After some hesitation, Blackwell had ended the enhanced student tour with a request for her to join him for dinner that night, which was then followed by another invitation for the next night, and again the night after. And, during a flurry of trips between Seattle and New Jersey, they had fallen deeply in love. In an unexplained miracle of fortunate timing, Captain Moore was able to give Caroline's hand to Peter at the Four Seasons Resort on the Hawaiian Island of Lanai between submarine patrols, and it was, everybody agreed, a most lavish wedding.

The quiet "I love you, Daddy," she had whispered into his ear, before moving into the arms of her new husband, stayed with him as the newly married couple cruised away to the Island of Kauai for their two-week honeymoon. When Peter could take a break from his work, the newlyweds then traveled extravagantly across the world, often on the *Sweet Caroline,* staying on the boat or in fine resorts, seeking new adventures and excitement as the software company thrived at home. In the next year, or maybe two at the most, Caroline had confided at their last Daddy-Date in a quiet Seattle restaurant, her father could expect that a grandchild might soon become an addition to the family.

And so now, without Caroline, there was really nobody left in the world for Moore.

He sat on the edge of his rack again, and then he stood and opened the bunk locker under his bed. Tucked behind the uniforms, the books, and the papers that seemed to control his life, was the magnificent *package*. It was thin, wrapped in plain white paper and tied with golden string. Inside the wrapping were the letters, all she had ever written to him, beginning after the death of her mother during the painful years in junior high school and high school, and then later as she moved east to Princeton for her four years in college. He carefully, almost reverently, untied the string, opened the paper holding the treasures within, and pulled out the first one, the one Caroline had written when she was just thirteen years old, now yellowed with age and faded with time.

It is not going so badly, Daddy, and I want you to know I am doing what you said. I am working to keep my grades up, Aunt Marcy is being very nice to me, and I am making new friends in school. I miss Mommy every day but I am able to stop thinking about her most of the time now, especially when we play soccer and during my piano lessons. I am also able to sleep okay, now, as I'm learning to turn off my mind at night—that was always the hardest time right after Mommy left us and I wish you could tuck me in like you did when we were all together. The really good news though is the piano recital Saturday night at the school auditorium went really good and I didn't get into a panic like I sometimes do when there is too much pressure. I wasn't really sure how well I had done with that Italian piece, Canzonetta, right after I finished, because the auditorium was silent. For about two seconds! Then everybody began clapping really loud, then they stood up and everybody kept clapping. It was kind of embarrassing because they just kept on clapping. I stood up and bowed a couple of times and then they clapped some more! Anyway, Mrs. Westwick, my piano teacher, was really happy and so now I am really happy too, except for your not being able to be there. I know you were at sea working on your submarine and becoming some kind of special officer, I think you said an Executive Officer?

I really missed you Saturday, but I understand and I know you really wanted to be there for the performance. I hope everything is okay with you and that you are safe under the ocean.

Now you are up to date. I love you so much.

Caroline

Chapter 3

Submarine Command Headquarters, Pearl Harbor

Before the morning sun rose above the shadows of the Waahila Ridge on Oahu's Mt. Olympus, three black United States Navy cars squealed into the parking lot in front of the COMSUBPAC headquarters building on Morton Street, several blocks from the pier that had welcomed the *Monterey* the night before. The headquarters was a tight cluster of offices packed with electronic systems that underscored their importance in the coordination of submarine activities throughout the Pacific Ocean. A Marine guard at the entrance snapped a salute as five men climbed from the cars and quickly flashed their identification. Led by Admiral Zehner, with Admiral Sullivan, Lieutenant Commander Martin Cooper, and two enlisted men rapidly following closely behind, they entered the building and briskly walked past empty secretary stations to Zehner's office at the end of the central corridor.

"This is Petty Officer Gary Smith from Naval Intelligence," Zehner growled, gesturing toward a short bespeckled man walking to the end of the table where an array of computer instrumentation awaited. Zehner narrowed his eyes and crossed his arms like a man tightly controlling an internal rage while Admiral Sullivan and the other men sat down around the table.

"Petty Officer Smith here has the CCTV recordings of the *Monterey* pier activity from last night and earlier this morning," Zehner said, looking at Admiral Sullivan and waving in the direction of the other two men. "Sully, you know the OOD at the Control Tower, Lt. Commander Cooper, and finally, this is Petty Officer Gene Broadman, the Yeoman with the Pearl Harbor records office holding the data on ingress and egress from the submarine base. Broadman, you got all the records from last night?"

"Yes, sir," a tall and deeply-tanned man in a second-class petty officer's sailor uniform answered quickly. "I got 'em all, including that woman."

Zehner turned to Smith. "Smith, link up your computer devices and get the pictures out here on the screen!"

"Yes, sir," Smith said, adjusting small round eyeglasses and opening his briefcase. He pulled five chips and connectors from the case and jammed the first one into a computer receptacle at the end of the table. An instant later, a large screen at the far wall of the room displayed a huge high-pixel electronic picture of a pier at night with a large nuclear submarine secured to the dark pilings with thick white ropes. As Zehner stood against the wall glaring at the screen, the picture quickly changed to a moving scene, showing a car occasionally passing by on nearby Hunter Street.

"This is the submarine base, Southeast Loch, and here is the topside watch standing there next to the *Monterey*," Smith said, looking at the screen that displayed a sailor with a pistol strapped on his hip, walking out of a small guard shack at the foot of the submarine gangway and wandering back and forth alongside the pier. "This was at 0017 hours, just after midnight."

"And that sailor would be Billy Bodine," Admiral Sullivan added. "He had the topside midwatch on the Monterey."

"Here comes the bad part," Smith said, rolling a wheel on the computer mouse, rapidly advancing the display. An older model Chevrolet pulled up in front of the guard shack and a sailor climbed out of the driver's seat, immediately followed by a blonde woman emerging from the passenger's side, wearing a Hawaiian blouse and shorts.

"Who the fuck is that?" Zehner asked, his booming voice reverberating off the wall as the men leaned forward to watch. The video displayed the topside watch walking up to the car's occupants and beginning a conversation.

"According to our records," Broadman said, "that is Petty Officer Cory Noonez, the military escort for the woman who calls herself Amanda Peterson. She came onto the base at around midnight and she wrote the purpose of her visit was to see her fiancée aboard the submarine *Monterey*."

"So, Noonez, Bodine, and this floozy are having a meeting next to the *Monterey*?" Cooper mumbled. "At least she's being escorted.... Oh shit," he added as the military escort jumped back into his car and accelerated away from the pier.

"That is a court martial event!" Sullivan exclaimed. "The escort is supposed to stay with his...."

"I want that Petty Officer Cory Noonez up for a Captain's Mast[9] no later than this morning!" Zehner roared.

The screen showed Bodine and the woman walking across the gangway onto the topside deck of the *Monterey,* and then over to the forward hatch dropping down into the boat.

"Somebody should be coming up to escort her through the boat, so at least she'll have an escort while she's on the boat…" Sullivan began, as a sailor popped out of the hatch. "There he is, who's *that*?"

Gene Broadman popped up his hand. "Again, sir, from our records, she came to the boat to see the *Monterey's* torpedoman, Fred Wilson, apparently standing his below decks watch that night. This guy who just popped out of the hatch is probably torpedoman Wilson. The Peterson woman had filled out his name on the sign-in sheet at the Main Gate when she entered Pearl Harbor."

The five men watched silently as Fred Wilson gave Amanda a ten-second kiss and guided her into the hatch, both of them disappearing down into the submarine. Bodine returned back to his guard shack area and again began strolling up and down the pier, guarding the submarine.

"Well, that is just fucking great, they *love* each other!" Zehner said. "Now we got a woman with no security clearance whatsoever, shacking up inside a Love Boat top secret nuclear submarine with her horny torpedoman…"

"Who's just come back from being out to sea for more than two months," Cooper said, shaking his head.

Sullivan glared at the OOD. "It comes with the territory, Cooper, for those of us who go to sea."

"It gets worse," Smith said, shuffling his stack of papers in front of him. "Much worse. Over at the Main Gate yeoman's office, I did a Google search on the Peterson woman after the submarine disappeared and discovered she's a student at the University of Hawaii, here from her home in Texas, now living in a dorm on the university campus." He turned and looked meekly at Admiral Zehner. "Sir, it may mean nothing, but from her Facebook entries, her roommate in that dorm is a woman named Ashia Jamila, a foreign exchange student from Iran on a student visa."

The room became completely silent and Admiral Sullivan heard the faint sounds of hyperventilation from Zehner behind him.

After a full ten seconds of silence, Zehner exploded, "Goddammit, Smith, speed up that YouTube or MP3 or whatever the fuck it is! And, when we finish, I want that Amanda Peterson's parents in Texas on the line and I want to dig out every subversive comment or action ever recorded on social media from this Middle East alien Asha Jamie or whatever her Goddamn name is!"

"Yes, sir," Smith said. "However, sir, I should point out that Amanda Peterson never did leave the boat…she came onto the boat, she smooched her fiancée, she went below decks, and she is still on the *Monterey*, at sea. If we call the family in Texas, sir, they will go bonkers, she will be declared officially missing, there will be a search, and all of that will hit the press, probably immediately." He held up his hands indicating quote marks as he envisioned the headline. "Missing Coed Trapped on Nuclear Submarine."

"Goddammit!" Zehner roared.

"Smith, move ahead with the recording," Sullivan said quietly. "What's next?"

Five minutes later, the recording accelerated to the rapid approach of a Corvette.

"That's the captain's car, Commander Gary Moore," Sullivan said. "Maybe he got the word about Amanda and is going to raise some hell on the boat."

"No, sir," Gary Smith said respectfully. "That would be nice but I already checked this out. It's going to get really weird, I couldn't believe this when I first saw it. The captain just salutes and then basically ignores the topside watch, immediately after which a man wearing a straw hat comes walking up out of the night to the pier. He chats with the captain and then *both men* cross the gangway and go down into the boat. Unbelievable!"

"The 'gangway'?" Zehner hollered. "You mean *the brow*?"

"Yes, sir, that's what I meant," Cooper said. "There he is!" he exclaimed as he pointed out a tall Black sailor with a straw hat walking up and intersecting with the captain.

"That's Doc Alan Wheat, the boat's hospital corpsman—he always wears that straw hat," Sullivan said. "What are they talking about? Is somebody sick on the boat?"

"Nobody's sick on the Goddamn boat!" Zehner exploded. "If anybody was sick, they'd be sent to Tripler Hospital or the base dispensary, or *somewhere else*! They wouldn't have a straw-hat-sailor come wandering onto the submarine at two o'clock in the fucking morning!"

Gary Smith glanced at the admiral. "Actually, sir, I think Doc Wheat just volunteered for the mission, for whatever it is they're doing," Sullivan said softly and turning in his chair to look at Zehner. "He probably heard some scuttlebutt about it and he's talking the skipper into letting him come along."

"Each of these guys is destroying his Goddamn career, Sully! Why the hell would they do this?"

At that moment, the screen showed a dark brown Jeep accelerating up to the pier and park immediately next to the Corvette.

"Now, who in hell is this?" Zehner said.

"SEALs, sir, SEALs" Smith said, advancing the display. "The *Monterey's* three SEALs, sir, and each of them willingly walked aboard."

"Correction," Sullivan interjected. "These are three *of six* SEALs currently assigned to the *Monterey.* There *were* eight SEALs, two were killed during its recent mission—the rest of the story is code-word classified."

Zehner nodded quickly and crossed his arms across his chest as they watched the SEALs gather their bags and walk onto the submarine. A moment later, a '57 Chevy pulled up, parked next to the Jeep, and two more men climbed out.

"We're working on the facial ID of these guys," Smith said. "The computer says they're probably petty officers Brian Robinson and Manny Munroe."

"Two nukes," Sullivan said. "A reactor operator and a machinist. The third nuke, the electrician Jules Baxter, was already aboard. That gives them three nukes, enough to run the entire nuclear plant if nobody hardly ever sleeps."

"Wonderful, now we're assembling a functional crew!" Zehner said. "What else ya got, Smith? Who takes the boat?"

"They *all* do, sir…."

"Jesus…."

The men watch as the SEALs and the man with the straw hat emerge on the submarine's deck and begin throwing the boat's mooring lines overboard. At the same moment, they see a cloud of black smoke surge out of the top of the sail as Chief Roy Berry climbs out of the hatch and strides toward the topside watch.

“That’s Chief Berry walking over to the topside watch, and they just lit off their diesel” Smith says, “Here’s the most remarkable part, coming up.”

“They’re talking with each other,” Sullivan said, “Why are they talking when Petty Officer Bodine already *knows* they’re casting off the lines!”

“Right about now,” Zehner yelled, “Bodine should pull out his fucking gun and start shooting them all! They’re stealing…”

“Sorry, sir,” Smith said, pointing at the screen. “Bodine doesn’t shoot anybody or call anybody on his radio! He actually *joins* them! He walks with the chief back onto the boat and they go below deck!”

“Holy Mother of God,” Zehner whispers to nobody in particular. “There they go…they go down into the boat, look at that! And the brow is pulling away from the pier and dropping into the fucking ocean!”

“Yes, sir,” Smith says. “They stow the lines and cast off the electrical cables, and then they all go below decks as the boat drops its brow into the harbor, then rotates, and finally disappears down the channel.”

The men at the table turned to look at Admiral Zehner who is angrily staring at the blank wall across the room.

“Sir?” Gene Broadman asked meekly. “Is there anything else that…”

“CLEAR THE ROOM!” Zehner hollered. “Except you, Sully, stay here.” He began waving his arms. “Everyone else, out, out, out!”

Smith, Broadman, and Cooper almost jumped out of their chairs and rushed from the room, looking relieved to escape. Zehner slowly walked around the table and sat down directly across from Admiral Sullivan, staring directly at the man. Sullivan looked back at him, waiting.

“We’ll be having a crew muster at 0600 at the pier…” Sullivan began.

“Where are we with the chase from the *Stout*?” Zehner asked quietly.

“Giving chase, sir, outside the channel now, giving chase.”

"They'll never catch them, Sully, you know that. Gary Moore is the best submarine skipper in the Navy. They're gone." He paused a few seconds, studying Sullivan's face. "Why?" he said softly.

Sullivan looked back at the man, thinking, and finally said, "Two things, Harris, that's all I can think of, two things."

Zehner stared at the man. "Go," he said quietly.

"The Dolphins Episode and the Indonesia mission, the one they just came back from…" Sullivan began.

"With two dead SEALs in the freezer, I know, Sully. Politics and the CIA came into…"

"Admiral, they didn't just bring dead SEALs back with them. They had brought the elite Special Warfare SEAL Team Six from the Joint Special Operations Command to the *Monterey* and to Indonesia for one particular reason. It would seem that they would have been allowed to finish their mission to take out the leaders of the Islamic insurrection in Indonesia. The Laskar Jihad movement is breeding across those Goddamn islands, the top jihadist, Jafar Thalib, is starting an Islamic theocracy…."

"I am aware of terrorism in Indonesia, Harris, I am aware of all that. But, now we know that Jafar Thalib had been starting an Islamic theocracy…"

"They were right there, Sully, the submarine was *right there in three thousand feet of water off the island*," Sullivan said with increasing intensity. "Thalib was right there in front of them, building his Islamic militia while the *Monterey* waited and was told to do nothing. We could have taken them all out! And while they waited, the submarine was vulnerable and the guys on the boat had to listen to some kind of Taliban deep water explosions going off every fifteen minutes." Sullivan leaned forward. "The crew sat out there, hearing the repetitive explosions, waiting for the SEALs to finish their Special Operation. And the SEALs knew exactly where he was, right there on the island where they could have fulfilled their mission," he said energetically. "Eight SEALs on the island, right up until…what was it? The CIA? Who lit off the whole thing *before they even got there*? The SEALs killed twenty of the Taliban and then they lost two of their own…they brought their bodies back to the boat and put them in the Goddamn freezer. And then they came home. The three SEALs who have disappeared in the *Monterey* were putting in non-vol chits, they were on their way out of the Navy, sir."

Zehner clenched his fists. "So, you think they're going back to West Papua? Going back to finish what the President, the SECNAV, the Chairman of the Joint…"

"Sir, why would they go back? Those men put their asses on the line and in the end, what they wanted to do didn't count for a goddamn thing. The CIA took over! All of that from all of them and *they never even got the go-ahead* order."

"Okay, maybe they're not going back to Indonesia, especially since the CIA has already eliminated the Jafar Thalib threat. You're friends with Captain Moore, Sully, since 'way back in the Academy days, you know him better than any of us. His entire career has been at the top of the game, Christ, a Battle Effectiveness E on his submarine's sail, two Presidential Unit Citations in his record, a silver star…." Zehner's voice dropped to barely a whisper. "Sully, where the fuck do you think they are going?"

"Admiral, I am quite certain that that crew is going wherever Gary Moore asks them to go. They are dedicated to whatever cause has entered the captain's mind, and the most dedicated of them all are the three SEALs and the three nukes."

"I got the SEALs! But, the three nukes? Dedicated enough to blow their careers, Sully? To risks their lives? You know, if they survive this, they'll all end up in Leavenworth for the duration…"

"Two of the three Nukes were at the end of their six years in the Navy. Baxter was the only lifer, but his wife had been driving him crazy, according to his fitness report. That said, for the SEALs and for the nukes, it was the Dolphins Episode on the *Gravely*, Admiral, about six months ago, that did it for them, on top of the debacle in Indonesia. After the Dolphins Episode, they would follow him *anywhere.* Do you remember what happened?"

Admiral Zehner looked thoughtful, and then slowly nodded.

It had been a covert undeclared mission in the dark of night at Pearl Harbor. The tiny rubber boat had moved slowly from the *Monterey* and across the black waters to the heavily-guarded USS *Gravely*, the guided missile destroyer, home to at least one admiral. As teams of Marines roamed the decks of the ship, on-guard for foreign invaders, the stealthy artistic talents of the submariners painted a 10-foot pair of golden submarine dolphins across her massive stern, shining brightly in the next morning sunlight as the captain had driven up to his flagship. One half-hour after sunrise, the entire crew of the *Monterey* had been mustered on the wharf in front of their submarine as the admiral from the *Gravely*, with the unfortunate name of Stucko, blasted Gary Moore who stood before them all with an unblinking stone-faced expression.

When the admiral finished his tirade and ran out of breath, Moore had spoken forcefully. "I will find the men responsible for this, Admiral Stucko," he had said, "they will be fined, they will be held accountable, and their service records will reflect this activity."

"And that will happen TODAY, captain?"

"Yes, SIR," Moore had said, snapping a sharp salute. "TODAY!"

And following that exchange, the admiral had spun around and stormed back to the *Gravely*, where a team of Marines had lowered themselves over the side for a 2-hour scrubbing removal of the insignia. Moore had turned to his crew, and doing everything he could to suppress a smile, had asked who might be responsible for graffiti such as a logo of the submarine service painted on the admiral's skimmer ship. The responsible men from the Monterey promptly raised their hands, including three nukes and three SEALs, they were each fined $500. One week later, when they had each opened the envelope containing their depleted paycheck, five $100 bills had been mysteriously attached to each check. And, during the months thereafter, nobody was able to discover any adverse reporting on any service record.

Soon the matter was forgotten to all except every submariner in Hawaii and at every submarine base around the world.

Speaking softly, Sullivan asked, "Harris, these guys just came back from hell. Two SEALs lost in action, our boat sitting there in the Indochina waters, exposed and waiting, the CIA intervening after this crew had risked their lives and were committed to what could have been successful." Sullivan narrowed his eyes, scrutinizing the senior officer. "I think, Admiral, this is the most pissed off crew in the history of the submarine service. I think, sir that it would be a very good idea, after our muster on the pier this morning, to bring the rest of whatever crew is remaining in Hawaii into the hands of a team of crack MD's for a full PTSD review. I believe there are some very unhinged minds here, sir."

Chapter 4

USS *Monterey*, Pacific Ocean

"Captain, we have high speed screws approaching, bearing 176 degrees relative." Berry's voice filled the stateroom, abruptly awakening Gary Moore from nearly an hour of deep sleep.

In an instant, the captain planted his feet on the floor and sat upright on his bunk, his mind alert, his senses engaged. The captain knew, the entire *Monterey* crew knew, they were being followed and that the search by the guided missile cruiser was underway. He reached over to the microphone clamped to the side of his desk and pressed the button.

"Engine room, this is the captain! Slow to four knots, do not cavitate the screws!" he ordered, seeking to stop the whirl of bubbles from high speed screws in the water, bubbles that collapse and create a crackling noise that can be heard for miles. He knew the *Stout* wasn't listening herself at that moment, no ship can listen while generating the "high speed screws" kind of noise. But the *Stout* had an ASW helicopter, and there was no way to know if it was now hovering over the waters ahead of the cruiser, microphone deep in the water, listening for submarine sounds beneath the seas.

He pressed the microphone to his mouth again after hearing the acknowledgement from Manny Munroe.

"Control, this is the captain, make our depth 800 feet, rig ship for deep submergence."

Chief Berry's voice immediately blared back, "800 feet, rig ship for deep submergence, aye, aye, captain!" Thirty seconds later, Gary Moore stood behind the ballast control panel, looking over the instrumentation as the submarine angled deeper into the ocean.

Chief Berry glanced at the captain. "Passive sonar, on the scanning array picked up the approaching ship, sir," he said, gesturing toward the sonar room where two SEALs were hunched over the panels, listening through their headsets. "Silverback and Jumpin' Jack are on sonar right now, tracking the bearings."

"That's the *Stout* out there," Moore said. "That Arleigh Burke AEGIS cruiser we passed on our way out of Pearl." "It's a Guided Missile Cruiser but the CO is, believe it or not, a junior officer, Commander Ralph Ginder, I know him. He's fresh up the ranks, trying to regain the ship's reputation after a disastrous five years of failures from their previous skipper—he's good, but he needs about five more years of salt. Chief, who is rigging the ship for deep submergence?"

"The Doc is doing most of the work, along with Fred Wilson, who has managed to break away from Amanda for a bit. Chainsaw is still up there in the bow compartment, keeping eyes on her…so to speak."

Moore scrutinized the two SEALs in the sonar room.

"Silverback! Frog!" he called, "one of you break away and man the sonar flank array and the spherical sonar. The COB will help you get it up and running. Do not go active with the sonar. We need to find a freighter, something making noise and heading west, anything, find it, and Berry will set the course after acquisition."

He abruptly departed the control center, moving forward through the watertight doors, walking briskly toward the bow compartment as he felt the ship angling further down, deeper into the ocean.

USS *Stout*, Pacific Ocean

On the bridge of the USS *Stout*, now ten miles away, Commander Ralph Ginder barked out his latest of a long string of orders to the men standing with him. He was a tall, thin man with a look of concentration on his youthful face, the intensity only slightly reduced by a remarkably rounded nose that looked like it had been transplanted from another face. His unfortunate drooping shoulders also detracted significantly from his desired demeanor of authoritative control. He straightened his back and peered into the dark waters ahead, as the sun slowly emerged behind him, from the east. In taking command of one of the most capable AEGIS Combat weapon vessels in the Navy, he had looked forward to this kind of chase his entire career—an honest-to-God real chase of a real nuclear submarine, aboard this fabulously complex ship complete with an antisubmarine helicopter and a Towed Array to be extended out behind the ship. And when they confirm the precise coordinates of that *rogue submarine*, Ginder thought, when they lock him into their electronic net, he can crank up his speed to the highest break-neck level possible, he can do *anything* he wants. That sub will not get away. He smiled, crinkling his strange nose, basking in the reality that he had an ASW helicopter, he had a Towed Array, he had the Navy's most advanced electronics systems for undersea surveillance, and he had the best-trained ASW crew in the United States Navy.

This will be a career-advancing exercise, he was sure of that.

"Slow to five knots," he ordered. "The Towed Array is deployed? How far out is the thing?" he asked, immediately answered by Adam Carter, the master chief on watch.

"Two point three kilometers, sir," the chief said, looking at the electronic information on the panel before him.

"Very well," Ginder said, quickly rubbing his nose with anticipation. "We've picked up his acoustic trail heading in the direction of that oiler, or whatever that is, ready to lock on. Launch the chopper."

"Launch the chopper, aye, aye, sir," Carter answered, leaning forward to his microphone communicating with the men standing by the SH-60 helicopter near the stern of the ship. One minute later, with enough noise to shake the windows at the front of the bridge, the black shape of the antisubmarine crown jewel thundered by and headed across the open ocean in the direction of the *Monterey*.

USS *Monterey*, Pacific Ocean

In the control center of the submarine, Bodine pulled back on the control wheel and leveled the *Monterey* at precisely 800 feet as Chief Berry quietly watched from behind. The helmsman reached over to the panel next to his diving station and flipped a switch, moving water through the boat with the trim pump, balancing the submarine precisely.

"That should keep her straight and level," Berry said to the young helmsman as Bodine turned back in his chair and adjusted the airplane-like steering wheel in his hands for precise depth control.

"Great, thanks," Bodine said. "I just got qualified on the boat four months ago and now I'm doing two jobs at once," he said, grinning broadly and pointing to the empty seat next to him. "Three months ago, I didn't even know how to spell Planesman, and now I *am* one!"

"Bodine, just watch your depth and we'll be fine."

At that moment the loud pinging sound of an acoustic challenge filled the control center, immediately followed by Frog's call from the sonar station.

"Captain, we're getting a sonar challenge, probably from the *Stout,* also now seeing the high speed screws from 187 degrees relative, starting to slow."

Moore heard the announcement as he reached the bow compartment. Pulling out the 7MC communications microphone, Moore replied, "Very well, sonar, continue to monitor."

Walking around clusters of huge torpedoes, Moore finally reached the torpedo tubes. Sitting on a bench at the side of the tubes, Amanda Peterson glared at the approaching man, then turned toward Chainsaw and scowled.

"This *Neanderthal* Mr. Chainsaw, hasn't moved for nearly a half hour," she complained as Chainsaw said nothing, watching her passively.

"Hello, Amanda," Moore said quietly. "I would like to ask a favor of you."

"YOU want to ask ME a favor?" she said, her eyes widening as her mouth dropped open. "Captain, are you *serious*? First, you kidnap me, then you imprison me under the ocean, and now *you* want a favor? Does it matter to you that I am getting *very claustrophobic*? And, do you care that when I tracked you down in the engine room, I passed a *voluminous* number of high radiation signs? *I am planning on having babies someday!"* She narrowed her eyes as she stared at Moore. "Finally, why should I do any favors for you?"

Moore met her gaze and after clenching his teeth for a moment, he finally said, "Mostly because your life depends on it."

She stared at him, waiting, and Moore continued. "I am going to need you to be absolutely quiet, do not drop or clang anything. They are looking for us, Amanda, but they are not trying to rescue you. If they find us, we will in all likelihood be attacked and sent to the bottom of the ocean."

"Jesus Christ, captain, what are…?"

"Second," he said, interrupting her and gesturing toward Chainsaw. "I am going to need Petty Officer Thor Ostrobothnia to help…"

"You mean Chainsaw?" she asked, looking back at the passive gaze of the SEAL.

Moore smiled quickly. "He almost never sleeps. But, when he does, he snores loudly, Amanda, kind of like a chainsaw. So his SEAL buddies labeled him 'Chainsaw' back in basic training in Coronado. The second SEAL is 'Silverback', he has gray hairs across his back.

"Good Lord."

"And to complete the story," Moore said, smiling again, the third SEAL is Jumpin' Jack Olson, or for short, 'Frog.' The word is that he outperformed his entire company of SEAL trainees, by jumping further than anybody during basic training. That's not too much information for you, is it?"

"Weird names, captain, thank you," she said, smiling.

"No question, but now you know the story behind the story of our SEALs. I am going to need Chainsaw to help with some valve lineups, Amanda. I will leave you free in the bow compartment, but please stay here and maintain complete silence."

"Free, like 'trapped' in the bow compartment? Thanks, at least Fred showed me how to work the toilet. *Jesus*, I never saw so many valves."

"You're welcome. We'll have a talk a bit later."

"I want off the submarine, captain," she said. After a moment and showing a slight trace of a smile, she added, "Fred snores also…but not too loud."

"I understand you want off the *Monterey*, Amanda. At this moment, we're currently 800 feet below the surface, but as soon as we're back on dry land, you're on your own."

"Okay, I accept that, where are we going?"

"I have work to do, Amanda, we'll talk later. Chainsaw, give Fred Wilson and the Doc a hand with the valve lineup."

"Yes, sir," Chainsaw responded immediately.

Moore beckoned for the SEAL to follow him, then turned and departed the compartment, Chainsaw following closely behind.

Two minutes later, they reached the control room where Berry informed him of a detected freighter ahead and to the South, a very large one with thundering screws. "From the ship's location," Berry said, "that would be the *Zaliv Amurskiy* if the logging of her departure from Honolulu is correct. Also, sir, the *Stout* is quiet now, she's listening."

"Very well," Moore said, glancing into the sonar room where the two SEALs continued to monitor the activity in the ocean. "The *Stout* has slowed to listen. She's probably already launched her ASW chopper. We'll be getting sonar hits soon, and we should pick up the screws of the *Zaliv Amurskiy* on her way to wherever she's going. Might as well give the *Stout* something to listen to. Send an active ranging ping at them."

Chief Berry, leaning over Frog's shoulder to watch the sonar screen abruptly stiffened and stared at Moore. "An *active* ping, sir? They'll pick it up and then they've got us."

"They already got us. Do it now, chief. They already have us if they're worth their salt, and I think they are," Moore answered. "Right now. I want them to know *exactly* where we are." He turned toward Bodine and ordered, "Ring up a new bell to the engine room--full speed ahead."

"Ranging ping shows the *Stout* is seventeen thousand yards and closing."

"Very well," the captain answered.

Bodine rang up a full speed order to the engine room, turning a knob next to his control wheel, and immediately the 7 MC loudspeaker blared, "Control, Maneuvering, we just got a full speed ahead bell, do you want us to cavitate?"[10]

Moore reached into the maze of cables and pipes above him and pulled down the microphone. "Cavitate! Cavitate! Make all the noise you want! Full speed ahead."

The entire submarine began to vibrate from the propulsion turbogenerators winding up to full speed, and a light above Bodine flashed red indicating the bubbles forming from the rapidly spinning screws were cavitating, generating a fresh cascade of sonar noise. Frog pulled off his sonar headset and turned his chair to look at Moore with a puzzled expression.

"I can't hear a damn thing but noise out there, captain," he said.

"Berry, can you launch an acoustic jammer from the signal tube, right now?" Moore asked. "We're going to give them some more noise."

"Yes, sir," the chief petty officer hollered as he ran over to the three-inch signal launching tube and fired the device into the ocean, creating a trail of intense sonar sound moving away from the *Monterey* .

"Making 44 knots," Bodine announced from his diving station, his eyes glued on the screen in front of him as the *Monterey* accelerated through the ocean. One small twitch on the control wheel, one movement forward or back, Bodine knew, and the *Monterey* would accelerate below her test depth or suddenly rise high enough to broach the surface, either a very bad idea.

"Steady as she goes," Moore said, looking at his watch. "Can anybody think of any way to make some more noise?"

"No, sir," Chief Berry said, his mustache twitching vigorously, his face showing increasing anxiety. "I think we are about as loud as any submarine can ever get."

"Great. Amanda may hear all the noise, let her know in another thirty seconds we rig for silent operations."

The *Monterey* continued thundering through the ocean as Moore waited and waited. He checked his watch a final time and suddenly hollered, "Bodine, make your depth 1000 feet, Chief of the Boat, confirm rigged for deep submergence, slow to five knots and do not cavitate. I need to hear SILENCE! Absolute silence!"

The men called back their orders and rapidly complied as the *Monterey*'s bow dropped down toward 1000 feet and her screws slowed to silence. Frog put on his sonar headset again, and with Berry reaching over his shoulder to adjust the sonar equipment, he suddenly sat upright. "Captain," he said, turning his chair to face Gary Moore at the periscope station. "We're picking up slow screws of the transport freighter, right…" He studied the screen in front of him. "Nearly right above us, sir."

Berry stood tall and smiled at the captain. "It's the oiler *Zaliv Amurskiy,* sir, just like you said."

"Correct, Chief, very good. And we're below what, three or four thermoclines[11] now, and *silent*? What is the heading of the *Zaliv Amurskiy*?"

"Looks like…." The chief turned more knobs, adjusting the sonar equipment to measure every quality of the ship nearly a quarter mile above them. "It appears to be bearing 274 degrees, sir."

"Very well," the captain answered. "Bodine, make our heading 180 degrees and stay rigged for silent operations for the next six hours. We're going to proceed *directly* away from its port side, under the layers." He looked at Silverback, watching the entire operation from the corner of the control center and said, "Silverback, would you head up to the bow compartment where our uninvited guest is, and inform her that if she makes a single detectable sound in the next six hours, she will *never* be allowed to leave this submarine?"

"Yes, sir, it will be my pleasure to tell her that," the SEAL answered with a big grin. "And on the way, captain, I will be sure not to slam the watertight doors."

"Thank you, Silverback, and I hope you can bring our guest an equal understanding about the big picture."

USS *Stout*, Pacific Ocean

On the surface of the ocean, now beginning to brighten with the dawn, the commanding officer of the USS *Stout* began to feel the warm glow of anticipation. Captain Ginder felt like a big game hunter, carrying his big game weapons, with the big game now moving into a trap from which there would be no escape. If the hunter's weapons were powerful enough, Ginder thought, and if the hunter was savvy enough, the outcome was assured. This submarine, manned by whoever had taken her, had shown some determination and that was good—who would ever want the object of the hunt just to lie down and give up; what fun was that? The captain of that rogue sub had tried to escape, even sending a noise generator to create an acoustic track that was immediately and solidly locked into the AEGIS computers. That, sure as hell, wasn't going to fool anybody. Besides, a submarine acoustic noise generator is supposed to divert incoming noise-homing torpedoes, not to confuse a modern AEGIS cruiser. Furthermore, *Stout* wasn't going to send any torpedoes in the submarine's direction, that was for damn sure—his orders had been to acquire and lock down the sub, not to sink her. Now, with her diesel generator shut off, she was almost certainly running on her small batteries, a short-lived process to be sure. Ginder rubbed his nose again with satisfaction and smiled.

It was now a waiting game, and the commanding officer of the USS *Stout* knew with certainty who could wait the longest.

Ginder looked through the windows of the bridge at the sea ahead. Now there is this big surface ship, he thought, a noisemaker itself, an acoustic barrier under which the prey thought he could hide…let the waiting game begin.

"Submarine signature now merging with the *Zaliv Amurskiy*, captain," Master Chief Adam Carter called out from the port side of the bridge.

"Very well," Ginder replied with enthusiasm. "Report on the *Zaliv Amurskiy*, chief, what is it?"

"Big sucker, crude oil tanker," Carter said. "Out of Honolulu, can make 15 knots, length 800 feet, tonnage deadweight 104,000 tons, enroute Singapore. Currently 31 miles out by GPS from mean low tide shore, Oahu."

"Very well. Bring them up on the radio, I want them stopped now."

Captain Ginder glanced at his data sheet and grabbed the microphone off the instrument panel spanning the bridge. He clicked in the maritime frequency and hollered, "Five Bravo Echo Victor Two. Do you read me?"

Immediately, the loudspeaker in the overhead blared, "This is the *Zaliv Amurskiy*, hear you loud and clear."

"This is the United States Warship *Stout*, request you stand-down. I repeat, stand-down, come to all stop."

"Negative," the voice answered. "We are in international waters. You do not have jurisdiction over this vessel."

Ginder squeezed the microphone switch again, aware that his hand was sweating profusely. "*Zaliv Amurskiy*, this is a request, and only a request. We have a nuclear submarine directly beneath you with an emergency, and we need it to surface. The *Stout* is requesting that you come to all stop. This is an international emergency and the lives on that submarine are threatened."

"Roger that, *Stout*. Will comply. Throttling back to all stop."

"Thank you, sir," Ginder radioed. "Stand by for more information."

The churning white water behind the freighter began to calm as the ship slowed its engines, and over the next seven minutes, the freighter came to a complete halt in the ocean. From the bridge of the oil tanker, the Greek captain and his first mate looked out the window, watching the guided missile cruiser approaching their starboard flank and the helicopter circling their ship. In the distance, on the horizon in the direction of Oahu, three more military helicopters from the Pearl Harbor area could be seen approaching the ship. Five hundred yards in front of the freighter, the helicopter from the *Stout* hovered over the ocean, and rapidly lowered two microphones into the water.

On the bridge of the *Stout*, Chief Carter listened carefully to the speakers in his headset and finally turned to the captain.

"Captain," he said. "The ocean is silent except for the whales and the fish. No sign of the *Monterey*."

Commander Ralph Ginder looked at his chief and then out the window at the huge shape of the *Zaliv Amurskiy,* lying dead in the water in front of their cruiser. He remained silent for nearly a half minute, deep in thought. He finally smiled and turned to Chief Carter.

"No, chief," he said. "The *Monterey* cannot just 'vanish' like that. Submarines don't just 'vanish' out of the ocean. It is right there, it *has to be* sitting right there, under this Goddamn rusted oil bucket. It is there, we heard it, its engines are idling, and we're all going to just wait for it to drain its battery, to surface, and then to surrender to the United States *surface* Navy. At that point, chief, at that point they will have surrendered, we will have them, and it will be done."

Pearl Harbor, Submarine Base, Southeast Loch

The submarine pier where the *Monterey* had been moored six hours before, COMSUBRON Rear Admiral Sully Sullivan and COMSUBPAC Vice Admiral Harris Zehner stood in front of a group of sixty-four very unhappy sailors. Some of the men wore dungarees, several were in Hawaiian civilian clothes, and only the executive officer, Lt. Commander William Smithers, stood out. Wearing a crisp white Naval officer's uniform, his gold dolphins in prominent display above his left breast pocket, his officer's hat in its precise proper position, the man stood stiffly at attention next to the lounging sailors, ignoring their grumbling and grousing. Thirty feet away, four black Navy cars had parked near the empty pier, and a group of officers stood by, watching the men.

Zehner's face scowled as he surveyed the men gathered before them. "Where the hell is everybody?" Zehner grumbled, glancing at his watch. "It's 0600 hours and thirty per cent of the crew is missing."

“They are the single guys,” Sullivan said. “Most of these men are married, Harris, they’ve all been at sea for the past two and a half months. We found most of them at home with their wives about 0500 hours this morning, and we ordered them here. We were banging on a lot of doors, they’re pretty pissed, to say the least. Their wives are also pissed, their kids are pissed, *everybody’s* pissed.”

“They are not *one-tenth* as pissed as I am, Sully. Where are the others who were not with their wives?”

“We couldn’t find ‘em yet. Probably somewhere in Waikiki or…”

“Waikiki or *somewhere*, got it.” Zehner’s eyes narrowed as he surveyed two sailors in rumpled civilian clothes staggering slowly down the pier, both of them obviously intoxicated as they navigated around the Dempsey Dumpster and the three cars still parked illegally on the pier. As one of them broke away to the edge of the pier to vomit into the ocean, William Smithers glared at the man with obvious disgust. At the corner of the gathering of men, three SEALs stood quietly in camouflage clothing, waiting for somebody to say something.

Sullivan looked at his watch. “Should we give the crew another five minutes?”

“Hell, no,” Zehner said. He walked over to stand directly in front of the men.

As Sullivan stood next to the admiral, Zehner cleared his throat and began to speak. “I know it’s early,” he said loudly, “and I know many of you have been abruptly awakened. I am sorry about that. Does any man here know what your submarine’s destination might be?” he asked.

After ten seconds of silence, he spoke again. “Does anybody know why your commanding officer, Commander Gary Moore, your engine room nuke, Petty Officer Brian Robinson or the Navy SEAL, Petty Officer Jack Olsen, left their cars here last night? Do you know what they did *before* they drove here last night, who they might have been talking with?”

After another prolonged silence, the admiral asked, “Okay, what about your COB? Anybody know what your Chief of the Boat…” he glanced at Sullivan.

“Berry,” Sullivan quickly said under his breath.

“What your COB, Berry, might be involved with?”

Several men looked at each other, a couple of them shrugged, and one of the men, a short balding man said, "We don't know what they are doing, admiral," he gestured behind him at the empty pier, "but could you tell us where our boat is?"

"Gentlemen, if I knew where your boat was, I would probably know where everyone else is, and we wouldn't be standing here right now! For your information, we may have its position pinpointed, about thirty miles off the coast, and we are waiting for it to surface. Do any of you know anything about any plan to move the *Monterey* to any other location?"

Silence.

"Okay, does any man here have any knowledge of anybody coming aboard the *Monterey* after your ship arrived at the submarine base last night?"

William Smithers raised his hand. "Go ahead, Mr. Smithers," Sullivan said.

"Sir, I'm not sure where the *Monterey* is or where any of the other men who assigned to this submarine have gone, but I can say there was some…uh…dissatisfaction after our last patrol."

"What was the problem, Mr. Smithers?" Zehner shot back.

"Well sir, several men didn't want to follow the orders we had from command regarding our special operations activities. They had other ideas and were not happy about the failed mission. I believe the captain was preparing a report about this." He hesitated a moment, and quickly added, "Sir."

"Okay," Zehner said loudly, ignoring the comments from the executive officer. "This pier is now a crime scene, and those men over there are from the NCIS, the Naval Criminal Investigative Service. They're going to be joined by the FBI and the NSA, and they are going to be interrogating each one of you. If any one of you has any information and refuses to divulge it to the investigating officers, you will be prosecuted under the UCMJ for being unforthcoming, concealing evidence, and impeding a formal military inquiry."

He paused while a sailor with crumpled whites and a sour expression on his face wandered down from the parking lot, looking as if he was lost, and finally joined the other men.

"Each of you will be interviewed. The remaining crew will be located and interrogated as well. You are ordered to remain in the barracks, or for those of you who are married, you are ordered to remain at home, and you are to see nobody else. You are ordered to not speak with the press. You are ordered to leave your computers turned off, to not discuss this problem about the *Monterey* with anybody, by telephone, by computer or by any other means—this incident is now classified as top secret and anybody breaking this order will be imprisoned in the brig at Pearl. Any of you holding orders to any other submarines or other duty stations are hereby advised that those orders are put on hold, effective immediately. Since about thirty to forty men are currently missing, if any of you know where any of them are, you are ordered to call the NCIS number you'll be given while we work to further determine who was aboard the *Monterey* at the time of her departure."

He glared at the men and said, "Do you have any questions?" Hearing none, he ordered Smithers to join with the boat's yeoman for a muster of each man present before finally turning away and motioning Sullivan to join him for the ride back to COMSUBPAC headquarters.

Pearl Harbor, Admiral Stephen Kent's Office

One hour later, the commander of the Navy's Pacific Fleet, Admiral Stephen Kent, sat alone in his palatial office across from Makalapa Drive, a short distance from Pearl Harbor. His door was closed, and two marine guards were posted just outside as he waited for the call. The red telephone at the corner of his expansive desk sat quietly, its single red light off, its importance defined by its color alone and the fact that when there was any conversation over the wires leading to Washington D.C. from that device, one of the most complex encrypting systems in the United States insured that *nobody* would ever know of the substance of that conversation. Scanners activated by the NCIS searched the room daily, looking for any transmitting devices, the Marine guard had orders to shoot anybody trying to enter the room when the red phone was activated, and at least in the mind of Admiral Kent and anybody else who had sat in that hot seat, there was an all-encompassing certainty of confidentiality when the door was locked and the red light was on.

His early morning call to SECNAV[12] had gone badly, very badly, and Kent had been subsequently informed by his personal underground messaging system in Washington that SECNAV's subsequent call to CJCS[13] Admiral Blankenship had then gone *exceedingly* badly. Then, as the morning continued to unravel, the SECNAV and the CJCS had both spoken with the President on their immediate conference call that had followed, and the operative word filtered back to Kent's office that "the President is speechlessly fuming and heads are going to roll." For the President of the United States to ever be speechless was a historical event, Kent knew, and he idly wondered what career opportunities, something like the manager of a yacht club somewhere, might be available to an admiral who abruptly had decided to leave the Navy.

Kent had spent most of his life with the jolting reality that he physically appeared to be, with an exactness that startled uninitiated officers meeting him for the first time, a nearly precise physical twin of the famed Fleet Admiral Chester A. Nimitz. From the firm jaw to the blue eyes, the white hair and the look of calm control, Kent appeared to be a clone of the most famous submariner in the history of the United States. His calm voice and his command demeanor, his gold dolphins above the ribbons on his dress uniform, and sitting at this desk, in this very setting where Nimitz had commanded the U.S. Navy to World War II victory in the Pacific, Admiral Kent left new visitors stunned by the similarity.

Also, Admiral Nimitz had once been court-martialed for running a ship aground had he not? If an officer ran a ship aground, how would that compare with an officer allowing a fully-armed nuclear submarine to be stolen by unknown thieves? There were similarities, weren't there, and didn't Admiral Nimitz end up as a fleet admiral with accolades for the rest of his life? Kent rubbed his temples, an activity that in the past had seemed to stimulate the brain cells deep within. There was always a chance that history might repeat itself, wasn't there?

Kent watched the telephone, knowing that his other telephone with twelve lines would not ring. There would be no interruptions to the impending dialogue, none was allowed by mandatory protocol. His attaché, Commander Dana Palmer, was busy connecting the encrypted call, and he knew that she would insure that nobody, absolutely *nobody*, would be penetrating the barriers of isolation for at least the next ten minutes. As he waited, Kent noticed that he was breathing harder, that his hands were developing that annoying tremor that happened about once per year, and that a tight knot was beginning to squeeze the depths of his stomach.

He stared at the phone, he placed both hands flat on the desk, and he waited. At the exact moment that Admiral Stephen Kent began to wonder what Chester A. Nimitz would do in such a circumstance, the red light on the telephone popped on and the speaker voice of Dana Palmer calmly announced, "Admiral, the President of the United States is ready to speak with you, sir."

Chapter 5

Seattle Headquarters, International Cyber Systems

At exactly 9 AM Seattle time, Dominic Mathews lifted his gavel and dropped it hard on the wooden block at the end of the long mahogany table, silencing the conversations in the room and bringing the meeting to order.

As Chairman of the Board of Directors for International Cyber Systems, Inc. (ICSI), Mathews revered two principles in each and every meeting at the top of the glass tower on Seattle's Columbia Street: punctuality and respect for Robert's Rules of Order. With seventeen Board men and women, each having his or her own agenda and issue, it regularly took a firm hand to maintain control and to keep the members from pursuing their own talking points. At the sound of the gavel, the room full of men and women turned to look at the Chair.

In the corner of the room, the company's founder and CEO, Randolph Blackwell, lounged back in an oversized leather chair, and quietly scrutinizing the proceedings. As the functional godfather of the company, Blackwell was a lean, sinewy man with leather-like skin that seemed stretched across his face, the lower half of which was concealed behind a well-groomed snow-white beard. His dark blue eyes, penetrating from beneath bushy white eyebrows, seemed to be watching everything and everyone at once as he sat silently while the meeting progressed.

Mathew's voice was deep, commanding respect, as he discussed the company's various subsidiaries around the globe and their collective business models and profit margins. At 55, he had been a fast-riser in the corporate world, with perfectly-groomed brown hair and sharp eyes that seemed to miss nothing in the Board meetings he regularly chaired. Mathews had been critical to the success of ICSI, working like a team with Blackwell, they had kept the company near the top of the Fortune 500, defining it as one of the most successful software companies in the world.

The agenda for the meeting was packed with presentations and management issues, with at least five voting matters to be covered in the two hours available. And so it was an annoyance when the massive wooden doors at the far side of the room abruptly opened, allowing the prim and proper Margarita Lindsey, the Chairman of the Board's executive secretary, to enter and briskly walk past the seated members directly to the head of the table.

"Miss Lindsey?" Mathews asked in a sonorous voice as he looked up at her, his expression radiating his curiosity at the unusual interruption to the meeting.

She leaned over the table and carefully placed a note in front of him. Mathews studied the note, his face blanching. He abruptly dropped his gavel, pushed back his chair and stood up. Without a word, he quickly walked across the room toward the older man in the overstuffed chair.

"Mr. Blackwell?" Mathews quietly addressed the man, "We have a bit of an emergency. Would you please come with us?"

The bearded man looked up at Mathews with surprise, his lined and leathery face showing little expression as he answered, "Of course, Dominic."

The ICSI CEO rose with surprising agility from his chair to follow them across the room and out the door as Mathews called back for the other Board members to take a break. As the two men tracked Margarita Lindsey's brisk pace down the hall toward a small conference room at the far corner of the building, Randolph Blackwell's voice boomed out, "What's this all about, Mathews?"

Mathews turned his head just enough for his deep voice to be audible as he answered, "The call waiting for us is from an undisclosed location in the South China Sea sir, and the caller wants to talk with us about a couple of people he found on a boat, *The Sweet Caroline*."

"That's Peter!" Blackwell's voice roared into the hall.

"Yes, sir."

Blackwell slammed the conference room door shut and they quickly pulled up chairs around the polished table in the center of the room. A single telephone with a digital recorder rested on the table in front of them, the telephone's flashing speaker light creating an ominous and pulsating rhythm as Mathews' hand reached out and stopped directly over the device. The chairman glowered at Margarita Lindsey, glanced at the weathered face of the company's CEO, and finally growled, "turn on the Goddamn recorder," as he slammed his hand down with unnecessary force on the speaker button, bringing the telephone to life.

USS *Stout,* Pacific Ocean off Oahu

In the calm early morning waters of the Pacific Ocean, thirty miles west of Honolulu, the massive oiler *Zaliv Amurskiy* lay dead in the ocean, the sleek shape of the USS *Stout* hovering nearby as four helicopters circled the ship with microphones hanging deep in the water. On the bridge of the *Stout,* the radios crackled the transmissions from the ASW helicopters, each seeking the sounds of something, *anything,* beyond noises from within the oiler mixing with the myriad of sounds from large and small fish. Captain Ralph Ginder paced back and forth across the bridge of the *Stout,* his frustration boiling over and nearly matching his increasing certainty that the *Monterey* had escaped…impossibly, absolutely and completely. They could remain next to the miserable slimy piece of junk oiler for all of eternity, he thought, but his career was not to be enhanced. Not on this day, not at this time, and not in the Goddamn foreseeable future…the submarine had won this one.

"Who are those guys?" Master Chief Carter asked quietly, breaking the captain's thought.

"Chief?" Ginder said, turning to the man.

"Those guys down there on the submarine. Who are they?"

A moment of silence passed as the two men stared out the front windows of the *Stout's* bridge. "I really don't know who they are, chief…." He took a deep breath as he watched the choppers expand their search beyond the tanker. "I don't really know, and I really don't care, but I can promise you one thing. Somehow, whoever is down there, somehow, they appear to have figured out how to fire off their nuclear reactor. So now we have a fully armed nuclear submarine loose in the Pacific for whatever awaits her…and us."

He abruptly turned to his master chief and added, "Get Admiral Kent on the line, now."

Seattle Headquarters, International Cyber Systems

"The price is one hundred million U.S. dollars," the voice said from the speaker phone in the Seattle skyscraper, speaking slowly and nearly mechanically with a heavy British accent. "The amount will be transferred within the next twenty-four hours to a numbered account in Zurich or Peter Blackwell will be executed. When the transfer is confirmed, he will be released."

Dominic Mathews looked across the table at the stone-cold face of Randolph Blackwell and raised his eyebrows ever so slightly, waiting for the response.

"With whom am I speaking and where are you?" Blackwell rumbled.

"Where I am is not important, with whom you are speaking is, I am Guleed Khalid," the speaker voice answered. "The conditions beyond the transfer, beyond the time limit imposed, include a complete absence of publicity and a complete absence of notification to the authorities including the CIA, the United States Navy, and Interpol. Do you understand?"

"What I understand, Mr. Khalid," Blackwell said, "is that you claim to have my son as your prisoner, you have made conditions, and you claim to want my money. Am I correct so far?"

"You are Randolph Blackwell, is that right?"

"Yes, go on."

"Good. I don't claim *anything*. I do, in fact, have your son, his life does, in fact, depend on your response and the absence of any publicity or notification. Is that clear?"

"Mr. Khalid, the only thing clear to me is that you want my money. I am familiar with pirating activities in the waters off the Philippines and your recent beheading activities. Your first name is 'Guleed,' which means 'Victorious,' correct?"

Mathews and Lindsey stared at Blackwell.

"Correct, but that has nothing to do…"

"Okay, Mr. Khalid, for you to be victorious on behalf of your band of pirates, I need proof of life, that is, proof of *healthy* life, of

Peter Blackwell and his wife, Caroline Blackwell. This will happen promptly by a *live video display*, and they both will need to be able to respond to my questions."

"The woman Caroline Blackwell has nothing to do with these negotiations."

"Caroline Blackwell is the centerpiece of my son's life, Mr. Khalid, and that makes her also the centerpiece of these negotiations. If she is not healthy and alive, these negotiations will go nowhere…you do want to be victorious, is that correct? You do want your one hundred million dollars, right?"

"We will not tolerate this kind of…"

"The fact is, for this amount of money to be released to you, I will be required to sell some stock. I will be required to sell a *lot* of stock in my company and that takes time."

"I'm telling you that you don't *have* time."

"You sound like an intelligent man, Mr. Khalid, you must know that a hundred million dollars of stock doesn't just get sold by the CEO of the company without completing a truckload of notification requirements. Finally, for this money to move into your hands, you will keep Peter and Caroline Blackwell healthy and alive for the days it takes to complete this process…"

"Days? That is unacceptable. I told you twenty-four hours."

"I know what you told me, Mr. Khalid. I am telling you the realities of business—this *is* a business deal we're completing, right?"

"It is a ransom…"

"We are now *both* in the ransom business. You will get your money, I will keep this quiet, I will get Peter and Caroline Blackwell, and you and I will be victorious in the end. Send my secretary your account number and show me the proof of their good health. Thank you for calling."

Blackwell's hand slammed down on the button cutting off the conversation and immediately stood up.

"Jesus…" Margarita Lindsey said softly. "You hung up on him?"

"They may execute your son." Mathews said. "You don't want to agree to their twenty-four hours? Don't you want to put a trace on the next call?"

"Call in the police and put a trace on a phone call from the Philippines? Watch my son get killed, watch Caroline get killed?

They will happily send us a video of that. Does that make any sense?"

"But what about the twenty-four hours?"

"They want a hundred million dollars," Blackwell said, looking at Mathews. "They will get it, don't you think?" He turned to leave the room. "But they won't get a cent if either of those two people is dead and now they know that. They will call back with their account number; I can assure you of that. Now, let's get back to the Board meeting. We have business to conduct."

USS *Monterey*, Pacific Ocean

At precisely 1,000 feet beneath the surface and eighteen miles south of the *Zaliv Amurskiy,* the *Monterey* silently moved beneath the thermal layers of water and increasingly away from the extensive antisubmarine warfare activities unfolding behind them. Within the control center of the submarine, Captain Gary Moore watched the men around him with admiration—Billy Bodine sitting at the helm, Chief Berry at the sonar station next to Frog, both men with headphones on, listening intently. The second SEAL, Silverback, was moving rapidly through the boat, helping anybody who needed anything. Amanda was quietly sitting in the bow compartment, fighting claustrophobia while her fiancée Fred Wilson worked with Chainsaw on valve alignment protocol in the lower level Control Center. The three nukes were in charge of the engine room, nothing to worry about there, and Doc Wheat...well, Doc Wheat was checking his medications, or whatever hospital corpsmen do on submarines when 90% of the crew is absent.

"Any cavitation?" the captain called out to Bodine.

"No sir, the engine room is holding us at four knots and we are *silent.*"

"Very well," Moore said as he contemplated what else could be done to remain undetected. They were nearly silent, since the *Monterey* had been retrofitted with the new Virginia Class silencing tiles. While that was helpful, Moore knew, they were still not yet entirely free from the ASW net expanding off the west coast of Oahu. Also, there were submarines in the 7th Fleet with enhanced antisubmarine capabilities that would be diverted to the chase, there were detonators that could be dropped that could penetrate the thermal layers above them, and there was the spectrum of ASW ships in the harbor, no doubt, now scrambling to leave Pearl for the search. But the Pacific was a very big ocean, and they were a very small submarine, and as each minute passed, the odds of their escape were exponentially improved. Another six hours, that's all it would take, he knew, and the vastness of their three dimensional arena of escape would allow them to continue their mission to the Philippine Islands.

"Chief?" he called out to the COB sitting at the sonar station. "I want us in the wardroom at 0945 hours—everybody not on watch. Would you arrange for that?"

"Aye, aye, sir," Berry said, removing his headset. "We'll be ready for you.

Chapter 6

Pearl Harbor War Room

The Top Secret Pearl Harbor War Room, a cold stone building at 251 Makalapa Drive, was a virtual masterpiece of electronic displays, with floor-to-ceiling flat panel Liquid Crystal Display screens in vivid color controlled by a series of consoles adjacent to the speaker's podium at the front of the room. The building sat next to the COMPACFLT headquarters at Pearl Harbor, and Admiral Sully Sullivan had been in the room only twice before since achieving flag rank. The first time was after the North Sea Fleet of China's People's Liberation Navy had conducted an aggressive and unprecedented exercise against submarines, and the second time followed an announcement from a conservative website declaring the presence of a fully-armed Russian Akula-class submarine in the Gulf of Mexico. Neither event had generated much steam, and an hour after each meeting had started, everybody had been dismissed without significant debate.

As Sullivan walked into the building at 0645 hours that morning, it was immediately obvious that this was going to be an exceedingly different event. The entire building was buzzing as the chairs in the War Room were packed with upper-level naval officers. The perimeter of the room was filled with a collection of suited men wearing earpieces with obvious weapon bulges under their coats. Serious and intense, they continuously scanned the room, their demeanor suggesting that there would be no distractions or interruptions from the central focus of an American nuclear submarine gone missing.

The commander of the Pacific Fleet, Admiral Stephen Kent, stood behind the podium, waiting and watching as the room filled. Each seat had a computer screen mounted on the table, the screens uniformly glowing with information about Naval operations in the Pacific. The trim and efficient Lieutenant Brenda Walker, sat down at the left side of her boss and immediately leaned over to whisper in his ear.

"The press corps has the news, sir," she whispered, "and the country is fundamentally freaking out. You currently have received," she paused to look at her computer screen, "two hundred thirty-seven calls and a couple thousand e-mails, as of ten minutes ago, asking for comments."

Sullivan looked at the woman and smiled. "Thank you, Brenda, and I apologize for waking you so early this morning. Would you and the remainder of our staff return all those calls and inform the callers that we do not comment on matters of national security?"

"Yes, sir, we've already mostly done that. In fact, all calls but one have been returned."

"All but one?"

"Yes, sir," she whispered as she noticed that, behind the podium at the front of the room, Admiral Kent was glancing at his watch and clearing his throat. "A Texan named George Peterson."

"Peterson? What does he want?"

"He wants to know where his daughter is. She is a 22-year old student at the University of Hawaii, and he says she has gone missing."

"Why is he calling me?"

"Something about her fiancé, a torpedoman…."

"May I have your attention, please?" the booming voice of Admiral Kent filled the room, just as the *Monterey's* executive officer, William Smithers, squeezed in a chair on Sullivan's right side, the man still wearing his crisp white Naval uniform and his eyes looking intently at the front of the room.

"As you all know," Kent said, "the Los Angeles class nuclear submarine *USS Monterey*, SSN-749, has recently returned from her final mission in Indonesia, and she was scheduled to be decommissioned and struck from the Naval Vessel Register. However, during the early hours of today, a skeleton crew initiated an unauthorized departure from the Pearl Harbor submarine base, and she is currently being sought by our airborne, surface, and submerged ASW forces in the Pacific."

The screen lit up behind him, showing a real-life display of a segment of Pacific Ocean with a huge oil tanker in the center of the screen, a guided missile cruiser a few hundred yards off its starboard bow, and four helicopters circling in position around the tanker.

"This is a real-time picture of our Guided Missile Cruiser, *Stout*, next to the civilian oil tanker *Zaliv Amurskiy* that has voluntarily stopped making headway about thirty miles west of Oahu where our ASW choppers are conducting an underwater search. The CO of the *Stout*, Commander Ralph Ginder, believes he has locked in the *Monterey* below the oiler and is looking for positive confirmation and acquisition. We think the submarine may still be running on its batteries and will need to surface or snorkel in the next several hours. There is no indication that its nuclear reactor has been activated although three nuclear-trained crewman are confirmed onboard. We have several other ASW ships departing Pearl for this position and our only sub within range, the *Indianapolis*, is being diverted from the north, ETA about 10 hours. We are in the process of launching sounding grenades for echo returns—as many of you know, the *Monterey* has been retrofitted with the silencing *Virginia* Class urethane tiles and she is going to be a bastard to find."

The screen behind the admiral changed to a recording of the USS *Monterey* underway on the surface of the ocean.

"This is a video of the *Monterey,* taken last year off Oahu," Admiral Kent continued. "At this time, we have no information about why she was taken. I have been informed that there has been no increase in the various communications from jihadist websites prior to this event, but we have deployed fully armed detachments of Marines to guard our other four subs currently still tied up at Pearl. The video tapes from every monitoring site in Pearl Harbor, including those at the pier that secured the *Monterey*, have been or are currently being analyzed.

"We have located all but about eighteen of the *Monterey's* crew currently ashore, and with CCTV review, we have identified the personnel aboard the submarine. Most of them appear to have voluntarily boarded the sub just before its departure. There is a single civilian onboard, a student named Amanda Peterson, who has a romantic relationship with a torpedoman apparently on-watch aboard the submarine. Why she came aboard, we do not know, but he actually escorted her onto the vessel. At this time, we do not know her role with the taking of this vessel. The CIA, the NCIS, and the NSA are all collaborating with this component. The commanding officer, Commander Gary Moore, and the COB, Chief Berry, are confirmed to have actively participated in the taking of the submarine. Three of the six SEALs assigned to the boat willingly went with them, and the remaining three SEALs have no knowledge of the reason or reasons behind their participation. The cars belonging to one of the SEALs, Petty Officer Thor Ostrobothnia, a Corvette belonging to Captain Moore, and a vehicle registered to the reactor operator, Petty Officer Brian Robinson, were all next to the pier; as I have stated, these men are on the submarine."

Admiral Kent paused as he looked around the room as if searching for anyone who could give him answers. "We have no ship's information about the watchstanders last night," he continued, "except for Petty Officer Billy Bodine, the topside watch; he was escorted onto the sub by the COB, Roy Berry. The CO met with *Monterey's* hospital corpsman, Petty Officer Alan Wheat on the pier, and then escorted *him* on the boat. The SEALs showed up as a group and escorted *themselves* on the boat." Kent scowled at the audience as he said, "Everybody seemed to escort *everybody else* on the boat—this is appearing to be some kind of a Goddamn collusion.

"Furthermore, we don't know why the three Nukes would collaborate in this theft…all three of them were involved in that graffiti incident on the USS *Gravely*, as were the SEALs, but the relationship of that event to this criminal activity remains undetermined. Brian Robinson, the reactor operator, was about to leave the Navy after putting in his six years, so his career would not be affected by his impending dishonorable discharge. Manny Munroe was up for promotion but he also was completing his six years obligated time in the Navy, and so we have no idea why he would covet a dishonorable discharge. Munroe is not married and we have nobody to interview except his parents on a farm in Nebraska. Finally, there is the Nuke electrician, Jules Baxter. This Baxter petty officer is a lifer, in the Navy nine years already, but word is that he's in the middle of a nasty divorce and his wife will soon be interviewed for any knowledge of a collusion.

"We have not been able to locate the remaining men who were assigned to the *Monterey* who didn't show up at the muster on the pier this morning and a state-wide search by the local police and everybody else is underway. Their pictures will be released to the media and the airport booking counters, and their locations will hopefully be identified soon. However, the men we could locate are undergoing an intensive debriefing. At this time, we know neither why these men colluded to steal a Goddamn nuclear submarine, nor how many others might be involved. We are concerned about China involvement, with Russia right behind."

At the right side of the room, a hand shot up into the air. Admiral Kent looked annoyed as he announced, "All questions will need to wait to the end, but I will entertain Ambassador Lieberman's inquiry at this time. Yes, sir?"

A slender man in an expensive suit leaned forward to his microphone and clicked the switch. "Thank you, admiral; has anybody located the submarine's executive officer?"

Immediately, before Admiral Sullivan could pull him back down into his seat, William Smithers stood up and loudly exclaimed, "Yes, sir, I am right here."

Admiral Kent looked at Smithers and dryly announced, "It seems that Lieutenant Commander William Smithers is here, Mr. Ambassador. Mr. Smithers, could you fill us in regarding why the commanding officer or others on the *Monterey* might have wanted to take the submarine?"

Smithers looked around at the staring faces, momentarily basking in this unexpected attention. "Thank you, admiral," he said. "Captain Moore and I talked many times on our recent patrol, which ended disastrously, and I might add, we certainly had a close working relationship. However, he did not reveal why he might have wanted to hijack the submarine. I would think, admiral, that since he was approaching the end of his career, it would seem likely he may have another agenda, possibly a submarine sale to a country such as China. I would suspect that such a covert sale would bring a great deal of remuneration...."

Admiral Sullivan immediately stood up and interrupted the man. "I take immediate exception to the comments of Mr. Smithers, Admiral, and I must interject a contrary opinion based on nearly twenty years of close association with Captain Moore. As you may be aware, I know him very well, sir, and I will tell you," he looked around the room, "I will tell *all* of you, that there is no way on God's earth that Captain Gary Moore would take any action that would be harmful to the United States Navy or that could be considered treasonous against the United States of America. I point out to all of you that he has led his submarine to multiple Presidential Unit Citations for bravery and success at sea, and he has earned the coveted Battle Effectiveness Awards for his submarine's extraordinarily capable performance under his command. During this past decade, since his wife expired, he has been one of the most dedicated and patriotic officers in the United States Navy. The fact that he is onboard that ship, admiral, should not lead to a presumption of his collusion with any foreign actors. I will say with certainty, sir, that Commander Moore would die before compromising the secrets of this nuclear submarine."

Sullivan sat down, his face flushed with anger as Smithers quietly sat down beside him. The two men pointedly avoided any eye contact with each other beyond a quick look of acknowledgement from the junior officer and his hushed comment, "I agree with everything you said, admiral."

"Thank you, admiral, for your character testimonial," Admiral Kent said into his microphone, "and we now will continue with the briefing if there are no more interruptions. I have been informed that the female aboard, Ms. Amanda Peterson, was living in a dorm with a student, one Ashia Jamila, from Iran, currently in the United States on a student visa. Her parents in Iran have not yet been located although this student will be intensely interrogated today; her affiliation with any extremist organization is being reviewed at this moment but no such affiliation has yet been recognized. Ms. Amanda Peterson's father lives in Texas and has recently contacted our COMPACFLT office, inquiring about the whereabouts of his daughter. Agents are on the way to his Texas home at this moment, and this student's classmates and professors at the university will be interrogated as quickly as the FBI can start the investigation this morning."

The screen behind the admiral switched to a world map showing the area around the Hawaiian Islands with segments marked off in an expanding array of blocks stretching from Oahu to South America, Alaska, and the China Sea. "If they escape our net under the tanker, we will have over sixty million square miles of Pacific Ocean to search," Kent said. "If we do not regain possession of the *Monterey* in the next four to six hours, the search will quickly move beyond the capacity of our surface and submerged ASW forces. The President will be notifying the diplomats and the leaders of every nation within missile reach of the *Monterey*. As you may know, she is fully armed with twelve Tomahawk missiles.

"Until we know more details about who is onboard and to whom those persons may have talked with prior to departure, it is likely that we will know neither the destination of this submarine nor its intentions until it is too late to do anything about it. At this time, she a potential threat to most nations of the world, theoretically including the United States of America. Within the next four hours, therefore, the *Monterey* will become identified as a hostile vessel, to be sunk by ASW forces at the earliest possible time."

Admiral Kent looked around at the silent room, his eyes narrowing. "A final comment. If the press calls any of you…and I promise you that the press will be calling *all* of you, your answer will be no 'comment.' That is all you will say, 'no comment.' I want this son-of-a-bitch story locked down tight. The President will be conducting a news conference later today where the press will receive the appropriate information he deems relevant."

The admiral looked around the room and finally growled, "Are there any other questions?"

USS *Monterey, Pacific* Ocean

Captain Gary Moore ducked his head through the control center's forward watertight door, and with Chainsaw following closely behind, and moving down the passageway, he squeezed around an array of equipment jamming the back half of the compartment. They found her, dressed in a dark blue submarine uniform, sitting on a bench immediately in front of a collection of warheads attached to a group of dark green torpedoes stacked all the way to the top of the overhead pressure barrier.

"Hello, Amanda," Moore said pleasantly, "Petty Officer Wilson has loaned you some clothing?"

She stood up and glared at the captain as Chainsaw quietly moved to the side of the compartment. "Fred got me this, Mr. Moore, and he called this thing a 'poopie-suit,' a rather revolting…"

Chainsaw immediately intervened. "This is the *captain*, Ms. Peterson, and he will be addressed as "captain," not "mister."

Moore smiled and said, "No worries, Amanda, did you get something to eat?"

"No, captain, I am not really hungry. Something about sitting around deep under the ocean, waiting to die, that seems to have taken my appetite. But thank you for asking. Since I am all alone up here, maybe you could tell me where my fiancé has gone?"

Moore glanced at Chainsaw who immediately answered, "Yes, sir, okay, Amanda, here's the deal on Wilson. He helped on the

Ballast Control Panel and with valve lineups, he then migrated to the engine room to help Munroe with the steam plant, and when he finishes that, he'll be working on the wire-guided system coming out of the back of one of those torpedoes, over there," he answered, pointing to the port side of the submarine.

"*Pardon me,* captain," Amanda said loudly. "I am happy Fred is basically working his tail off, since he is trapped here with me. However, I am *also* a human being, and still trapped under the ocean with all of you. As a human being, I have certain rights which my lawyer shall inform you about at the proper time. This Neanderthal," she looked up at Chainsaw, "continues to have me under house arrest. How long are you going to keep me *trapped* on this submarine?"

Moore looked at the woman and thought about his answer. Her blonde hair was frazzled, her mascara was smeared, and her eyes looked wild and frightened. The captain had seen the look from an officer's eyes long ago, when he was training on one of his first submarines out of New London, Connecticut. It had happened more than twenty years before, when a young Naval Academy graduate taking his first submarine indoctrination cruise during his junior year became claustrophobic. It was the look of raw fear, the kind of mind-numbing terror seen in the eyes of people who feel trapped and can find no escape. The captain of that boat was informed of the man's condition and he had been evaluated and treated by the submarine's hospital corpsman.

Amanda looked like she was bordering on becoming one of the claustrophobics in the world, the people who suffer from a kind of rising internal terror within their mind when held in confined spaces. After *exactly* the correct dose of Ativan, swiftly injected into the frightened Naval officer's left deltoid muscle, "kinda like a flu shot" they told him, the corpsman had informed the man he would be fine. The officer had calmed down and they returned to port. The man's emerging career remained intact and unblemished in the surface Navy, but he was never to cast a shadow in any submarine throughout the remainder of his career.

"Amanda," the captain said calmly, "You are not under any kind of 'house arrest.' I am sorry that you came aboard, that should not have happened. However, I cannot release you from our boat, as much as I would like, because we are deeply underwater and we are moving away from the Hawaiian Islands."

Amanda let out a gasp, quickly suppressed, her eyes widening further.

"Even though you didn't volunteer," Moore continued, "you have become a part of a submarine mission and as unfortunate as that may be for you, we all would appreciate your help this next week or two."

"*Week or two?* I am being held prisoner for *a week or two more,* and *you* want *my* help?"

Moore smiled. "Maybe just a week or so, I'm not sure. I repeat, you're not being held 'prisoner,' you just won't be able to leave for a bit, because of the circumstances.... I would like to ask for your help, perhaps giving Wilson and Bodine some help in the galley. You could also help Frog feed and take care of the two dolphins we have onboard, that would be a big help. In the meantime, I will allow you to remain with Petty Officer Wilson here in the torpedo room, you may alternate the use of the head with him, you may take your shower there, and you may dine with the remainder of the crew that has become a part of our mission. I would also ask you to use discretion in your relationship with Wilson...he is, in fact, your fiancé?"

"He is my fiancé, but we did not plan our romance to be underwater. Furthermore, there is nothing very romantic about a torpedo compartment with all these torpedoes with nuclear symbols on their warheads, and I do not like your implication of possible impropriety. I'm a very *proper* girl, I just wanted to visit him, since I haven't seen him for more than two months...."

"I am sorry about that, but that is the nature of submarine duty. *Somebody* has to be on watch and the patrols can be lengthy."

"Okay, okay," Amanda said, taking a deep sigh. "Fred has told me 'the needs of the Navy comes first' and all of that, about a thousand times. Did he volunteer for this new mission and not tell me?"

"No, he did not know about this until it was too late. With you in port, I am certain he would not have volunteered. Fred Wilson just happened to be in the wrong place at the wrong time."

"Like, he happened to be on the submarine?" she exclaimed. "He had the damn duty. How could he *not* be here? More than two months at sea and he gets the damn duty watch on the night of arrival? If it wasn't for Billy Bodine, I wouldn't have even been able...."

"Billy Bodine broke several topside watch naval regulations when he let you onboard last night." Moore smiled. "The Chief of the Boat, Roy Berry, negotiated an agreement after he unlawfully let you aboard. For that reason, as you know, Petty Officer Bodine is *also* with us. He was, in fact, volunteered for the mission last night and as a result, he came along quite willingly."

"He '*was* volunteered*?'* That doesn't sound very voluntary, sounds like he was blackmailed to me, under some kind of awful threat. I really need to talk with my attorney." She hesitated and glanced at Chainsaw. "With all due respect, captain. What is this, some kind of covert mission, an espionage kind of thing?"

"We're on a rescue mission, Amanda, a military rescue mission, and as I have said, if you could help us, we would all be most appreciative."

She looked at the captain in silence, her jaw muscles alternatively clenching and relaxing. "A rescue mission?" she finally asked, her voice becoming small. "We are the rescuers?" She glanced at Chainsaw, her eyes taking in his powerful biceps, and she turned back to Moore. "Who is the rescuee?

"We are trying to save my daughter, Amanda. My daughter Caroline. We are going to rescue her. We are going to the South China Sea to get her, in the vicinity of the Philippines Archipelago."

"The Navy is sending you to the South China Sea?"

"No," Moore said quietly. "That is not exactly correct. The Navy is *not* sending us, and the Navy does not know why we are going. All they know is that we are, in fact, *gone.*"

Amanda stared at Moore, her eyes wide, her mind grinding through a jumble of thoughts. "Holy mother of God...." She said. "How many of the crew are with us?" she finally blurted out. "Isn't the crew supposed to be one hundred and twenty..."

"Initially, there were eleven, but with you here, now, there are twelve."

"Okay..." she started, hesitating for a moment before looking up at Gary Moore, her eyes beginning to glisten. "Okay," she repeated. "You are doing this for your daughter, Caroline. I can understand that.... It happens that I also have a father, back home in Texas, who also loves me. I really do think that if I were in trouble, he would be there for me, that he would come to wherever I am to help me. I believe he too would try and save me." She hesitated then added, "I *hope* that he would try and save me."

She brushed her hand across her face, wiping away the tears that had filled her eyes, and she looked up at the captain again.

"How can I help?" she asked in a voice that was so quiet that it was nearly drowned out by the noise of the first explosion from the sounding grenades launched by the USS *Stout* in the waters behind them.

Chapter 7

Pearl Harbor, Hawaii

Admiral Sullivan's driver stopped at the Kamehameha red light, waiting to cross the intersection and enter the Makalapa gate into Pearl Harbor and the submarine base. His brain was buzzing from intensity overload mixed with the fog factor that always occurred when there had been interrupted or no sleep the night before. His mind churned the facts of the past eight hours as he struggled to make sense of the briefing and the activities of the *Monterey*. Captain Moore had seemed normal the night before during their brief and aborted debriefing at SUBRON 1. The man had been deeply angry, that had been obvious, but he had demonstrated a willingness to accept and to adapt to the nonsense from Washington that had been driving most of the submarine leadership crazy these past several years.

The aborting of the Indonesia mission was a problem for all of them, that was certain, but like any good commanding officer, Moore had seemed ready to just move on. In any event, his time as a submarine skipper was up, his command years were over. He was finished with this part of his life, but the man had a shower of accolades from every level of the submarine service to smooth his path to Washington and to future promotions where he himself could influence policy in the right direction during the years ahead.

So what, exactly, the hell was going on?

"Sometimes this signal takes forever," the driver said as they waited and watched convoys of tourist buses passing in front of them.

"So, in the Aloha spirit, we wait," Sullivan said, trying to *will* his mind back into a clear state of thinking. Maybe another cup of coffee would help…he knew Brenda Walker would have a full pot waiting at submarine headquarters. Another cup of coffee on top of the six or seven already consumed throughout the night, that may help….

His cell phone abruptly rang as the light turned green and their car accelerated through the intersection. "Sullivan," he barked into the device, watching *two clusters* of Marines holding M27 automatic rifles peer into the front and back windows of their black

Navy car before saluting and finally waving them through the submarine base gate. The orders had been followed, he noted, and *nobody* with even a pimple out of place would be granted access to the sub base until everything got sorted out.

"Admiral, sorry to bother you, sir, this is Lt. Walker," his attaché's voice said over the telephone.

"Go ahead, Brenda."

"Yes, sir. I have Mr. Peterson on the line, calling from Texas."

Sullivan hesitated for a second, then finally said, "Okay, put him through."

"Yes, sir," she answered and after two loud clicks, she purred, "The Admiral is on the line, sir," as the booming voice of a man with a strong Texas drawl immediately blasted into Sullivan's ear.

"Where the hell is my daughter, admiral?"

"Mr. Peterson? Could you stand by for a moment, sir?"

Sullivan directed the driver to park in a shaded area in front of the COMSUBPAC headquarters on Morton Street and to go find a cup of coffee somewhere. All he needed at this point was for some enlisted driver to be telling his friends at O'Malley's that somebody from Texas had lost a daughter aboard a nuclear submarine.

"Go ahead, Mr. Peterson," Sullivan spoke into the telephone as he watched the driver depart the area.

"Admiral, is this conversation confidential?" Peterson asked, sounding like a cowboy who had just climbed off his horse.

"This is an encrypted line at this end, Mr. Peterson. However, your local telephone system is not necessarily confidential and could be accessed by any of several hackers or government agencies. What can I help you with?"

"Sir, I received a call from my daughter's roommate, Ashia Jamila, this morning that Amanda didn't return back to the dorm last night."

"Yes, sir, and she is a civilian? How can I help with that?" Sullivan said with just the correct measure of interest.

"Well, sir, my daughter…like I said, her name is Amanda…she has a final exam today, she never misses a class or exam, and she has not shown up after visiting her fiancé last night, a Mr. Fred Wilson, stationed aboard the nuclear sub, *Monterey*. Mr. Wilson does something with torpedoes on the submarine."

"Okay, have you contacted this Mr. Wilson?" A brief flash of guilt passed through Sullivan's mind.

"Well, sir, that's the problem. I can't contact *anybody*. Furthermore, it's not like Amanda to not be in her dorm room or in the library the night before an examination. She's very diligent, working to get good grades for nursing school. I think something might have happened to her…I can't reach her on her cell phone and she *always* answers when I call. Is there any way you or I could contact Mr. Wilson or is there anybody out there who knows where he is? Hasn't the *Monterey* come back into port?"

"I can't talk about submarine deployments, that's…."

"Admiral, my daughter went to see her fiancé, a man on one of your submarines. Your submarine was supposed to arrive in port yesterday. Sir, she is now missing. The Hawaii police require a 24-hour wait before they will even *start* an investigation, and *hell*, I don't trust them to do anything right. I would call Hawaii 5-0, if there *was* such a thing! And then, twenty minutes ago, I received calls from men claiming they're with the CIA and then a call from somebody who claims he's with the NSA—all of them are coming up from San Antonio to visit me, right here in Fredericksburg, Texas, to talk about Amanda. Why the hell do they want to talk with me? Has something happened to my daughter?"

"Mr. Peterson," Sullivan said, the cell phone feeling increasingly heavy in his hand, "I do not know where your daughter is right now, and I do not know the location of Petty Officer Fred Wilson. However, I understand your concern…"

"Oh, *really*, admiral? Do you *really* understand? Do you have a daughter?"

Sullivan hesitated. The man was going to hear it all on the news soon, probably within the next hour, and then all hell would break loose. He pressed the telephone tightly against his ear.

"I do not have a daughter, sir. But I believe I understand what you're going through. There will be many more issues involved here, and I will do everything I can to keep you informed. I will tell you, sir, that Amanda's future will be the future of many others with the *Monterey*, and…"

Peterson's voice became louder. "Admiral?" he said, his voice becoming agitated. "'Many others with the *Monterey*?' what the hell are you talking about? Is she okay?"

"Mr. Peterson, can I give you a number?"

"Jesus Christ! Are you going to shuffle me off to somebody else, like everyone has done today?"

"No, sir, I am going to give you my direct cell number…and I will tell you, sir, that *nobody* has my direct cell number. I am going to ask you to cooperate with the NSA and with the CIA. I am going to promise you that I will contact you, or my attaché Brenda Walker will contact you, with every piece of available information regarding Amanda as this continues to unfold…."

Five minutes later, as Admiral Sullivan walked past the busy offices at COMSUBPAC, Brenda Walker called out that one fuming Admiral Kent was holding on his telephone. He walked into his office and noticed that all eight of his telephone lines were flashing. "He's on line six," Brenda's voice carried over the speaker system as Sullivan dropped into his chair and picked up the telephone.

"Sullivan here," he said tersely.

"Sully? This is Kent. We've just completed a geek-enhancement process of your video surveillance tape analysis of the sub base and there is no question that your man, Commander Gary Moore, walked *willingly* aboard the *Monterey* early this morning with the boat's corpsman, Petty Officer Alan Wheat. We have confirmed from the video tapes that there are three SEALs onboard, and that there are three nukes, the COB Berry is aboard, and we presume that Petty Officer Fred Wilson is there as well. Furthermore, we confirmed the topside watch, Petty Officer Bodine, allowed a female college student *who dorms with that Goddamn Middle East foreign national*, to board in the accompaniment of Petty Officer Fred Wilson.

"Yes, sir, we understand from our review that there's twelve on the boat…. Any others?"

"Jesus Christ, Sully. Are you something more than a fucking adding machine? Your *Monterey* has eleven men qualified in submarines—that is enough, not counting that Goddamn female civilian. That is more than enough. That is enough to command the sub, to fire the torpedoes, to run the reactor, to launch covert ops anywhere in the world, or to fire any or all twelve Tomahawk missiles at anybody they want. Those eleven people are enough to start World War III. And now that Goddamn skimmer skipper on the unguided missile cruiser *Stout* has just informed me they are going to let the

Greek tanker continue on its way, since nothing seems to be hiding under it except whales and Goddamn octapussies! We now, therefore, have no idea where the *Monterey* is. We have lost the son-of-a-bitch!"

Sullivan looked out the open door at his attaché at her desk, her firm and compact body sitting upright, staring back at him with just enough insider knowledge for the pale look of shock to register across her face.

"So, now, Sully," Kent's voice blasted from the telephone, "what I gotta know now, *what we all gotta know now*, is where in hell are they going? Do you think you could start working on that, sometime before we are all relieved of our fucking commands?"

USS *Monterey, Pacific* Ocean

The Sonar Room of the USS *Monterey* was Captain Moore's favorite compartment. Throughout any patrol, the room was nearly always stunningly quiet and dark as sonarmen scanned their green screens, listening, searching, and logging all the sounds in the ocean around the submarine. Chief Roy Berry hunched over the center screen, his earphones clamped tightly against his ears, his eyes watching the display screen as he waited for the next blast from the surface. The chief glanced up as Moore entered the area and asked, "How far away from them are we, captain?"

"Approaching nearly fifty miles now, still at one thousand feet, picking up any cavitation, chief?"

"None, sir, the nukes in the engine room are holding us to nearly dead-silence," Berry said, flipping a couple of switches on his display screen. "The skimmers up there are bombarding the waters with noise, using the damnedest combination of systems from their electronic inventory. Then about every four minutes, they light off another one of those Goddamn explosive detonators, which everybody in the universe can hear and that are driving everybody nuts. The grizzled chief petty officer turned to look up at the captain and smiled. "It sounds like they're getting desperate up there, sir. I can't say for sure but I think they *really* want to find us."

"It seems that way," Moore said dryly. "We're under several thermoclines which should help reflect the echoes away from the boat. No indication they have any directional alterations, is there?"

"You mean do they know where we are? No, sir," Berry said. "I think they still think we're under the tanker back there…which, incidentally, has been dead-in-the-water for at least two hours now although it sounds like its screws are starting to rotate again. That guided missile skimmer thing is moving around the tanker, pulling its towed array, like a fuckin' drunk tiger looking for the deer he imagines must be close-by."

"Captain?" a voice from the sonar room doorway turned Gary Moore around. Wilson was standing just outside the door, watching Moore carefully. "Captain, could I speak with you for a moment?"

Gary Moore stepped out of the sonar room and moved to the corner of the control center to face the torpedoman. Fred Wilson had been attached to the *Monterey* for nearly four years, and the captain knew, the man had more capabilities in the torpedo room than probably any other man in the submarine service. Standing an even six feet tall with dark black hair and olive skin suggesting an Eastern Mediterranean background, he appeared to be solid, capable of wrestling his beloved torpedoes directly into the tubes without the mandatory hydraulic loading systems.

"Captain," Wilson began, "I'm sorry about Amanda, I know…"

"Wilson," the captain interrupted him, "it's done and so we move on. Has she filled you in about our little mission here?'

"She did, sir, and, hell, I would have volunteered to go if you hadn't already *acquired* me, so-to-speak." He smiled. "It is nice to have her with me, sir, but again, I'm sorry about sneaking her aboard."

"Like I said, it's behind us now. I'm going to need your help since we're about 90% short of trained crew. You've stood helmsman watch and the ballast control panel watch, you'll need to take six on and six off, alternating with Bodine, during our transit…"

"Yes, sir, no problem, port and starboard watches, been there, done that. Amanda and I can help with the food preparation—that will give me a primer on future domestic skills, capabilities that I sadly lack. She's also working to become a nurse, in the real world, if any help is needed there."

"The Doc will appreciate that."

"Finally, captain, if any torpedoes are needed, sir, we have a full load. I'll have them ready to go."

"Not likely, unless the Chinese come after us."

"The *Chinese*?" Wilson's eyes widened. "Jesus, where are we going? I thought your daughter was somewhere in the South Pacific."

"Most of our crew, that is, those who had volunteered to join on this mission have been briefed by the COB. To bring you up to speed, Caroline is in an area of the South China Sea, somewhere near the Philippines although we don't know precisely. Her boat was taken over by pirates, and we'll be gathering intel with the SEALs through satellite acquisition as soon as we can safely get up to periscope depth, probably in about six hours. We are going to find her location, and we're going to rescue her."

"The South China Sea?" Wilson stepped back slightly. "Jesus.... We have enough fuel for that?"

At that moment, another detonation from a sounding explosion carried into the submarine, stopping the conversation as Chief Berry cursed and ripped off his headset. "Goddamn skimmer pukes!" he hollered from the sonar room. "If they keep doing that, the bastards are going to make us all go deaf."

Waipio Gardens, Hawaii

The ring of the doorbell at the apartment caught Claudia Baxter by surprise. Watching the reruns of the daily soaps, she had not expected any visitors, nor did she have any interest in sharing her Doritos with any relatives who might have found their way to the remote reaches of Oahu's central valley where she had taken refuge. She popped the biggest tortilla chip she could find into her mouth and pushed mute to silence the love scene radiating from the television. Peering through the tiny peep hole in the door, she could see two large men wearing suits, *wearing suits in Hawaii, for God's sake*, standing outside in the narrow corridor.

She swallowed the chip, opened the door, and asked, "Are you from the IRS?"

The men glanced at each other as the bigger one pulled out his wallet and held up a badge and said, "No, ma'am, I am Agent Tanaka, this is Agent Ramirez, we're from the NSA. We would like to have a chat with you."

“The NSA?” her eyes darted back and forth between the men. “Am I in some kind of trouble? And…if you wouldn’t mind telling me, what does NSA stand for?”

“Mrs. Claudia Baxter?” Ramirez asked, turning his head slightly to look behind the woman and into the apartment.

“Yes, sir, that’s who I am,” she answered, stepping back, allowing them to enter the apartment after squinting her eyes to scrutinize their badges. The men sat on the sofa, facing her as she pushed the tortilla chips across the coffee table.

“Wanna chip?” she asked. “They’re really good.”

“The NSA is the National Security Agency,” Tanaka said, gazing at the woman. She might have been a blonde bombshell, ten or more years ago, he thought. “Your husband is Petty Officer Jules Baxter, a nuclear-trained electrician serving aboard the submarine USS *Monterey*?”

She snorted and said, “He *was* my husband. No more now, thank God.”

“So you are now divorced? We noticed your house out in Pearl City is boarded up.”

“That’s right, I boarded it up myself, to deliver a message when he returns from the latest of his many, many trips to sea. I think he’s supposed to come back soon…I’ll let him figure out how to divorce me, I don’t have the time.”

“Yes, ma’am, you’re expecting him back soon?”

“Hell, yes, any day now, and I think he’s going to get the message.”

“When was the last time you saw him?” Tanaka asked, opening his portable computer and rapidly hammering at the keys.

Claudia looked surprised. “Are you serious? I *never* see him, that’s why I boarded up the house. I got tired of waiting for…”

“Ma’am,” Tanaka repeated, “it is very important. When was the last time you saw him?”

“Okay, okay, I was coming to that, about two and a half months ago, last time he left. Gone off in that Goddamn submarine to God knows where, again, leaving me to take out the trash, pay the bills, mow the lawn, clean up after the dog, and every other damn fool thing he should be helping me with, at least *once in a while*. Does that answer your question?”

“Yes, ma’am, that must have been difficult,” Ramirez said. “By the way, would you mind turning off your television?”

The three looked at the television where a game show host was yelling something about prizes and discounts to a screaming audience.

“Sorry,” Claudia said quickly, grabbing the remote and turning off the screen. “Why are you asking me all these questions? Is Jules in trouble?”

“You will hear it soon enough,” Tanaka said. “Petty Officer Jules Baxter, after returning to port, is now gone again on the submarine for reasons unknown.”

“You mean they just came back and then the crew took the submarine out to sea again?” Claudia asked. “Already? Where are they going this time?”

“Well, ma’am, that part is still confidential. Can you tell us if he has had any recent problems with finances or with anybody causing him any problems?”

“Problems? What kind of problems?”

“Threats, calls from unknown people, calls from overseas. Visits from anybody who might have appeared threatening? Was he worried about anything?”

“His paycheck came regularly, and with submarine pay and hazardous duty pay, we didn’t have any bad money problems. But he never let me spend any money for anything I wanted, and he was pretty pissed off about everything else,” Claudia said, squinting at the men.

“Did your husband ever gamble?”

“Gamble? Like in some kind of Indian casino at a reservation near Waikiki? Are you guys nuts?”

“No, ma’am, like cards, or….”

“Cribbage on the boat! That’s all he ever played, is that illegal? You guys are from the government, right?”

“That is correct,” Tanaka said. “The NSA is a branch of the government.”

“Well, then, you should know, he’s pissed off at you guys, all of you guys. He had no problem with anything excepting for the government interference with submarine missions.” She thought for a moment. “And, he was always pissed off at me. That’s why I left him.”

"Thank you, ma'am," Ramirez said as the two men stood up. "We're having a couple of people come by today to pick up whatever computers you have in your home for analysis, and we'll be conducting a study of your telephone records in the central office, if that's okay with you."

Claudia stood and placed her hands on her hips. "And, if it's *not* okay with me?"

"I'm sorry, I know this is disruptive. We have to do these reviews in any event…it's a matter of national security."

Claudia protruded her lower jaw. "Well, that is not fine with me. I am hereby announcing that I am refusing to allow you to do any of these things." She suddenly brightened. "Do you have a warrant for this, a search warrant?"

"Ma'am," Tanaka said patiently, "before we do anything, the NSA has requested that I read the following to you and to your attorney. Do you have an attorney?"

"Just read it, Mr. NSA, and then I'll decide if I want to go out and try to find my attorney."

"Thank you, ma'am," Tanaka said as he pulled out a stack of pages. "In 2002, after reviewing a 22-year-old precedent, the Federal Intelligence Surveillance Court of Review, the court that oversees the process whereby the President authorizes the wiretapping of foreigners, ruled that: The president has the inherent authority to conduct warrantless searches to obtain foreign intelligence information ... We take for granted that the president does have that authority and, assuming that is so, FISA[14] could not encroach on the president's constitutional power."

Tanaka looked back at the woman. "The President has ordered this search, Mrs. Baxter. This is an international crime, ma'am, your husband is involved, we are concerned about foreign threats against the United States, the President has authorized this and so we are going to search this home and the home you boarded up near Pearl Harbor, we are going to analyze all your computers and any computerized storage systems, and we are going to search your mail and all of your telephone records."

"You *bastards*!" Claudia hollered.

"If your husband or you is not guilty of anything, then you have nothing to worry about," Ramirez said. "Now, we'd appreciate it if you'd fill out the answers to these questions. Some of them are kind of personal, but please answer them the best you can. We'll be staying here until after the computer people arrive."

"Okay, then," she said, looking back and forth at the two men and taking a deep breath. "So, I have no choice and this is a pretty big deal. You're going to stay here watching me until your computer people come? That's really great, and you didn't even call and make an appointment to see me. Now I know why Jules hated the government so much. I have just one more question. If anything happens to Jules, if he doesn't come back from whatever it is he's doing…." She hesitated a moment, seeking the right words. "If he doesn't come back or is killed or something like that, do I get survivor benefits?"

USS *Monterey, Pacific* Ocean

Deep under the Pacific Ocean, Captain Gary Moore realized that, for the first time in the past thirty-six hours, he really had nothing to do. They had escaped the rapidly assembled net cast over the waters west of Oahu, of that he was certain. The *Monterey* was running smoothly and quietly, 1000 feet below the surface, as she expanded the surface Navy's search zone and as the detonations had faded and finally disappeared far behind them. The nukes had the engine room running smoothly and Chief Berry was busy like a good Chief of the Boat, pacing in and out of the Sonar Room, watching the depth gauges like a nervous mother, and watching the sonar displays when he wasn't scrutinizing Bodine's steady hand on the helm. The SEALs had huddled in the corner of the central control room, on the far side of the periscopes, awaiting the NSA download that would be coming in a few hours, and Amanda had migrated down to the galley to start hunting for some food to prepare for dinner.

As the distance separating the *Monterey* from the guided missile cruiser and ASW choppers had increased, Captain Moore slowly accelerated the speed of the submarine. A little cavitation here or there would not be as easily detected as it would have been, closer to the pursuers, the bubbles not generating enough crackling noise to reveal their position to any searching sonar systems. And, blessedly, as the distance from Oahu increased, the detonations from the armada of submarine-detection devices became a distant memory. Now, with the near-silence of the ocean surrounding them, the submarine's interior became a quiet and deceptively peaceful environment that suggested there was no movement, no threat, and no crushing pressure outside the submarine's pressure hull.

Moore ordered Bodine to lessen the *Monterey's* depth to 800 feet as they reached over a hundred miles from the escape point beneath the *Zaliv Amurskiy*. The Navy, Moore knew, would be highly challenged to effectively search the expanse of ocean now extending out for more than a thousand square miles from where the freighter had been. They would lay out their grids for the continued search, expanding out from the tanker like ripples from a stone in a pond, seeking the maverick submarine, using every available P-3 Orion aircraft, every ASW chopper, combined with an ever-increasing flotilla of surface craft. All of them, in a coordinated search for a magnetic variance or the hint of a sound from something other than the creatures of the sea, would be looking for them. The biggest threat, Moore knew, was from other American submarines that could conduct their searches from the deep, greatly increasing the probability of the *Monterey* being detected. To find his submarine, Moore knew, anybody out there would have to get reasonably close, and he was not going to let that happen.

The *Monterey* had escaped, everybody in the Navy knew that now, but the search effort would continue if for no other reason than the fact that the men in pursuit needed to tell everybody in the world that they were trying to find the submarine.

To make the search even more difficult, the men in the control center of the *Monterey* had already detected how sonar sound would move through the Pacific waters they inhabited. A half hour before, Chief Berry had launched the boat's advanced temperature probe, the "Sexy Butt"[15] probe through the boat's countermeasures tube. That marvelous robotic device created a perfect map of thermoclines for the submarine, the changing temperature hiding spots of the ocean. Moore hoped that, deeply beneath the surface of the Hawaiian waters, the magical thermoclines would continue to hide them, like pulling dark curtains in front of the stalker's eyes. Hopefully, there would be no sonobuoys ahead and no P-3's buzzing the skies above, but there was really no way to be sure. While a little bit of luck would always be welcome, it was the one element that could never be relied upon by any submariner under the sea.

With Chief Berry's help, Captain Moore established a Plan-of-the-Day to coordinate everybody's watchstanding assignments, meals, and sleep. The three nukes would run their own system with one man sleeping on a mattress laid out on the engine room deck, the other two men rotating between watch stations. As soon as the specifics of their target were established, the three SEALs would devise a plan and practice repeatedly right up to the last moment. There would not be much free time in the days ahead, and the beginning of the next intensity, the training exercise, was to follow their response to the retrieval of the coveted satellite information.

Pearl Harbor, Hawaii

As the day passed in Pearl Harbor without positive reports from the aircraft and ships searching the ocean west of Oahu, Admiral Sullivan joined the gathering of men and women from multiple government agencies searching Commander Moore's home. It was a small rental house in Pearl City, with a patio and weeds in the yard emblematic of the owner's absence for prolonged periods of time. Although no roadblocks were in place, the cluster of black SUV's, government Fords, official Navy cars, and spectators gave almost a festive atmosphere to the street in front of Moore's residence.

The house was not much different from others up and down Annanue Street. There was a simple wooden exterior, a small porch in front of the home, windows with drapes fully drawn, and a three-foot brown wooden fence surrounding the property. A small empty garage sat fifty feet from the main house. Men carrying boxes with protruding electrical cords walked back and forth, depositing their computer loads into the SUV's.

Wandering through the house, Sullivan watched the holes being created in walls behind bookshelves, the drawers from two desks dumped upside down on the floor, an answering machine and telephones wrapped in bubble wrap and ready for the next box, and pictures of various family members clustered together and set aside for another departing box. The man had had a wife who had died about eleven or twelve years before, Sullivan knew, expiring from some kind of cancer. He also had a young daughter, someone named Carol he thought, who had married a year ago to a man living in Washington State. He expected that she would be calling Pearl

Harbor shortly as the news of the submarine hijacking spread, a call seeking to discover where her father had gone and even whether or not he was aboard the *Monterey*.

Commander Moore had had few hobbies—there simply wasn't enough time between missions to become good at anything beyond the professional challenges aboard the submarine. There was a faded picture of him in Western clothes riding a horse near some sugarcane fields. There was a set of golf clubs with a thick layer of dust standing in the corner of the bedroom. Everywhere throughout the home, men with flashlights and invasion tools searched, pulled up boarding beneath sinks, and punched more holes behind cabinets, looking for any information to explain the *so far* unexplainable.

He was about to ask one of the men with tiny "NSA" letters on his gray shirt a question relating to the magnitude of the disassembly of the house when his cell phone interrupted his thoughts.

He pulled the device out of its holster and barked, "Admiral Sullivan."

"Admiral, this is Brenda with a report I thought you'd want from Hawaiian Telcom Wireless, the carrier of Commander Moore's cell phone."

"Go ahead, what have they got?"

"What they have, sir, is two and a half months of silence, no calls coming in and certainly no calls going out during the time he was at sea."

"There are no cell phone calls from a submerged submarine."

"Yes, sir. After the *Monterey* returned, there were two calls out—one to a dry-cleaning service, presumably to leave a message about his uniform, and one to his mother's nursing home in Southern California."

"His mother is alive?"

"Yes, sir, I called the home, someplace called Benevolent Care of San Dimas just to check up on it, just said I was calling on behalf of Mr. Moore. The clerk there told me the captain's mom has advanced dementia but that when her son calls, she always brightens up for a few days. The ward clerk also mentioned that Mr. Moore had called her last night."

"Okay, nice work. I never heard him mention her. Any incoming calls?"

"Yes, sir, that's where it gets interesting. Does Commander Moore know anybody in India?"

"India? Who called him from India?"

"Somebody named Mombo, sir, M-o-m-b-o, not M-a-m-b-o, don't know anything more than that."

"Mombo? What kind of a name is that? Where in India did the call come from?"

"That's the problem, sir. Mombo is the name on the cell phone account but it's a nickname or a cover name of some kind. I think the Indians must really love their cell phones, currently there're more than a billion of them. However, their cell towers mostly burn diesel fuel for power and they're running out of polluting…"

"Brenda, can they locate the call or not?"

"Not yet, sir. They're towers everywhere across India but they're unreliable and going down all the time. Satellites are being used but India has a national policy with cell phones that can block location."

"Brenda, get to the…."

"Sorry admiral. This Mombo guy used an Iridium 9555 handheld device, with Iridium Extreme location (GPS). The thing needs three satellites at the very least for triangulation. The LEO[16] system has 66 satellites in polar orbit passing over at various times lasting from about four minutes to fifteen. As luck would have it, there were only two satellites overhead during the call and so the cell phone location is one long line running across two thirds of India and, believe it or not, out across the Indian Ocean and through the Philippines. Said they couldn't triangulate with two satellites but they could biangulate, creating a very long line rather than a pinpoint dot on the map."

"Wonderful. So, you mean the call came from somewhere on that line? What time was the call made?"

"Yes, sir, it was definitely somewhere on that line. The call was made at 2037 hours, almost 2100 hours, Hawaiian time. It lasted about 1 minute and was terminated by Mombo. We tried calling the Mombo number and got nothing, no response. Commander Moore then tried to call this Mombo back, five times, without success."

"Does this Mombo person have some kind of account?"

"No, sir, it's some kind of a joint satellite-based account somewhere in India, a part of a system with about 1500 other account-holders who…"

"No calls to the other ten or eleven men on the submarine? Nothing to the SEALs?"

"No, sir, but I'm coming to the good part."

"I was hoping there would be a good part."

"Yes, sir, we got Chief Berry's cell phone records—he was the COB on the *Monterey*. They show he called Baxter, Robinson, and Munroe, all three nukes, about fifteen minutes after the captain got his Mombo call."

"He called the nukes right after the Mombo call? Okay, recruitment calls. Very nice work, Brenda. So, it appears the SEALs were probably blowing off steam down in O'Malley's or somewhere with Berry and maybe Moore. And then, the captain gets a call from this Mombo character and tries to call back. That call won't go through and so the Chief of the Boat then recruits the nukes, somebody recruits the SEALs, and away they go to God knows where. The other three, Wheat, Bodine, and Wilson, were probably innocent captives or volunteers as they all gathered and went to sea."

"Along with that chick…sorry…that woman from Texas you told me about, the one with the Jihadist terrorist roommate at the university."

"Brenda, you are so severely politically incorrect…."

"Sorry, again, sir. That *Muslim* roommate, that Ashia Jamila woman, who might be exactly the very person behind this whole thing."

"Right. The NSA is tracking her down…that'll lead to another thousand telephone messages to decipher. Brenda, bring the NSA up to speed about the Mombo call from India. Maybe Mombo and Ms. Jamila had some kind of relationship."

"Yes, sir. What do you want me to do about the line across India?"

"Unless you have any better ideas, see if there are any other Mombos in India and whether they might live on the LEO line? This will be one of those long-shot kind of things. What we really need to know is how a one minute call from a Mombo telephone somewhere in India could trigger a group of men to steal a nuclear submarine. By the way, check Commander Moore's service record for his daughter's married name, if it's there, and find out where she lives. She needs to be notified about his absence, if she doesn't call us first."

Columbia Center, Seattle, Washington

In the center of Seattle, rising high above the masses of cars and buses on the streets below is the tallest skyscraper in the state of Washington, the prestigious Columbia Center. At the top of the building, where the rooms are sealed by massive oak doors and the windows stretch from the plush carpet to the soundproofed ceiling, are the rooms for those who covet privacy, for those belonging to the club, by invitation only, the esteemed Columbia Tower Club. At the corner room of one of the office suites, with windows that looked toward Vancouver, the San Juan Islands, and the Pacific Ocean, Randolph Blackwell and Dominic Mathews sat at opposite sides of a massive wooden table as both men looked at the speakerphone system in the center of the table between them. The room was silent except for the sounds of breathing as the two men waited for the call.

"Have you told your family yet? Doesn't he have a sister?" Mathews asked politely, subconsciously bracing himself for the answer.

"Hell no." Blackwell growled back. "You think I want to create a nervous breakdown in that woman?" He looked disgusted. "Christ, that's all we need."

"No, sir," Mathews said. "I just thought..."

"This is one of those things where thinking could get you into trouble," Blackwell said, his leathery face turning to the huge copper clock ticking off the minutes on the wood-paneled wall. "Lead you down the wrong pathway. They said *nobody* gets notified and that includes the boy's sister, his wife's family, the police, the CIA, the NSA, and every other agency you've ever heard of, Dominic. If we screw this up, Peter dies, his wife Caroline dies, their Wally will be sunk, and we all go into mourning. I'm not going to let that happen."

"No, sir," Mathews said quickly.

Blackwell looked at the clock again. "They should be on-time, if they really want one hundred million dollars. We have one minute to go."

"Don't you think we should try and negotiate them down to fifty million?"

Blackwell's deeply tanned face winced. "With negotiations, Dominic, you need *leverage*. We have no leverage except for money. Do you know of any other kind of leverage we have that balances against their threats to kill my son and his wife?"

"No, sir, I don't," Mathews said at exactly the instant the telephone in the center of the huge executive desk began to ring.

Blackwell hit the desk's recording machine button and immediately turned on the telephone's speaker button.

"Randolph Blackwell speaking," he said as both men leaned forward, listening intently.

"This is Mr. Khalid, and good day to you, sir."

"Good day to you, Mr. Khalid," Blackwell said. "All we need is proof of health and life and the routing numbers for your account in Zurich."

"Are you on speaker phone?" the British voice answered.

"We are on a speaker phone. The company's Chairman-of-the-Board, Dominic Mathews, and I are the only two in this room. Nobody else is listening to this conversation."

"That is good, Mr. Blackwell. Unfortunately, there has been some conflict with your son, and the ransom price for his release has just increased to…"

"Mr. Khalid!" Blackwell roared into the telephone microphone. "You have set a price, and we are preparing to pay it. We are negotiating in good faith, sir. If you raise the price, then this conversation is ended."

"The price is going to be raised because your son…"

"Then this conversation is ended," Blackwell shot back as he reached over to the telephone and shut off the call.

Blackwell sat back in his chair, his leathery face reddened, his breath coming quickly as Mathews stared at the man in disbelief.

"They'll call back," Blackwell said. "I am quite certain they want their ransom. We'll give them a few minutes."

Within ten seconds, the telephone rang again and Blackwell answered. "Mr. Khalid, are you back with us again?"

"I am back and do not hang up on me again or your son and his wife will…"

"Don't ever raise the price that you have set, and that I have agreed to, or you are negotiating in bad faith. That is a waste of my time. Is that understood?"

Mathews looked at the CEO as he realized that Blackwell was beginning to sweat profusely.

"Okay, I will accept your counter-offer, and we will lower the price to the original one hundred million. We have now been in possession of these two prisoners for nearly thirty-six hours, when will the money be ready?"

"The money is available as soon as the stock is sold."

"Mr. Blackwell," the voice said with intensity. "I told you twenty-four hours and now it is…"

"Sir, one hundred million dollars does not just exist in a truck filled with hundred dollar bills. It exists in stock, it is my stock that I am selling as soon as the EDGAR filing is accepted by the SEC. Do you understand these terms or do you need an explanation?"

"Explain."

"To sell the stock, an EDGAR filing must be made, that is an Electronic Data Gathering Analysis and Retrieval form with the SEC, the Securities and Exchange Commission. Are you with me so far?"

"Go on."

"This is a public filing, and once it is approved by the SEC, then the sale can happen. Only when the approval is given can the sale be initiated. When the sale is accomplished, you will get your one hundred million. I will tell you, sir, the SEC will approve of my selling my stock as soon as they've reviewed the filing."

"And when will that be?"

"As soon as they reconvene next week."

"*Next week?* I told you twenty-four hours."

"You need to look up two things, Mr. Khalid, then you need to explain it to your colleagues. You sound like an intelligent man and you certainly have access to a computer."

"I have a computer, and I do not expect to be insulted…"

"Go to the Internet and look up Thanksgiving in the United States, a day of *thanks*, a day of celebration we have, every year, *during which time the SEC is closed.* Then look up the EDGAR filing required for the sale of stock to obtain your money. You will see the filing has been made in good faith, as we have agreed, and you will see the request is awaiting approval. If you will again confirm the life and health of Peter and Caroline Blackwell, you will have your money next week, just before the transfer. After our United States

Thanksgiving holiday, Mr. Khalid, you are going to be a very wealthy man. Is there anything about the transfer you do not understand?"

There was no answer. Mathew's eyes widened as the CEO reached across the desk and slammed the telephone to silence.

War Room, Pearl Harbor Headquarters

The electronic display screens in the War Room next to the COMPACFLT headquarters remained dark as Admiral Stephen Kent turned on his microphone from the front of the room. It was going to be a brief advisory updating, the military memo had said, an updating that would bring the gathering of upper echelon officers up to date with the information gathered...what little of it there was. It was not going to be a strategy meeting, for strategy depended on knowledge, information, and insight based on probabilities—at that moment, the matter of the USS *Monterey* departure from Pearl Harbor left everybody with virtually no knowledge of substance.

Admiral Sullivan sat down next to his attaché, Brenda Walker, and nodded a quick greeting.

"The executive officer, Lieutenant Commander Smithers, won't be making this briefing, admiral?" she asked with just a trace of a smile as she watched him closely.

"Lieutenant Commander Smithers was not invited to this briefing," Sullivan replied with a brief look at her eyes to confirm she understood.

As the officers standing near the entrances shut the doors, Admiral Kent glanced at his watch and his voice boomed into the room, "Thank you for coming this evening for this briefing. The *Monterey* is now gone, she escaped our grasp in the waters off Pearl Harbor."

There was a muted reaction by the officers filling the room as everyone waited for the admiral to continue. On the left side of the room, near the front, Vice Admiral Harris Zehner wrote furious notes to himself as Kent continued to speak; the remainder of the officers in the room sat intently quiet.

"I also thank each of you for your "no comment" to the press and for allowing my office and the White House to remain the only sources of information for the public. I finally thank you for not recording any of this meeting; as you are aware, everything discussed here remains top secret and notes are not to be removed from this room." He glared at Admiral Zehner who promptly closed his notebook and put down his pen.

"We do not know where the *Monterey* is going and we do not know why she was taken," he continued, looking at his notes on the podium. "However, right now, I do have some NSA input from their investigation that at least sheds light on who is doing this. Within the past six hours, the President has been in direct contact with the ambassador of virtually every country within the range of the *Monterey*. At this moment, the only countries moving their armed forces up to alert status are China and Japan. As you know, these countries have both already been on a modified high alert because of their territorial disputes over the islands near Yonaguni in the Okinawa Prefecture. Also, the *continuous* conflict potential of North Korea has kept Japan's military and alert system on a very high level.

"About one hour ago, the Chinese ambassador announced his country's intention to attack the *Monterey* if they can locate it in their territorial waters, and he indicated they will be intensively searching for the submarine. This announcement is highly problematic because of our other subs in the area near the waters south of Hong Kong and near Cambodia. As you know, precise identification of any detected submerged submarine is uncertain and an aggressive posture of attack without certainty of identification can lead to a disaster. The British have also been notified because of the proximity of the Falkland Islands to the Strait of Magellan where the submarine may be headed, around the southern point of South America."

Kent looked around the room at the assembled men and women. "Basically," he added, "we have no information about why the *Monterey* was taken or where it is going—we therefore, unfortunately, have to assume the worst."

The bags under his eyes that had been present for the past several years seemed about twice their normal size, Admiral Sullivan noticed, and the man's face was pale and drawn. But the strong voice and command characteristics were the same as always, and Sullivan focused on the continuing summary.

"Using Pearl Harbor security tapes and interviews with about one hundred people so far," Kent continued, "we have identified the twelve people who are on the sub. You are already familiar with the details; the data sheets you have before you summarize the

Monterey's current stock of weapons, standard for a Los Angeles Class submarine. I remind you, she had just returned from patrol a few hours prior to the hijacking and the offloading of her missiles and torpedoes had been scheduled for the next morning.

"The tape shows the previously identified University of Hawaii civilian female, the woman we have identified as Amanda Peterson, walking without escort aboard the sub and allowed to move below decks by the topside watch. The interrogation of the woman's father in Texas by the FBI has now been completed and no subversive or jihadist affiliations have been uncovered. As they all walked aboard the submarine, as far as we can tell from the review of the pier-side tapes, the topside watch did not discharge his firearm during the initiation of the hijacking."

Kent scanned the room as if looking for anybody who might want to create a break in the stream of continuously bad news. He glanced at Vice Admiral Zehner who was sitting rigidly upright, both hands clasped together on the desk in front of him.

"We are not aware of any covert conspiracy," he continued, "between the crewmembers who have hijacked the sub and any foreign government. As you have been informed, Amanda Peterson's roommate of Middle Eastern heritage, a woman named Ashia Jamila is being questioned. She is currently undergoing an extensive NSA investigation. She is not on the TSA No Fly list."

Admiral Kent looked up from his notes. "Is there anybody with any questions or comments?"

Several officers in the room raised their hands, and for the next five minutes, a broad spectrum of questions was asked by the audience and answered by the CINCPACFLT admiral. Admiral Sullivan finally raised his hand and stood up, turning to the audience to address them directly.

"It would be of interest to this audience," he said, "that I met with the *Monterey's* commanding officer briefly after the submarine's return to Pearl, and he appeared to be harboring some considerable displeasure about recent government command activities affecting their operations in the…."

"Admiral," Kent's voice barked over the loudspeakers from the front of the room. "I remind you this submarine's covert activity remains code-word Top Secret…"

"Yes, sir, I am well aware of that," Sullivan replied. "My comments relate to the captain's dissatisfaction with the curtailing of his submarine activities during a special operation, a dissatisfaction that is possibly playing a role here."

Admiral Kent looked down at his notes again and said almost as an aside, "Very well, Sully, thank you, your comments are noted." As Sullivan waited patiently, Kent studied the pages before him for an additional moment and finally looked up at the audience. "On that subject," he said, "tomorrow, the President will be announcing the death of al-Shabaab by undercover CIA operatives, eliminating the al-Qaeda leadership from Indonesia. Should that element have been the source of any discontent to Commander Moore, I would expect this may eliminate the concern."

"Yes, sir," Sullivan responded. "I suspect it might although the SEALs on his submarine, and everybody else on the *Monterey*, may have concerns about why they could not have done it themselves sooner, while they were there. There had been American deaths on this operation, a further cause of the crew's discontent. The problem will be, of course, the best way to let the captain know the goal of his mission was accomplished…after the fact, so to speak."

"We can't exactly call him on the telephone," Kent said with irony as Sullivan sat down. "We will, however, add this information to the next NSA submarine downlink."

As the audience mulled the report, there was only one final question. It came from Vice Admiral Harris Zehner, it was loud, it was succinct, and it did not have an answer.

"How are we to know," he asked, standing up and turning to face the audience, "that the captain of this submarine is not threatening the West Coast of the United States with this hijacking? Do we have any uncertainties about his patriotism at this point in time, especially with this disaffection just noted by Admiral Sullivan?" He paused to let that consideration sink in. "Would it seem prudent," he asked, "for us to expand our ASW search across the waters off Washington, Oregon, California and perhaps Alaska? What are the chances that this man, who appears to have lost his capability for rational thought, might threaten the United States of America?"

Kent looked at his admiral from the podium, hesitated for a moment, and then said with his deep and commanding voice,

"Everybody in this room is aware of the downgrading of our Naval forces these past several years—it would seem appropriate for us to concentrate our *limited* anti-submarine forces in the areas most likely for this submarine to go, until we know more about where they are going." He looked back at the audience. "Now, are there any more questions?"

Sullivan stood again, his face reddening with anger. "If it would please Admiral Zehner, his comments deserve a response…." He looked at Kent, waiting.

"Go ahead, Sully, I was thinking you might have a response," Admiral Kent said into his microphone. "Say your piece."

"Admiral Zehner raises a good point about the patriotism of Commander Gary Moore. I would like to make my own point *again* to this body that the captain of the *Monterey* has repeatedly demonstrated the highest levels of competence and patriotism to this country during the many years I have known him. When I talked with him a few hours prior to this event, he was one hundred per cent lucid and coherent in every respect. This man has spent more time *under* the ocean than many here have spent in the Navy, his skills are legendary, his dedication to the United States Navy and our country has gone beyond, *far beyond*, the dedication expected, and I will add, much of this dedication has been with great expense to his family."

Sullivan tried to slow his breathing. "I will therefore ask this body to not attack this patriot's character and to accept there is a Goddamn good reason for what has happened. I do not know the reason, but we will find it. He knows the price he will pay, and the others who are with him know the price they will pay from this activity. Finally, I ask all of you to leave no stone unturned, leave no question unanswered in our collective effort to bring this nightmare to an end and return these good sailors safely to Pearl Harbor."

He sat down to the silence of the room, the unexpected smile from his attaché, the scowl of Admiral Zehner, and the final words of Admiral Kent. "The next meeting will be in two days," he said quickly, "*irrespective of the Thanksgiving holidays*, and everybody is expected to be in attendance." There were no further questions, and the meeting was adjourned.

USS *Monterey*, Pacific Ocean

Aboard the USS *Monterey*, the three SEALs, the commanding officer, and the Chief of the Boat sat back in their chairs and studied the huge plasma display screen in the officer's wardroom. Under normal operations, the room was a meeting and dining place for the submarine's officers, with a full-length table spanning most of the interior of the compact room. Several chairs surrounded the table, five of them now filled with the men facing the display screen. On the port side of the room, a large painting of a slender and beautiful naked woman hung as a majestic display of real-world beauty; the starboard side held the electronic screen, linked to a variety of inputs from periscope visual and infrared imagery to sonar displays, video recorders, communication equipment, and satellite images.

In the dark of night during the previous twenty-four hours, the submarine had travelled hundreds of miles southwest of Oahu in the direction of the Mariana Islands and the Philippine Sea beyond. At precisely 0207 hours, under the black sky of a moonless night, Berry had slowly moved the submarine to periscope depth where the Chief of the Boat had raised the periscope's antennae just above the surface of the ocean to intercept the programmed broadcast from the NSA satellite release. Each broadcast from the agency, lasting just a trace more than a millionth of a second, carried a vast volume of data, delivered to the multi-layered encryption systems aboard the *Monterey*. All that was needed for decoding success was the appropriate top secret encryption codes, the correct time of each scheduled micro blip of release, and an AN/BRA-34 antenna that could receive the information.

Thor Chainsaw leaned his huge shape forward in his chair and adjusted the screen's contrast as the men watched the recording of the Philippine's blue ocean waters spanning the display. Captain Moore toggled the switches on his hand-held controller in an attempt to locate and lock on the presumed position of *The Sweet Caroline*. "This time-delay recording is right on top of the *Sweet Caroline's* approximate location at the time of Caroline's call, just north of Busuanga Island, almost got it, almost got it," Moore said, moving a small ball in the center of his controller. "She had said about 100 miles north of Nablag."

"Yes, sir," Chief Berry said. "At that point, they'd just be in the vicinity of the Mindoro Strait. Christ, they were barely 100 miles south of Manila…. We need to zero in on her yacht about twenty minutes before the call came through to your cell phone, captain. 2314 hours, right?"

"Exactly," Moore said as he watched the screen

On the screen in front of the men, the blue waters fast-forwarded across the screen, tiny blips of boats appearing at one side of the screen and quickly disappearing off the other side.

"Here it is!" Moore exclaimed as the screen froze, the outline of a miniscule sleek white boat visible near the edge of the screen. Moore looked at the numbers on his controller. "This is about where they must have been and this is about the time, 2300 hours Hawaiian time and 1700 hours Manila time," he said.

"It's a hard call," Silverback said, pointing at a white image in the upper right corner. "The view is pretty fuzzy, it has a white deck but it's hard to tell what kind of boat that is."

"It could be damn near anything, but I don't have any idea what her boat looks like," Captain Moore said as he adjusted the knobs on his controller. "I don't even know its color or size—they were supposed to pick up the boat in Manila, three days before. However, it would seem likely that there are not that many luxury yachts off the coast of Mindoro Island."

"If they were heading south, why didn't they take the protected route through Tayabas Bay, down the Tablas Strait?" Silverback asked. "They sure as hell didn't want to go into the Sulu Sea, with its infestation of pirates from the eastern coast of Palawan Island."

Moore studied the map for a moment of silence. "The Tablas Strait is too shallow, fathometer readings down to less than 100 feet, too much risk of broaching. They took the western route around the island, trying to stay in waters thousands of feet deep."

"Keeping to the northwest, probably heading toward Nablag Island or Malalison Island in safe waters, a tourist diving mecca."

"It's all speculation," Moore said dismissively. "Chainsaw, move the time ahead, track 'em."

Chainsaw adjusted the screen again, increasing the contrast, allowing the white railing and wooden decking of the boat to barely become visible. "There are a hundred fishing boats here," he said.

"But this one here has white decks, and from the wake it looks like it's cruising at five or six knots."

"That's it," Berry growled, "that's gotta be them. Can we get a time sequence, make it move, on that TiVo YouTube thing of yours, captain?"

"I'm going to advance the sequence," Moore said. "This recorded time from the NSA is about seventeen minutes before she called. My cell phone says the call was precisely at 2314."

The men watched intently as the wake behind the vessel came to life and the boat started moving more rapidly across the water. Abruptly, the small waves spreading out from across the stern began to show white flecks.

"Look at that," Chainsaw said, pointing at the screen. "It's speeding up, they're changing course. Something's starting to come after them. Can we zoom in a little? Give us little more magnification?"

"Sure," Moore said. He carefully turned a knob on the side of the controller.

The view of the boat moving through the water moved closer, and at the edge of the screen two small dark shapes with a trail of violently splashing white water became visible from the west.

"There they are, the bastards," Berry said, glaring at the monitor.

"Fuckin' pirates, no question, hot after the yacht," Chainsaw added, sitting back in his chair to watch.

The men sat silently, watching the pursuers and the victim racing as a unit across the ocean, the distance between them gradually closing. It was almost a surreal scene, like they were watching some kind of movie, Moore thought, a movie with a known ending. Suddenly flashes from the pirate boats became visible and almost instantly, the yacht became dead in the water as the two boats circled.

"They crippled the boat, shot out its engines," Frog said from the end of the table, his slender body leaning forward, his arm pointing at the wake that rapidly disappeared.

Gary Moore found himself grinding his teeth and breathing harder. Like a deer hobbled by an attacking animal, he thought, the yacht was now wounded and unable to move, remaining motionless as the two skiffs circled, flashes of gunfire now coming from all three vessels. There was no way to see people on any of the vessels, Moore realized, the resolution was too low. The men watched the silent scene from the satellite images before them, almost spellbound as the flashes stopped, first on the yacht and finally from the two skiffs.

It was a torture to his mind that cried for relief.

As his stomach tightened during the time he knew they had come aboard, into the world of his daughter, during the time they were seeking to harm her even as she called him from the satellite phone, he felt the rising surge of blinding anger. He couldn't ignore that it was Caroline's wealthy husband, the kind of man every woman had dreams about, who had taken his daughter into his arms and into his life with vows of love and promises to protect her. Peter Blackwell was the man who had brought his daughter onto his yacht, he was the one who brought her to this sea and delivered her to the terror of the pirates. Moore wanted to strike out at something, *at anything….*

The fury that continued to surge through Moore's mind began to diminish as Thor Chainsaw said softly, "I think the battle is over now, they've captured the ship." There will be accountability, Moore resolved, accountability is on its way to these waters, and it will bring a swift justice to the creatures who would do this.

For the next five minutes, there was no activity from the South China Sea as the yacht continued to remain still, the two dark shapes of pirate boats attached at her side, like black tics clinging to a beautiful body. The men watched quietly from their chairs, nobody saying a word. Then, one of the dark boats began to pull away, a fuzzy dark shape, creating white water behind it as it accelerated. One minute later, the second black spot pulled away from the yacht and accelerated to join the first boat. They both moved further from the yacht, each churning up more white water, each creating a significant wake, each heading west, out of the Mindoro Strait, back in the direction from which they had come.

Suddenly, the screen went white with an explosion on the yacht followed by the hazy flickering of an intense fire that burned for not more than thirty seconds.

"Jesus Christ…" Silverback murmured as they watched in horror. "They've just blown up the yacht."

"Is there any way to get a better resolution on this Goddamn thing?" Chainsaw asked, reaching out to the screen again to increase the contrast. The images of the two boats moving away from the fire became fuzzier and then sharper, as the yacht sank into the ocean and virtually disappeared from the screen.

"It's the distance of the satellite from the sea," Berry said. "The yacht is sunk and so we now have a different target, they're taking them away, if anybody actually was taken prisoner."

"Oh, they've taken prisoners, I can promise you that," Moore said grimly.

"They are doing this for money," Berry said hopefully. "All we need to do now is to follow the two pirate boats back to wherever they're going, to the shore or to a mother ship and we got 'em."

Berry turned to the captain. "Sir," he asked, "can you remember *exactly* what your daughter said when she called?"

"Of course," Moore said. "She said, 'They're killing us all, they killed the captain and most of the other men, Peter is trying to hold them off,' or something like that."

At that instant, the screen suddenly went blank and cryptic notations appeared across the screen.

"What happened?" Berry asked, spinning around to stare at the screen. "Can we get the recording going again? Can we advance it? We need to follow them."

Gary Moore rapidly re-set the timing of the sequence, jumping back to the explosion and the fire, following the two fuzzy spots as they moved away from the burning yacht. He accelerated their movement right up to the spot of a blank screen again at exactly the same moment as before.

"It ends here," Moore said, "the filming and recording ends right here. The satellite probably moved out of position."

"Jesus…" Chainsaw said softly. "Where did they take them?"

The slender body of Frog took a deep breath and whispered, "If we can't follow them, do we even know if there is a mother ship or if they took them to the shore? Also, there are probably a thousand ships and hundreds of ports in that part of the ocean. They're all involved in commercial fishing or transporting products, no way to tell which one is holding potential hostages."

Moore stared at the empty screen. The increasingly probable failure of the mission had suddenly become more apparent and the death of his daughter more probable than at any time since her frantic capture and the killings. There would be no going back to this day or to this time for a second chance. Even if the mission completely failed, even if they had to surrender to some U.S. Navy fleet ship, even if they were all court-martialed and locked up forever, they could at least say they had tried to save Caroline and her husband.

The captain suddenly bolted upright. "I'm going to turn this Goddamn thing around," he said, his fingers racing across the controller device. "We're going to put this computer in reverse. I'm going back in time, back to before the attack, before the chase. We're going to follow those two boats *backwards*, across the South China Sea; back as far as we can, back through the clusters of boats closer to land, if that's where they came from. Because," he said with certainty. "*Where they came* from is probably exactly where they must have *gone* after the attack…with their hostages. That is where we'll find them."

So quietly that nobody heard, Thor Chainsaw added in a voice that was no more than a whisper, "Fuckin' genius," he said, "and, that will be where they've taken Caroline." He turned to Captain Moore. "Captain?" he asked, "Did your daughter say anything else, anything about the pirates?"

"No," Moore answered. "Just that the people on the boat were getting killed and that the captain had been killed." He thought intensely, forcing himself to remember every element of the call. She had been terrorized and unable to give him the precise coordinates of their chase and capture. She had given them as much information as possible, but she had been stopped.

"There *was* one more thing," Moore said, his mind pulling up the sound, the terrible voice, from the telephone. "It wasn't what *Caroline* said. It was what somebody else said. There was another voice I could hear over the cellphone, a man's voice, telling Caroline to hang up the phone. He said for her to drop the phone or that…." The five men in the room turned and stared at the captain as he said the final words, "…that, if she did not drop the telephone, the man's voice said something like '*Peter Blackwell will be killed.*'"

The room was silent as the words sank in. It was the Chief of the Boat who finally spoke, his raspy voice filling the compartment, his bushy eyebrows drawing together as he asked the obvious question they were all thinking.

"*How did the pirate fuckers know they had just captured Peter Blackwell?*"

Silverback asked, "Somebody told them the wealthy guy named Blackwell was heading south from Manila?"

"Everything can be a conspiracy issue," Moore said, a quick and terrible thought flashed through his mind. *If Peter Blackwell was the wealthy man to be held for ransom, of what value was his wife?*

He shifted around in his chair and finally said, "More likely he just identified himself to them when they took over the boat."

Silverback grunted. "I don't know, sir. I think they knew exactly who he was, at the time of the attack, and I think they knew exactly what boat he was on. Maybe somebody in Manila, somebody noting their departure…."

"Somebody now waiting for a share of the ransom," Chainsaw said quietly.

There was no response and the men watched as Moore moved the controls to run the sequence in reverse, backing the attacking ships away from *The Sweet Caroline*, moving them back in time across the South China Sea. His hands rapidly jumped across the controller, moving the black ball in the center, twisting a couple of knobs, pausing every few seconds to scrutinize the screen's display of the waters near the Palawan coast. They followed the skiffs' wake to the south, through the waters of the South China Sea, past clusters of other small boats, around fishing boats, and near a couple of larger boats that looked like transport boats. After another minute of surrealistic backwards movements, the small skiffs finally and slowly backed up to a huge dark freighter at least a hundred times the size of Caroline's boat. They stayed attached to the boat for at least five minutes of reverse filming before the movement of the satellite created a blank screen again.

"There's the mother ship," Chainsaw said softly, "probably less than five miles off the western coast of Linapacan or Palawan Island, anchored in about 200 feet of water."

"That sucker is *big*," Silverback said, staring at the screen. "Probably snagged right out of the shipping lanes in the South China Sea. Nice for us to have a big target, if they don't have too many terrorists onboard," he added. "It's big enough to get a clear identity, it probably is anchored…. Can we get the coordinates?"

"Locked in, got it," Moore said, writing down the numbers from the screen.

"Good," Chainsaw said, "let's go get the miserable sons-of-bitches."

Chainsaw stood up from his chair, quickly joined by Silverback and Frog. "We are going to identify this ship and then we are going to build us a model," he said as the three SEALs headed out of the wardroom toward the forward compartments of the boat. "We are going to build us a micro *mother ship*."

"And some micro hostages and pirates," Frog added with a smile.

Four hours later, Berry's voice carried throughout the submarine, over the 1 MC system, announcing that breakfast was being served in the crew's dinette. The food, served by the torpedoman Fred Wilson and Amanda, was a combination of eggs, rice, canned peaches and water. The water tasted suspiciously rusty and stale, but most of the diners drank some and they found the food to be reasonably tasty. There was no milk, there hadn't been milk on the submarine for over a month. Everybody on the boat, except Bodine at the helm and Robby at the nuclear reactor control panel, sat at the cramped tables and eagerly devoured the food, the enlisted men noting that the captain ate with them rather than off in the officers' wardroom as was the norm. Spirits were up, especially now that everybody knew the precise target at the end of their voyage, the *mother ship*, and the enthusiastic conversation reflected the sentiment to proceed as quickly as possible to the goal.

Sitting at the starboard dining table with the three SEALs, the captain marveled at the quantity of food each man consumed, often asking for seconds and then thirds as Amanda eagerly made the rounds and scooped additional eggs and rice onto their plates. She seemed to be happy with her new job, as chef, as server, and as dishwasher, working side-by-side with her torpedoman lover, almost like she was practicing for the domestic years as a wife with children. It seemed to Moore she had adapted to the submerged existence quickly, after the first day or so, observing like everyone else in the boat that, while under the ocean, there was no sensation of movement, no feeling of the water surrounding them, no sense of the pressure that put them all at risk.

After breakfast and an enthusiastic compliment to the two chefs, Moore returned to his stateroom, closed the door, washed his face and climbed into a fresh dark blue one-piece jumpsuit that covered him from his shoulders to his feet.

He lay back in his rack and slowly untied the golden string around his white packet of letters again with a gentle reverence, almost like he was performing a religious rite, as he opened the white paper enclosing the treasures from Caroline. He had kept the letters in sequence, marking a kind of historical series of events that could bring him some comfort, blending with a profound and deepening sadness. The next letter was a happy one, he knew, it was the letter of optimism, a letter written when she was just fifteen years old and ready to start high school.

It was a letter he had almost memorized since he had received it at the end of one of the longest patrols of his career.

Hello again, Daddy, from San Diego.

I am sorry it is so long since I've written to you but I've been crazy busy here with studies and my friends in school. Everything is fine with Aunt Marcy (I would let you know if it wasn't), although she tells me almost every day that I have too much energy. If you were here, I know you would be telling me that the 10th and the 11th grades are the most important in my life, that they will determine where I go to college, who I end up marrying, and how smart my kids are going to be—all of which will determine how happy I am going to be. Right now, I need your advice about what I should do about all these boys who seem to have become interested in me. I won't get conceited, Daddy, don't worry, I just don't want to do the wrong thing and a lot of the boys are really nice. I also know you would warn me about all the sailors in San Diego—again, don't worry, since it's the high school boys that have me worried. Anyway, I didn't want to write about boys, I just wanted to let you know that I miss you and that I'm keeping my grades up. I have found that, unlike most of my girlfriends, I like science a lot. A couple of the boys helped me with my science project, a synthesized photosensitive mimicry system, similar to what is found in nature, proving survival like Darwin predicted—I won the Sweepstakes Award for San Diego County and I actually had to give a speech at the university auditorium. It went fine, Marcy was there and everybody seemed happy until a professor in the audience asked me what I wanted to do with my life…and I didn't have a clue. Embarrassing, for sure, but I think you would have liked the speech. They kept clapping forever and ever! I love you Daddy, and I'm sorry you have to work so hard in that submarine, wherever you are. I hope you can come back home for a while, and maybe we could go to that ice cream place we used to like on the pier—then we can talk and talk. I have so many other things to bring you up to date about and most of the time I really REALLY miss you!

Love,

Caroline

Chapter 8

Cho Ying Atlas, South China Sea

The steel decks of the anchored tanker *Cho Ying Atlas* creaked as the dark swells from the South China Sea rolled beneath her. Beyond the repetitive groaning of steel in the early morning hours, the footsteps of the three men briskly moving down her port passageway on the B level alerted the skinny Filipino sentry that Guleed Khalid and his bodyguards were approaching. Khalid was the biggest of the men by nearly six inches, a startling contrast to the diminutive body size of almost everybody who lived on nearby Palawan Island. His voice, his presence, his *authoritative manner* regularly demanded respect from those around him. And his oversized mouth filled with bad teeth, surrounded by a landscape of scarring and pockmarks, caused revulsion and fear among those prisoners he regularly tortured and often executed.

"Any problems?" Khalid growled as the sentry, a thin man with curly black hair standing in front of the steel door, quickly lowered his Kashtan automatic rifle.

"Nothing but babbling from the last three hostages you delivered, until Macuha ordered them to be silent," the man answered, stepping aside and opening the massive door to allow Khalid and his guards to enter.

"Stay alert," Khalid ordered the sentry as they entered the bastille of failed protection for the tanker's crew, the citadel[17] safe room of the *Cho Ying Atlas*.

They walked around the mattresses scattered on the floor, ignoring the disheveled men rising up to fearfully watch Khalid. The Filipino guard in the corner of the room turned on the bright overhead lights. Most of the men on mattresses were Chinese, and except for a woman between a well-dressed Caucasian and an Indian man at the far side of the room, they wore greasy and torn t-shirts pulled over the top of filthy trousers. Sitting upright on her mattress in the far corner was Caroline, her long hair disheveled, her fiery eyes staring directly at Khalid.

"Don't look at me, Caroline," Khalid said to the woman, waving his gun in her direction. "You and your husband's crew killed three of my men a couple of days ago, and it is only because of Peter that you are still alive. And you, what's your name?" He glared at the Indian man sitting next to her.

"My name is Mombo, I am from India, and…"

"Mombo," Khalid repeated harshly. "My name is Guleed Khalid. It is a good thing you know how to surrender perfectly, or *you* also would be dead." Finally he turned to the Caucasian man. "Peter," he smiled at him, "you are a lucky man. Very lucky because you are the most valuable person in this room…"

"Go to hell, and keep your hands off…" Peter Blackwell began.

With a quick movement, Khalid reached over and grabbed Caroline's hair, jerking her to her feet. "I may lay a hand on anyone *or anything I like*, including your precious Caroline, and you have forgotten that you are not in charge?" Khalid said quietly, as he threw her to the mattress. "Chain of command, Peter, chain of command. This is *my* ship, not your little boat, I am the captain here, do you understand that?"

"Peter," Caroline said, moving her hair back from her face, "I'll be fine. We really have no choice…."

"Listen to your wife, Peter," Khalid said, pausing for a moment as he patted the top of her head and his huge mouth opened with a smile. "And, if you do everything right, Peter Blackwell, and if your father does everything right, you may find freedom awaits you." He turned to walk toward the door with his two men. "The same cannot be said for Caroline," he called over his shoulder.

"Khalid!" Peter's voice boomed out into the room, stopping Khalid abruptly. The man slowly turned and faced Peter Blackwell who was now standing and pointing his finger at the man. Khalid said nothing as he began caressing the pistol in his holster.

"We are a *package*, Khalid," Blackwell said firmly. "Caroline and I are a package, have you got that? I go nowhere without her…nowhere…."

Khalid's huge mouth closed tightly as he glared at his hostage. His hand lifted away from his gun and he crossed his arms across his chest, staring at the captive.

"You go where I tell you to go!" he said harshly.

Without another word, he turned away, and as the two guards followed, he walked out the door, slamming the steel barrier behind him, sealing the hostages again in the dark citadel of the captive tanker, *Cho Ying Atlas*.

USS *Monterey*, Pacific Ocean

For the SEALs to gather all the necessary information about the tanker they had seen on the screen, Captain Moore had to break one of the most fundamental rules of submarine protocol, the rule of *absolute silence*. From their high-resolution screen, the photos of the tanker demonstrated a visible deck conforming to the *Seaphoto Maritime Photography Catalogue* image of the *Cho Ying Atlas*. The crude oil tanker was almost big enough to be seen by the naked eye from outer space. From the coordinates, she was resting in 156 feet of ocean, 4.9 miles off the northern third of Palawan Island, her displacement of more than 82,000 metric tons creating an enormous transport capability that had routinely moved massive amounts of oil along the central shipping lanes of the South China Sea. The crew could see in the slow-motion time frame that she was rolling in the slow swells of waves moving toward Palawan and Linapacan Islands, her steel sides were rusted and covered with algae since her anchors had been attached to the offshore island shelf after her hijacking. It had been a violent day of death and capture that had barely made headlines around the world.

There were no sources of information about the tanker in the *Monterey's* archives and it quickly became obvious that they would need to interrogate Google in a search for the schematics of the ship. However, it was impossible for the SEALs to study the Internet for random information about a specific ship without sending signals to the satellites to narrow the search. After a half hour of hearing the SEALs' case and seeing their need, Captain Moore launched what he liked to call "The International Cruise Ship Internet Option." Only a single commercial cruise ship needed to be identified, to activate the option. It was a simple task in a sea filled with cruise liners and their passengers, the ships loaded with thousands of people continuously interrogating the Internet about everything from pornography to the correct temperature for roasting a turkey.

The *Marco Polo* was easy to find, her lights blazing across the Western Pacific night, her huge screws churning the ocean, her antennae transmitting and receiving trillions of bytes of data every second in the continuous interaction between her passengers and the satellites above. Shadowing the ship through the night, checking her course from time to time, Captain Moore prepared for the inquiry, a quick 3-second transmission buried in the business and personal transmissions from the passenger liner. For the answers to his three questions, the inquiry from the submerged *Monterey* would have to be quick and to the point:

1. Find all pirate hijackings in the past two years off the Philippines.
2. Provide all specifications relating to the exterior and internal structure of the *Cho Ying Atlas*.
3. Identify any news information about Caroline and Peter Blackwell.

Hopefully, Captain Moore thought, there would be no triangulation from listening military ears, triangulation that could pinpoint the *Monterey* as the source of the inquiry.

From the periscope peering into the night lights of the *Marco Polo*, Gary Moore gave the thumbs up signal, Chief Berry at the other side of the control center keyed the information request, and within eight seconds, all the data in the world about those three questions was in the possession of the SEALs. After a final GPS fix to adjust the submarine's inertial guidance system for precise navigational confirmation, the captain dropped the periscope, and ordered Bodine to dive to five hundred feet. The SEALs confirmed the *Cho Ying Atlas* had disappeared a couple of months before, and as they started their model-building work, Captain Moore headed toward the engine room.

Although the submarine was rigged for silent cruising, the engine room was filled with a spectrum of whining and rumbling noises from the machinery filling the compartment. The propulsion turbine, the air conditioning systems, the various drain and trim pumps, and the turbogenerators, all spinning with humming, grinding, and screeching noises, created a cacophony of noise that made normal conversation more of a yelling match than speaking. The outside of the submarine may be silent, and most of the inside of the submarine was silent, but within the engine room was a bedlam of noise, most of it muffled by buffer cushions at the machinery attachment points. In contrast to the usual clusters of men roaming around the upper and lower levels of the compartment while at sea, the entire engine room now contained only three nukes, and two of them were sequestered back in the air conditioned Maneuvering Room where the huge control panels allowed operation of the submarine's nuclear and electrical systems.

With the noise-silencing ear plugs jammed into their ears, Robby sat stiffly upright in front of his beloved nuclear reactor control panel while Baxter watched his electric control panel like a mother hen, both men facing their meters with focused concentration. Manny Munroe, covered with grease and oil stains, hustled up and down the ladder connecting the compartment's upper and lower levels, continuously rushing around the steel deck, inspecting his machinery and, from all appearances, appeared to be happy with how his equipment was performing. The entire compartment was hot and humid from the steam hissing through the large insulated pipes and leaking out through connecters, as well as from the shimmering heat from the high speed turbines. Moore noticed each of the two men in the Maneuvering Room had arranged an air conditioning pipe aimed directly at the tops of their heads, while Munroe's shirt was drenched in oil and sweat as he clamored around the engine room.

"Hello, captain," Robby said, taking his eyes off the reactor control panel for a moment. He was a lean man, with an unusually slight frame for a submariner, his curly red hair covering the top of his head and kept as long as the Navy would allow. "It's five days out now, sir, making some progress for your daughter?" he asked.

"We are," Moore said quickly, moving his position slightly to one side of the Maneuvering Room to insure cool air descended from a ventilation pipe above his head. "We are east of the Philippines, and we have identified the probable mother ship—an empty tanker, the *Cho Ying Atlas*, taken from the South China Sea shipping route. The SEALs are working on our attack plan; they now have all the information they need. We'll be transiting the Philippine Sea for the next couple of days."

Moore looked around at the men. "You guys okay back here?" he asked.

"Yes, sir," Baxter said, crossing his arms in front of his chest and scowling at the maze of electrical meters in front of him. "We're doing port 'n' starboard watches, six hours on watch, six off, rotating among the three of us. The duty mattress is around the corner for us to zonk out between watches, and we gotta call-schedule all set up. Food's not bad, either, and that gal—what's her name?"

"Amanda…." Munroe said from behind the captain. "Sweet Amanda." He looked at Moore and smiled broadly. "The latest experiment with women-in-submarines."

"Amanda," Baxter said wistfully. The girl is a great cook, she makes the best eggs and boils the finest rusty water I've had in a long time. Beats the holy hell out of my Claudia back home who burned my eggs and didn't even know how to boil water." He paused and grimaced. "Actually, I should have said," he added, "my Claudia who *used* to be back home."

"Right," Munroe said. "Now that Amanda has settled her soul--think we could make her a nuke? I could use some help in the engine room, and it just doesn't seem fair that, with a total of only one woman on this *entire* submarine, that she should have to stay up front with a forward puke."

"The 'forward puke' is *engaged* to her," Moore said with a smile, "and she's not 'staying' with him. I also don't think she is interested in becoming a nuke, especially since she hasn't yet joined the Navy. She did say she wanted to be a nurse but has not yet expressed any interest in nuclear power. By the way, Doc Wheat has ordered her to remain forward of the nuclear reactor compartment so you shouldn't be seeing her around the engine room much. Something about her having babies some day and ovarian exposure to radiation."

"Wonderful," Baxter said. "Another reason to show up for the evening meal. If I get a cut or something, will Amanda bandage it up?

"No," Moore said, smiling, "Doc Wheat will bandage it up."

Baxter winced. "That's no fun, guess I won't get a cut."

Munroe rushed up from the port side of the engine room, reached over to the throttle controls, and moved one of the wheels slightly to increase the propulsion power as Baxter reached up to his electric control panel and adjusted a knob regulating the flow of electrical current from the starboard turbogenerator.

Moore looked at Robby. "I'm going to be needing the best possible calculation about how much reactor we have left," he said. "Obviously, we're approaching the end of core life—do we still have enough to get out there and back?"

Robby suddenly became dead-serious. "Captain," he said, "we have not been exactly cruising in a power conservation mode. If we continue at this rate of power consumption, we'll be at maximum depletion in about seven or eight days." He pointed at the Reactor Control Panel. "Notice where the control rods are, sir? At that depletion point, we'll start to lose power. At some point, depending on how long we're at full speed, we will barely have enough power to come up to snorkel depth and light off the diesel." He looked back up at the captain. "Which we can do, of course, if nobody is worried about our being identified by everybody out there. Can we get back to Papa Hotel by then?"

"Depends on what happens when we get to the *Cho Ying Atlas*," Moore said. "On our return trip, when time isn't so critical, we can slow down and conserve some power. Right now, we have to get there as soon as possible."

Baxter swung his chair around and looked up at Moore. "Captain, is your daughter being ransomed or anything like that? Has there been any word since her capture? Do you know if she's okay?"

"We just scanned every major newspaper in the country. As of a half hour ago, there is no word about her or her husband. If there is any kind of ransom consideration, it is not being reported to anybody."

Pearl Harbor, COMPACFLT Office

Whenever Rear Admiral Sullivan was urgently summoned to Admiral Kent's office, it was automatically bad news. In Sullivan's office at Pearl Harbor, his attaché Brenda had *whispered* to her boss that Admiral Kent wanted to see him across the highway at the COMPACFLT office "immediately" and then she promptly held out his coat and hat before he rushed from the building to the car. There was no time to find a driver and the admiral quickly jumped into the driver's seat and accelerated to the Pearl Harbor exit. Sullivan had discovered during the past several years, that the signal outside the Makalapa gate is consistently an accurate indication about the good luck or bad luck he was about to experience—if it was red, impending activities would go badly, and if it was green, it was probable that a blessing of good fortune was about to come his way.

The light turned red just before he reached the intersection and he screeched to a stop. He waited and he waited, his fingers drumming on the steering wheel, as three different groups of pedestrians needed to cross the street in front of him, walking painfully slowly, *aloha style*, as the admiral fumed inside his car.

Three minutes later, he screeched his car to a halt outside the COMPACFLT building and rushed inside. Kent's collection of secretaries and aides motioned Sullivan into the admiral's office where the white-haired man sat calmly behind his desk, his hands resting on the spotless desktop, his blue eyes looking as if he wanted to talk about the beauty of the flower clusters growing around the grounds of the command center. Remarkably calm, Sullivan thought, just like Chester Nimitz during the dark days of the War in the Pacific. He swung the door behind him and promptly sat down in the chair across the desk from the admiral, attentively waiting for the man to speak.

As the door clicked shut and the silence came to an end, Kent's eyes seemed to become colder as his deep voice boomed, "Where the fuck is our submarine, Sullivan?"

"Well, Stephen, I'm working on that..."

"The President wants to know, the CNO wants to know, the SECNAV wants to know, and I want to know."

"Yes, sir…"

"Furthermore, Vice Admiral Zehner wants to know, the Brits, the Japanese, the CIA, the NSA, the entire fucking world wants to know! The Goddamn Chinese want to know *very very* badly and, as you are aware, they are now committed to sinking the *Monterey* if they can find it. They might very well find it."

Kent's tanned face grimaced as he added, "All of this shit comes down to you, *admiral*, are you making any progress?"

The way Kent said "admiral" left no doubt in Sullivan's mind that his career was not quite as certain as it had been before the *Monterey* disappeared. Kent's scowl created a further sense that his own future, and the future of Kent, harbored a spectrum of events that would likely include a court-martial and dereliction of duty kinds of things. Isn't that what they did to the admirals overseeing the fleet when those Navy ships collided in the waters off Southeast Asia?

Sullivan swallowed hard and tried to match the stare of his senior officer.

"We are trying to find out why his daughter has not yet called us, sir. It seems very unusual, with news about this in the press, that we have not heard from her. We're trying to find out why, when we're getting calls from everybody's families about the hijacking, calls from homeless people about the submarine, calls from the curious, calls from *everybody on the entire planet.* And, sir," Sullivan said quietly, "we are trying to find out why there has been no contact from Caroline...whatever her last name is, about the captain."

Kent stood up behind his desk, appearing to Sullivan to be at least a foot taller than he had appeared the last time he saw the man. "For God's sake, follow the NSA's search of Facebook, go *somewhere*, find out what her name is, and if 'Caroline-whatever-her-last-name is' should actually call you," Kent said with dripping sarcasm, "would you please tell her we *also* would like to find her dad and the submarine, but *we don't know exactly where to look.*"

"Yes, sir, I will tell her that," Sullivan answered quietly. "She had a wedding, a high profile wedding, about two years ago, and I was invited by Captain Moore. It happened when we were in Washington working on funding for that covert Indonesia project—I couldn't go. I've looked everywhere for the invitation but it appears to have long ago been discarded. The NSA is looking for a record of the marriage—we don't even know who the hell she married or where the hell she was married, and the only person who can tell us for sure is the captain of the *Monterey.* We've extended the search net across the Pacific, we've looked for any debris suggesting her sinking, and we've even blocked the Strait of Magellan along the southern tip of South America..."

"I *know* where the fucking Strait of Magellan is!"

"Yes, sir, and in spite of the government bullshit with no funds left for anything, we now have the tightest ASW net we can assemble. We've got the seventh fleet deploying the towed linear assortments and the VDS[18] array across the South Pacific, and we're using the Thales Underwater Sonar System.

"Finally, the NSA is closing in on information from the Middle East family of that roommate of the Amanda woman who snuck aboard the boat, that Ashia Jamila female at the University of Hawaii. She is under intense interrogation and there are apparently some radical Muslim family elements back in Iran. We don't know how many weapons Amanda might have taken aboard. This last element is a smoking gun, sir, and we're monitoring the chatter from..."

"Sully, the *Monterey* has been gone four days and you're monitoring the chatter?"

"No, sir, well...yes, sir," Sullivan said, finally standing up, taking a deep breath and looking straight into Admiral Kent's eyes. "The only way out of this thing, Stephen, is to find out *why* they took the sub. There has to be a fundamental reason for this, a damn good reason, and honest to God, the way it unfolded, a hijacking by force seems unlikely—there was no gunfire and a whole group of *Monterey* sailors willingly came aboard. They brought the nuclear reactor on line and made it operational, and the CO has exhibited his combat capabilities to escape our net."

"Okay, great," Kent said. "I got all that, and I already *know* all that. Moore is the most talented commander in the fleet, and they must have had a good reason to do this. All that is wonderful, but I will tell you, it does not make sense for eleven men to willingly destroy their careers, to take the chance of the submarine being compromised, sunk, or captured, to face the long prison sentences they will get should they survive this escapade." He paused, and slowly sat down. "Okay," he continued, his voice softening, "Sully, would you do me a favor and go find the reason they took this submarine? If you haven't done it by this evening, would you do it in the next day at the latest? We're having another combined briefing on Tuesday, the fucking press is going to be there..."

"The press? Sir, I don't think..."

"I know, I know, let me change the way I said that. The President thinks the press should be updated at this briefing, the President is going to be monitoring the satellite feed on this briefing, and the President is going to hold a Presidential briefing in the White House at the conclusion of the briefing. On top of that, the CNO and the Secretary of the Navy will be flying out to Pearl. They are going to scrutinize my ass, they are going to scrutinize your ass, and they are going to scrutinize every ass on the line of the United States Navy submarine command structure at Pearl Harbor. They will, and I will, very likely be talking with the President, *again*, immediately after the briefing."

Kent leaned across the desk, staring at Sullivan, his jaw muscles grinding.

"*Would you bring me something good to tell these people*?"

International Cyber Systems, Inc., Seattle

The howling wind blowing across Seattle buffeted the windows of the towering glass building on Columbia Street as Dominic Mathews gaveled the Board meeting to order. Sitting around the long table in the center of the room, none of the seventeen members appeared happy to be at a Board meeting on a Saturday morning of Thanksgiving weekend. In the corner of the room, sitting straight in his overstuffed leather chair, the white-bearded Randolph Blackwell watched the Chairman of the Board, his narrowed eyes looking around the room as if he was seeking to enter the minds of each Board member, looking to assess the probability of the acceptability of the information soon to be brought before them.

"Thank you for coming to this emergency meeting," Mathews said to the men and women facing him, "your attendance today goes beyond the call of duty and far beyond your normal obligation as Board members. I know many of you traveled significant distances to be here, and I thank you for that. I also assure you, this will be the briefest Board meeting on record." He glanced down at a page of notes. "In fact, the purpose of the meeting is to go on record, as a courtesy to each of you and the fulfillment of the regulatory environment, about a business matter about to be consummated. There will not be an opportunity to vote on this and no vote is required. At this time, without going into more detail, I will turn the meeting over to Mr. Blackwell."

He turned toward Randolph Blackwell and added, "Sir, the meeting is yours."

Blackwell's slender frame stood up and stepped away from his leather chair. He walked the length of the room, his white hair hanging over his forehead, his eyes looking straight ahead, seemingly unaware of the silence and the stares from everybody in the room. At the end of the long table, standing behind the seated chairman, he turned to face the group as he brushed his hair away from his eyes.

"I'm sorry," his voice rumbled, "that my son, Peter, could not be with us today, since his stock in our company will be affected by what you are about to hear. All of your stock will be affected, and there is no way I can change that. I will be selling shares when the markets open on Monday for the generation of funds in the amount of one hundred million dollars. These are my personal shares, the sale or purchase of which I'm sure you realize needs neither your approval nor the SEC's approval."

Ignoring the faint gasps from several Board members, he looked at an overweight man near the head of the table.

"Bernie, as Chief Financial Officer, you are directed to sell an amount of my shares to generate this revenue and you are furthermore directed to notify me as soon as the trade has been completed. " Blackwell looked around the room at the other Board members. "Provided as a courtesy to you today, the minutes of this meeting will record this information. The minutes will be confidential, and each of you will maintain strict confidentiality, no matter how compelling the media may be, no matter how many news corporations may call each of you, *and they will*, and no matter how many friends or relatives ask for information. If significant stock trades occur from any of you prior to my sale of stock, the SEC will quickly and properly confirm that you all possess insider information, and it will be confirmed that this information was used for stock trades prior to my sale. If this information to you, by subpoena of the minutes of this meeting, results in your own trading of stock before Morningstar, Reuters and others report the sale to the public, be assured you will be removed from this Board, you will be investigated for a Class B misdemeanor, and you will likely receive a prison sentence. That is all."

As everyone in the room watched in silence, the elderly man walked back across the room. As he opened the door, one of the females sitting near the end of the table called out, "Mr. Blackwell, is our company in some kind of trouble?" The only answer from the CEO was a vigorous slamming of the door.

That sound was immediately followed by the sharp crack of Dominic Mathews' gavel striking the wooden block to signify that the Thanksgiving weekend Board meeting for ICSI had come to an end.

USS *Monterey*, Pacific Ocean

As the *Monterey* cleared the Mariana Islands north of Guam and moved into the middle of the Philippine Sea, Gary Moore decided to take the submarine near the surface for a breath of fresh air. They were approaching the Babuyan Channel, above the Philippine's north island of Luzon, as Doc Wheat reported some carbon dioxide buildup slightly above the usual ten-fold increase common for submarine air. The oxygen for the boat had been supplied by the "Bomb," a contraption that separated oxygen from hydrogen in ocean water. It was located in one of the auxiliary machinery spaces behind a thick curtain of steel to protect nearby humanity from the potential explosive capabilities of the device.

If everything worked well, which everything did most of the time, all was fine for the supply of oxygen to humans enclosed for long periods within the confines of the submarine. However, odor often became an annoying factor, increasingly noted on the *Monterey* by Amanda, who wondered about that "hissing" sound that lasted about twenty minutes each night, accompanied by the foulest odor she had ever had the displeasure to inhale. "It is like a mixture of unknown toxic lethal substances," she had complained to Wilson, "combined with concentrated fragrance of skunk, rotting vomit, and dog dung. *Submariners actually put up with this sort of thing*?"

"They're just blowing the head," Wilson had casually explained, clarifying that each day, Bodine, and sometimes Munroe, had to flush the sanitary tanks below the toilets by blowing the contents into the deep ocean waters under very high pressure. "After each blow," he further explained, "they have to vent off the pressure *somewhere*. They can't vent it *outside* the boat, makes too much noise. So they vent it *inside the boat*, so we can use the toilets, and..."

Amanda had cut him off, telling him she'd leave the details to the submariners. From this point on, she would just think about other things until she went to nursing school, when such items resulting from things like human waste might become, by necessity, more acceptable.

The buildup of toxic odors was slower than usual with only twelve persons on the submarine, Moore was happy to notice, but he reasoned a little fresh air pulled in through the snorkel would be welcomed by everybody. After Chief Berry declared from the sonar station the complete absence of engine noises from any nearby ships, Bodine carefully brought the *Monterey* up to periscope depth. Berry raised the starboard periscope and Captain Moore raised the port 'scope for a direct visualization of the surrounding ocean. Moore began rotating his periscope for a quick 360 degree rotation, as Berry did the same, searching for any ships or surface objects that might spot them or collide with the snorkel.

Moore suddenly hollered, "Full left rudder, NOW, full left rudder! Dive! Dive!"

Berry saw the small fishing boat an instant later and both men immediately lowered the periscopes as the *Monterey* quickly submerged again. The surface craft, dead in the water, had been not more than a thousand feet away from their periscopes. It was a small and very silent wooden boat with bright colors on its side, balanced by outrigger floats. In the middle of the boat, three men had stared directly at the periscopes. Their eyes had been like saucers, their mouths had dropped wide open, and two of them dropped their fishing poles into the water as the submarine immediately disappeared.

"'Scopes are down!" Berry yelled, adding, "Bodine. Make our depth 300 feet."

The two men watched the depth gauge unwind as the *Monterey* quickly moved down into the ocean.

Berry turned and looked at the captain. "Fishermen," he said. "They're going to report us. They're going to report us to somebody."

"They will, no question," Moore answered, "probably to the Philippine government. Do you think we snagged their nets?"

"Didn't see any but they were fishing and God knows, we probably snagged *something*."

Moore looked at the gauges at the diving station and then looked at his Chief of the Boat. "You saw the last NSA download, didn't you?" he asked quietly.

"The Chinese wanting to sink us? Hostile little bastards...."

"They just don't know," Moore said. "They don't like pirates any more than we do."

"Right, but they're still looking for a reason to attack us."

"That may be correct but they're not going to find us."

"Agreed," Moore said. "However, we still have to get across the Philippine Sea. Remember the Chinese didn't pay any attention to the international 12 mile territorial waters definition when they attacked the Navy's EP-3 operating off their island of Hainan awhile back."

"Right. That was a fun experience, especially for the Chinese pilot who crashed into them. That attack was well outside their territorial waters."

Berry looked hard at the captain. "I think the South China Sea is potentially the biggest military flashpoint in the world, and the Chinese will simply sink us if they find us."

Moore looked at the chief and smiled. "They're going to come after us if they can. So, we better be good, don't you think, Berry?"

"Captain, if we're going to be good, don't you think it would be a good idea to be locked and loaded? Permission to load the torpedo tubes?"

In the torpedo room, Petty Officer Fred Wilson looked at Amanda with increasing appreciation. He moved his black hair off his forehead as he straightened up next to the long steel Mark 48 torpedo at his side, greeting her as she returned from the shower. She was now beginning to look extraordinarily sexy with her borrowed dark blue boomer suit, her wet hair hanging over her shoulders, her breasts pushing seductively against the front of the garment. She even smelled good, he noticed as she came close to him, a clean soapy feminine kind of smell that created an excitement—remarkable, he thought, considering that such an experience had never previously occurred in this compartment on this submarine.

He reached over to the torpedo, shut the panel allowing access to the electronics within, and had just started to compliment her when the loudspeaker above his head suddenly blared, "Torpedo, control, load tubes 1 through 4, do not flood tubes."

Amanda looked up at the speaker with a startled expression as Wilson immediately grabbed a microphone and answered, "Load tubes 1, 2, 3, and 4, do not flood tubes, forward torpedo room, aye, aye."

For the next ten minutes, Amanda stepped back and watched with amazement, as Wilson raced back and forth through the compartment, activating the torpedo fire control system, activating hydraulic moving systems, opening torpedo tube doors, and finally rolling four sleek torpedoes down their rollers and into the tubes. He shut the door of each tube, turned and smiled at Amanda as he grabbed the microphone from the maze of pipes in the overhead and said, "Tubes 1, 2, 3, and 4 loaded and locked, ready to fire after flooding and opening outer doors."

"Very well," came back through the speakers as he sat down next to Amanda and informed her that all had gone exceedingly well considering that the usual five men involved in the process of loading torpedoes were not aboard.

Amanda reached over and gently placed her finger across Wilson's lips, silencing the man.

"I'm here," she said. "Although I may not be qualified in submarines, and I may not be qualified on torpedoes, and I may in general be clueless about all these complicated systems," she smiled, "I know how to follow orders and I am qualified in *some* things."

He studied her face, thinking about her beauty and what he could say at this time and in this place. Wilson finally took a deep breath and said, "You are very qualified in many things…thank you for putting up with all of this." He waved his left arm toward the machinery and the stacks of additional torpedoes surrounding them. "Thank you for coming here to be with me, and for helping me throw some chow together for the crew."

"And for being a nurse in early, early, training, and for helping you with the dishes, too?" she said, her eyes becoming moist.

"Yes, and for all that too, thank you."

"You're welcome," she said. "With my help, you are getting so domesticated, Fred. At least we can be together even if this is not the most romantic environment and even though we are under the…deeply submerged under the...whatever part of the ocean we're in."

"Philippine Sea" he said quietly, smiling. "Think of this like an engagement cruise, sorta...."

"In a suite with torpedoes and little cramped racks."

Wilson sat up straight and smiled. "Did you say you're willing to take orders?" he asked.

"I am..."

"Okay, then, Miss Amanda Peterson, putting aside all the orders I would *like* to give you right now, I am ordering you to kiss your fiancé, do it quickly, and to make it very, very nice...."

"Yes, sir," she said with a salute. As she moved into his arms, she whispered, "don't take all my Chapstick."

Chapter 9

Captain's Stateroom, USS *Monterey*, Pacific Ocean

Within his darkened stateroom, Captain Gary Moore couldn't get the moment out of his mind, not when he was awake, and repeatedly, not when he was asleep. It was almost like some kind of post-traumatic stress syndrome, he figured, the kind of thinking process burned into his mind that would not go away, not even after twelve years, recurring as vividly as if it had happened the day before. It often came to him at night, or in the early morning hours, when he was in an environment that actually had evening hours and morning hours, in a place of the *real* world where sunlight and night occurred on a regular and predictable basis. Within the submarine, continually deep under the ocean where hours of the day or night had no meaning, it would often come to him after four or five hours of sleep, and every time, with every recurrence, the memory of *that day* was always the same.

They had stood there together, a father and a daughter, side by side. Thirteen-year-old Caroline in her yellow summer dress, and Captain Gary Moore in his white officer's uniform, gold dolphins and other medals above the left breast pocket, officer's hat pulled down over his forehead, shoes shining with a mirror finish planted on the freshly-cut grass. The gravestones stood before them, facing them, the fresh flowers in the dark red soil in front of Meredith's headstone with colorful petals moving back and forth in the trade winds of Hawaii, the winds that blew across the expansive pristine grounds of the Nuuanu Memorial Park. They were the winds that could never cleanse the torture of her death. There were no words and there was no experience that could erase the reality of her fulminant departure, her presence taken away as if by a vicious pariah of nature, forever gone from their lives.

There was the sense that she had lifted up from the red Hawaiian soil at that moment and said to him, said *to both of them*, "I am so sorry, I am so terribly sorry."

Caroline had stood there holding his hand for ten minutes on that dismal day of her burial, each silent with the thoughts that would never leave them for the remainder of their lives, each feeling the presence of the other and knowing that everything had changed forever. As he had turned to look down at her with reddened eyes, she had spoken to him quietly and seriously, in a voice that could barely be heard, a message from her heart. There would never be a time in the future, she had told him, that her father would ever leave her, *as her mother had just done*, to never return. She would just not allow it, she had said, and then after fighting back her own tears, she had said it again while squeezing his hand, her voice choking.

In a voice deepened by the intensity of the moment, with his wife bearing witness from the grave, he had replied to Caroline that he would always be there for her, no matter the circumstance, no matter the challenge, and no matter the distance. There were only two of them, now, a father and a daughter, yet to be separated by the oceans of the world, while forever linked by the love and memory of Meredith Moore.

When he suddenly awakened and opened his eyes to look around his cramped stateroom, as he *always* did at that very moment, he cursed to himself as he swung his legs over the side of the bed and sat up, clutching his hands together as he noticed, how remarkable it was, that his dark blue boomer suit was, once again like always, completely soaked with sweat.

Engine Room, USS *Monterey*, Pacific Ocean

As the *Monterey* moved across the middle of the Philippine Sea, heading for the waters north of the island of Luzon, Petty Officer First Class Brian Robinson studied the power meter of his nuclear reactor control panel. The meter, *the power*, was becoming a problem. As he flipped switches, started or stopped main coolant pumps, activated circuit breakers throughout the engine room or adjusted control rods, everything behaved, the systems complied as directed. Everything behaved except the power meter.

They were accelerating through the water in the direction of the Philippines at high speed, the rod configuration set for 100% nuclear power, the pumps thrashing main coolant through the core, the boilers blasting steam into the engine room, and the turbines screaming out their power as Manny Munroe babied his mechanical devices. But the power meter continued to be a problem. The indicator, pegged at 100% for the past several days, pushed by all the systems to remain at 100%, was now 97%, down another percentage point in the past six hours, down from the peak level in just the past forty-eight hours.

The power level of the nuclear reactor was beginning to drop, and nothing Robby did seemed to have any effect.

He reached out to the rod control system and bumped the control rods against their stops. No movement, no way to get back up to 100% no matter what he did. The reason for the problem, Robby knew, was as simple as the reason this submarine was supposed to be enroute across the Pacific for the shipyard in Bremerton, Washington—after so many years of service, she was now depleting her store of uranium. They were, in summary, very slowly running out of fuel.

Robby wiped the sweat from his brow, and speaking loud enough for Baxter to hear through his ear mufflers, said, "Any ideas how to get us back up to 100%, Jules?"

Baxter glanced away from his electric control panel clusters of meters to glance at Robby's power meter.

"97%?" He frowned. "Can't you crank the rods a bit?"

"Of course I can 'crank the rods,' Jules, I've been 'cranking the rods' all day or night or whatever it is.

"We're gonna need to conserve power...."

"Right, turn off the air conditioning, shut off the lights?"

Baxter smiled. "Nice thought," he said. "120 degrees in the engine room, sitting here in the dark?"

"Or, we need to light off the diesel."

"Fine, except that, right now, we would need a 500 foot oxygen intake pipe at this depth."

"Drain the battery?"

"You're not draining *my* battery."

"Or, we need to slow down."

"Nope, like the captain says, we gotta get there."

"So, we can't do anything, we're screwed." Robby pulled out the iPad-like computerized log sheet and began recording the numbers off his panel.

In the *Monterey's* Auxiliary Machinery Space, the three SEALs huddled over the table holding an evolving miniature model of the *Cho Ying Atlas.* The oil tanker replica was a virtual precise duplication of the full size ship, the details gathered from the most recent Internet interrogation from the naval architecture site where her length, her compartments, and the location of rooms could be precisely identified. The pieces of wood for the model came from the plywood used for Doc Wheat's recent medication delivery. A variety of miniature objects were placed on or around the small ship, each representing various people, from SEALs approaching the vessel to potential pirates on the ship, all positioned to various locations in the scene as the men began the process of mentally preparing for the assault.

The three SEALs worked well together, their relationship cemented during the previous Indonesia operation, their reliance on each other enhanced by the deaths of their two fellow SEALs and the unexpected premature extraction from their suddenly-terminated operation. They exercised together, six times each day, grunting and sweating as they hollered out the count of pushups, pull-ups, running on the treadmill at six miles per hour up ten to eighteen percent slopes, and sweating their way through the weightlifting and resistance conditioning. The hulking figure of Thor Chainsaw served as their leader. Silverback had his vast knowledge of languages. Frog had the unusual combination of a comprehensive biological knowledge of dolphins mixed with a broad experience with explosives…especially the kind that could be carried by dolphins. Each man's independent capabilities, when merged together as a team, allowed for an impressive efficiency that greatly improved the probability of a successful mission.

Captain Moore had shown them the recent NSA download, outlining the CIA's success in killing al-Shabaab, their undercover operatives moving in within weeks of the *Monterey's* preliminary SEAL operation in Indonesia. Because of the CIA, and not because of the *Monterey*, the terrorist bastard was dead. That, they all acknowledged. The al-Qaeda leadership was damaged, but the SEALs' efforts in the final analysis had been for nothing. The CIA had finished the job the *Monterey* had started, the mission to Indonesia was a waste of time, two lives had been lost, and the covert operation of the SEALs was without value. They hadn't failed, but the CIA had made sure they wouldn't succeed, pulling them out before they could take the final action against al-Shabaab.

Yet the three men had maintained an air of professionalism, even in their diminishment. The one central factor that stimulated them was that now the CIA would be forced to just sit back and watch the results from *their* attack on the *Cho Ying Atlas*, the kind of anticipated success the SEALs should have enjoyed…perhaps the CIA operatives stationed in Manila would enjoy the show.

"What are you boys doing?" Amada asked as she stepped through the watertight door leading into the Auxiliary Machinery Space. She smiled. "Looks like some kind of weird miniature doll house."

The three SEALs straightened up from the table holding the evolving model of the *Cho Ying Atlas* and gazed appreciatively at the woman.

Chainsaw smiled. "We're building a little play ship," he said, "kind of like the big ships skimming the waters above us."

Silverback grimaced. "I don't think she's cleared for…" he began.

"Ah, yes, a "play ship," Amanda said. "Looks like fun, could I build the little hostage people on the play ship?" she asked innocently. "Or would you like me to create the terrorist people? Maybe some little play SEALs? I'd be happy to place them on the cute little decks, maybe one in front of that sweet little anchor chain?"

"Jesus…" Chainsaw said slowly.

"Okay," Silverback said, resignedly, "this model here, this microship, defines our plan of action, Amanda, this lays it out for us, makes it easy…."

"Great, got it," Amanda said. "I already figured that out, obviously. A practice format. Like with Osama bin Laden. Are we going to go there in our tiny submarine? I just fed the two little dolphins, will they be going with you?"

"Amanda," Frog said, studying her face. "Your help actually would, in fact, be greatly appreciated since we are running short on time. Here are some sticks, please create a few hostages, put them…"

"In the citadel?"

"Goddamn it, Amanda," Chainsaw interjected. "How much do you know? Have you already qualified on this submarine?"

"Nope, haven't qualified on anything, yet" she said, smiling again. "But I am a straight-A college student, so I know *everything*," she added. She took the sticks from Frog and her smile slowly disappeared. "And, would you boys do me a great big favor? When you encounter the terrorists who took Caroline, it would make me very happy if you would kill every single one of those bastards?"

"Thank you, Amanda," Frog said. "However, we are not going there to kill pirates or terrorists or whatever they are. We are going there to rescue Caroline and any other hostages, plain and simple. If we bring them back alive, we have succeeded."

"And you have only one chance to get it right," Amanda said forcefully as she sorted through the sticks. She looked up at the three men and added, "Let's get this thing together and pray to God that Caroline is still alive."

Admiral Sully Sullivan's Home, Honolulu

At nearly two o'clock in the morning, Admiral Sully Sullivan climbed into his bed, exhausted, next to his sleeping wife, Martha. She stirred as he moved under the covers and asked sleepily, "Everything okay, honey?"

"Everything's a mystery, honey, go back to sleep."

A moment of silence was followed by, "A mystery?"

"I can't find things. Moore's daughter's wedding invitation, for example, I've torn the house apart…"

"Oh, Caroline's wedding? That's down in the cellar, in the back closet, inside the fireproof safe, second shelf, next to all those tax forms that we stored. Do you want me to get it for you?"

Two minutes later, Sullivan stood in the cellar closet, the safe open, the Caroline and Peter Blackwell wedding invitation in his hand. He leaned up against the wall in the quiet room, studying the gold engraving and the ornate script—the wedding would be "on the beautiful Island of Lanai," of a Peter Blackwell and a Caroline Moore, and "the pleasure of your company" was requested. The gold engraving and the formality of the invitation left no doubt that this would rank among the top weddings of the year in Hawaii, and the Blackwell dynasty would be further enhanced. He now had a starting point after which everything began to make sense.

Thirty minutes later, Sullivan lay in bed next to Martha, staring at the ceiling, his mind racing through the thoughts that seemed to move in circles, always returning to the same starting point. A man had stolen a submarine, his name was now internationally famous, and his one and only child had not called to find out what had happened. She had not flown to Pearl Harbor, she had not shown up in a tearful interview on CNN News, and she had not broken down the doors of the COMPACFLT headquarters demanding answers.

He tried to picture the woman...he had only seen her once as a beautiful and confident teenager accompanying her father at a change-of-command ceremony...but he hadn't seen her again for several years. She had been sent to San Diego after her mother had died, he remembered, but Gary Moore rarely mentioned her other than the fact that Caroline had subsequently enrolled at Princeton five or six years ago. The wedding invitation itself had been a surprise, and he had just assumed that Moore had asked the admiral's name to be included on the guest list, fulfilling the protocol of inviting a senior officer, even while knowing he probably would not attend.

So, the real question was, the admiral's brain almost shouted into the night, what was the ongoing relationship between Commander Gary Moore and his daughter, Caroline? The questions and answers swirled, like a dance with the devil of ambiguity. Had she gone down some kind of tortured pathway after her marriage and disappeared? Had Caroline's marriage gone badly and she had moved to some distant location or a distant country? When her mother had died, of some kind of medical problem, Sullivan remembered, had Commander Moore abandoned his daughter, perhaps become estranged from her? And, after that, he had simultaneously thrown himself into his work to become one of the best executive officers and then commanding officers the American submarine service had ever seen?

What happens to father-daughter relationships when the mother dies and the father goes to sea for long patrols?

Sullivan rubbed his eyes as the central question returned to him, again and again. The relationship goes to hell, right? For twelve years, there had been no mother, for five days now, there has been no father and no daughter. But, when the father disappears, why is there also no daughter? A whole family cannot just disappear, can it?

Since the only person on the planet known to Sullivan who could answer the questions had disappeared with his submarine, there were, therefore, no answers.

He was clenching his teeth with a dark and disappearing dream at the first moment of sunlight when the bedside telephone rang and Sullivan caught it on the first ring. He glanced back at the bed and saw Martha was already up and gone from the bedroom.

"Sullivan," he almost hollered, sitting up at the side of the bed, tightly pressing the receiver against his left ear.

"Admiral, this is Wong, from the NSA."

"What have you got?"

The voice on the telephone, remarkably mechanical, confirmed most of what Sullivan already knew but left gaps of critical information. Peter and Caroline Blackwell's home in the prestigious Medina outskirts of Seattle was empty, and the whereabouts of the Blackwells was unknown. Other than vague references by a neighbor about a long-planned vacation to multiple exotic locations in the world, nobody had any idea where they might be. Airline records were of no value since they flew private jets, and with thousands of private jet flights each day to remote locations, which jet they might have been on and where it flew remained uncertain although the investigation was continuing. Finally, NSA interviews with the senior members of the Blackwell family were notably unrewarding.

When it was all said and done, it kept coming back to the same result.

Sullivan's mind raged. *Nobody seemed to know anything, why are you bothering to call me now and tell me you know nothing?*

The NSA was now moving on to more potentially rewarding investigations, looking into the background of Amanda Peterson's Middle East roommate, Wong told Sullivan, and they've started examining Captain Moore's potential for blackmail or escape, seeking anything that might have driven the commander to steal a submarine.

Admiral Sullivan hung up the telephone, cursed silently to himself and pulled out his dress uniform. After a steaming five-minute shower, he quickly dressed and said good-bye to his wife.

"You're not going to have breakfast?" Martha asked from the kitchen where freshly-cracked eggs simmered in a pan.

"There is no time," Sullivan answered as he pulled out his car keys.

"You're not going to call for your driver, honey?" She smiled at her husband. "He can be here in a couple of minutes."

Sullivan kissed her quickly, and as he moved toward the door, he called back, "I'll be driving myself this morning. I may be late getting back."

The Nuuanu Memorial Park was a stone's throw from the Pali Highway, and Sullivan shrugged off the chill of walking into the early-morning environment of bodies incarcerated within the ground. After scanning the large directory of names, the words Meredith Moore stood out on one of the larger tombstones, almost like she was calling out to him. It was a snow-white marble stone, rich with blood-red veins from the Carrara quarries in Italy. The name had been centered within the stone, the dates of her birth and her premature death centered below the name. The admiral stared at the stone, scanning the dates and the words below. He glanced at a smaller nearby headstone carrying the name of a baby Alexander. He read the names and dates twice, the sentences bringing an essence from the hearts of the survivors.

His right hand reflexively reached to his telephone as he would to a holster with a powerful handgun. He activated the camera app and focused the device on the words across the tombstone in front of him. A record of this must be kept in his possession, he knew, it was too important to just look and then move away. On the face of the stone was a message to the deceased from a husband and a daughter, the most profound statement a human could say to another. It was a message at the time of death, always with the hope the thought would be seen somehow by the departed, would be *felt*, and often with just a hint of regret that the words had not been spoken sooner.

By your departure, you have intensified our love and bonded us closer together. We are now richer for knowing you, and stronger for what you gave throughout your life. Our love for you and our love for each other will increase with time. It is our treasure and it will last forever~~~Gary and Caroline.

Sullivan pressed the button. He saw the flash as the words burned into the device's memory chips. He tucked his telephone into its holster and turned to walk briskly toward his car, now with the knowledge, now with the *certainty* about why Gary Moore had taken the submarine.

It all had to do with the daughter.

As he climbed into the car and started the engine, he punched the numbers on the telephone and she immediately answered.

"Admiral Sullivan's office, may I help you, sir?" Brenda Walker said.

"This is Sully, Brenda. Call Bentley at the 19th Fighter Squadron at Hickam and get me the fastest plane they have. I need to be in Seattle before the sun sets."

USS *Monterey*, Pacific Ocean

Aboard the deeply submerged *USS Monterey*, accelerating across the Philippine Sea at thirty-seven knots, Captain Moore and Chief Berry hunched over the navigation table, scanning the charts of the ocean around them. The control center of the submarine remained almost empty, except for Bodine at the helm with Wilson relieving him from time to time, and Doc Wheat standing watch at the sonar station. The *Monterey* was in hostile waters, everybody knew that, with the NSA intercepts having already warned all the Pacific submarines in the American fleet of China's aggressive intentions against any vessels deemed to be in their "territorial waters."

Furthermore, Moore had intercepted orders to the Navy vessels in the western Pacific, clearly indicating that a ring had been established across the East and South China Sea by American submarines to prevent the *Monterey* from moving closer to the Chinese mainland. It was clear that the command center had decided there was a reasonable chance the *Monterey* was being taken to a foreign country, and the country needing nuclear submarine technology more than any other in the world was China.

"If the Americans don't get us…" Moore began as he moved his calipers across the navigation chart.

"The Chinese will," Berry said, finishing the sentence.

"The perfect enigma. The Americans think we want to sell our submarine to the Chinese and the Chinese think we want to attack them. Nice."

"Yes, sir," Berry said. "Very nice. Everybody wants to kill us. It's becoming a real combat situation, but we've been through this before. The sooner we clear the Philippine Sea, the sooner we watch the Babuyan Channel disappear behind us, and the sooner we get to the mother ship."

"Amen," Moore said as he studied the ocean chart spread across the table in front of them. "We're about fifty miles west of the Luzon Ridge and the Balintang Channel access point to the South China Sea."

"Yes, sir," Berry said, the unspoken concern of a collision with an underwater Balintang mountain peak hanging in the air for both men. The charts looked reassuring, but they knew the charts had looked reassuring for the crew of the USS *San Francisco*, nearly 15 years ago, before she slammed into a seamount with a peak barely 200 feet beneath the surface, killing one man, severely injuring more than twenty others, and nearly resulting in the sinking of the submarine. According to the charts, the peaks of the Balintang waters remained greater than a thousand feet below the surface. But the submarine was blind to the bottom of the ocean, and everybody knew there could be no pinging from the boat's sonar system to determine the exact depth of the ocean bottom below; a single sounding ping would carry for hundreds of miles and would immediately alert the searching world of the precise location of the *Monterey*.

So they pressed on at near-flank speed, hoping the charts were correct.

"Captain, I'm picking up something out there," Doc Wheat suddenly exclaimed from his seat in front of the sonar system. The corpsman stared at his sonar display screen, watching the snow of incoming noises move down the screen, with intermittent white spikes. His ears were enclosed with a powerful noise-cancelling headset, and each time a spike showed on the screen, he visibly flinched. "Sir, somebody out there is conducting a search."

As Moore and Berry rushed into the sonar room and watched the screen from behind the man, his black face began to show a fine sheen of sweat. "I may have qualified on the sonar station when I qualified on submarines," Wheat said, "but nobody mentioned the fine points of Chinese sonar while I was vaccinating the crew."

"It's one of those French high-frequency searchlight sonar systems, maybe the variable depth Thomson thing," Berry said, studying the image.

"I don't think they carry any of these searchlight sonar systems on their submarines," Moore said. "It's probably from one of the *Jianghu* frigates, one of their ASW ships."

"Well, that's a good thing and they sure as hell don't have us," Berry said as he picked up a pair of headsets and sat down next to the corpsman. "This is just a random search, they're just pissin' pings around in the ocean."

Captain Moore watched the sonar return for another couple of minutes as the two men adjusted their sonar receiver instruments to fine-tune the received signals. He finally straightened and walked back into the control center to the diving station where Bodine sat alertly, the airplane-like control wheel in his hands.

"Everything okay, captain?" he asked, his eyes remaining fixed on the depth gauge.

"We're on-track, Bodine, so long as nobody drops any wrenches," Moore said, looking at the gauges in front of the sailor.

"Yes, sir," Bodine said as he reached over to the ballast control panel and adjusted one of the trim settings.

"Just to add some insurance and to add a couple of thermal layers above us, let's rig ship for deep submergence and go down another three hundred feet to 850, same course."

"Down to 850, aye, aye, sir," Bodine called out, gently pushing forward on his control wheel. Immediately, the *Monterey* angled downward toward the new depth, further under the sea, and further below the sonar interrogation signals radiating out from the Chinese fleet.

Berry walked out of the sonar room and grabbed the 1 MC microphone from the overhead area. "Rig ship for deep submergence. Rig ship for deep submergence," he said, notifying everybody in the sub to close off all unnecessary ocean water piping. At the moment the submarine reached 850 feet, the captain ordered all stop.

"All stop, aye, aye, sir," Bodine answered as he transmitted the order to the propulsion station in the engine room.

Ten minutes later, as the three Chinese ASW ships passed within eight miles of the *Monterey*, the submarine was directly over the western entry into the Balintang Channel. The returning echoes from the ocean floor blended nicely with the miniscule spike from the submarine, now silent at all stop and hovering quietly at precisely 850 feet. Everybody in the submarine waited, knowing the Chinese were above, looking for them, listening for them, and ready to take immediate action if any detection occurred. Nobody slammed any water-tight doors, nobody dropped any equipment on the steel decking, and nobody flushed any tanks or rotated the screws. Hovering above the Balintang mountain ridges, the *Monterey* remained silent as Doc Wheat and Chief Berry listened intently for anything signifying detection, especially the banshee scream of incoming high-speed screws from a homing torpedo, signifying their imminent destruction and death.

In the engine room, Manny Munroe stood next to the three-inch auxiliary piping, staring at a seawater pipe that connected directly to the ocean pressure. The piping was getting old, another reason for the decommissioning and demolition that had been pending, but this particular pipe had developed a specific and new problem: it was beginning to hiss and drip high-pressure seawater into the bilge. The water, a fine mist with a tiny jet of spray, was coming from a bend in the pipe, where a threaded angle joint allowed the pipe to run up into the starboard condenser. The seawater pressure within the pipe at this depth, Munroe knew, was enough to blow him all the way across the engine room, and it appeared to be leaking in progressively larger amounts as the depth of the submarine had increased.

Great, now we have a choice, Munroe thought, a black-and-white do it or don't do it kind of a thing. He knew that, no matter what he did, he was going to drown, or sink, or get captured, or he thought, get fucked by *somebody* with decades of naval legal training who would second-guess and criticize his actions if they survived. And, it was really a minuscule thing, right now, just a little hisser of a leak in a pipe connecting a submarine at great depth, surrounded by a high-pressure frigid ocean outside the pressure hull of the submarine. Just a little ocean water pissing into the bilges, he thought, to be quickly pumped overboard by the drain pump.

He studied the pipe closely, his eyes narrowing as he watched the dripping and the hissing of high-pressure sea water into the submarine. If he did nothing, and the pipe blew open, the blast of water would be a flooding disaster for the engine room that would almost certainly include a shutdown of the reactor and the drowning of all men in the compartment. We would have to surface, if the saving of life was important, the saving of the remaining crew, all of whom, if they didn't drown first, would be immediately captured by one of the pinging Chinese ships above.

Munroe's mustache twitched at the thought…while surfacing would be better than drowning, being captured by the Chinese would be the worst of all possibilities, especially with no support from the American side. Also, a capture would probably be followed by a long prison sentence or death by a bullet in some stadium somewhere. The pings from the Chinese had become louder over the past half-hour, and as they had slowed to a soundless operation, Munroe had been listening to them in the nearly-silent engine room. It had become almost like a Chinese water torture kind of thing, a ping every five to ten seconds, a pause, a wait, and then another ping. The control of his imagination became a compelling effort, the kind of imagination that makes one hear the distant incoming sounds of high-speed screws, the kind of screws that accelerate torpedoes directly to their target.

The choices all seemed bad, very bad. Even minor flooding would make considerable noise and would lead to surfacing of the submarine…a victory for the Chinese and a disaster for them all. On the other hand, if there was uncontrolled flooding, they would rapidly drop *down*, deeper and deeper, finally reaching, and then exceeding, the submarine's crush depth where bulkheads would collapse, pipes would rupture, and the final result would be a sudden end of life for everybody on the *Monterey*. That would also make a lot of noise.

That event would give the bastard Chinese skimmers some real entertainment…. Munroe's black mustache finally stopped moving.

With the Chinese above and a crushing death below, Munroe made his decision and quietly shut the valves connecting the leaking pipe to the ocean. The results on the secondary nuclear plant were predictable as the chain reaction of machinery malfunction followed. As the vacuum in the condenser dropped, the starboard turbogenerator immediate began to wind down, resulting in rows of high-voltage circuit breakers snapping open with flashing arcs of electricity, alternate lights going out throughout the entire boat, as red warning lights flashed on across the nuclear reactor and electric plant control panels. Battery-driven battle lanterns glowed with the loss of power, and came on in the overhead spaces as Brian Robinson jumped off his chair in the Maneuvering Room and hissed, "Jesus holy Christ! What the hell is going on?"

Jules Baxter stared at the reactor operator and said, "*Shit, I don't know*. We just lost half our power plant. Where's Munroe? Get somebody to check the engine room."

The headsets tightly clamped to their ears carried the crackling voice of Captain Moore. "Engine room, this is control, report," followed by Munroe's voice in the lower level engine room announcing through the headsets, "Maneuvering and Control!

Munroe here. We have a flooding threat, lower level engine room, starboard auxiliary main seawater piping, isolated, repeat isolated."

Baxter stood up and spoke quickly into his mouthpiece. "Captain, flooding threat from starboard auxiliary seawater piping," he said. "Now isolated, lost starboard propulsion turbine and starboard turbogenerator, cross-connecting electrical system!"

"Very well," Moore's voice returned into his ears. "Maintain silent operations, cross-connect, now."

The captain would also be on his way back to the engine room, both men knew as they rapidly adjusted their controls for an electrical system now half-gone. The battleshort switch was on, there would be no automatic shutdown of the nuclear reactor.

Keeping the reactor operational is my priority, *my number one priority*, Robby thought as his hands raced across the panel, energizing back-up pumps and secondary power supplies to the reactor control system. He knew, and everyone aboard the submarine knew, that without an operational reactor, they would quickly drain the batteries, they would then have to climb up to snorkel depth, light off the diesel, and generate an acoustical signature that would broadcast their location to everybody for hundreds of miles.

Standing in front of his electrical control panel, Baxter mumbled, "Easy peezy," as his hands flew across his electrical control panel, matching voltages, synchronizing electrical equipment, and bringing power from the port side of the boat to the entire submarine. He had done it a thousand times, first in training fourteen years ago, and then under operational conditions, over and over again. Now, here he was, doing it again, to help save the submarine and to support the man in the lower level engine room, the man who had just single-handedly protected the *Monterey* from sinking or falling into the hands of the Chinese.

By the time Captain Moore arrived in the engine room, Manny Munroe had already pulled the offending joint from the seawater piping, and while cursing with great passion, had quietly lowered it down into the bilges. As Moore moved down the narrow passageway of the starboard engine room, he spotted Munroe intensely searching for a substitute piece of pipe.

"What's the story on the Pearl shipyard, Skipper?" Munroe asked the captain, "that they would X-ray and certify a piece of crap like that thing I just shitcanned?"

"This is an old boat, Munroe…"

"Well, captain, it seems like this elderly submarine might be trying to kill us."

At that moment, a replacement piece of pipe rolled into sight from the stacks of replacement pipes, Munroe grabbed it, walked around the captain and back to the site of the open seawater piping. Cursing at the pipes with a vernacular that suggested that most of the offending piping was engaging in active and continual sexual intercourse, he threaded the new segment, pulled out two connectors, and began joining them together, the muscles of his massive arms sweating and his mustache twitching. Munroe finally pulled out his wrench and began to tighten the new segment into place, creating a perfect match, a solid joint that could withstand whatever pressures the *Monterey* might experience with even deeper dives.

The captain had not said a word during the entire process, until he started to leave. When it became apparent that the replacement pipe would hold the pressure, he stepped around his engine room machinist mate, and before walking away, he told the man, "Nice job, Munroe, thank you."

As Moore walked away toward the ladder leading up and out of the engine room, Munroe watched his departing figure silently until he was almost gone, and he then quietly said, "Thank *you*, sir, my pleasure." He hesitated, and then hollered after the departing figure, "Captain?"

Moore turned around to look at the man. "Munroe?" he said.

"Captain…anything new in the downloads about your daughter?"

Chapter 10

Dry Deck Shelter, USS *Monterey*, Pacific Ocean

Sitting in the Dry Deck Shelter (DDS)[19] next to the water containers holding the dolphins Taser and Domino, Frog gently splashed saltwater over their backs and sides. He could see them moving their eyes as he stroked their skin, and the air flowing through their blowholes seemed to move in and out more rapidly than usual. That could be, he knew, a sign of metabolic distress. Even more worrisome to Frog, neither of the dolphins had eaten their fish dinner with their usual vigor that evening, another indicator of distress. He pulled out a couple of pieces of squid from his frozen packet, their favorite treat, and both dolphins quickly and neatly snatched them from his hand. He had noticed Amanda had taken a liking to both mammals, and had been providing for most of their feedings; she had reported no problems.

However, although Frog couldn't be certain as he listened to the rumbling vibrations around him as the submarine picked up speed, it seemed likely that what Taser and Domino really needed was some time in the ocean.

Growler Jet, Whidbey Island Naval Air Station

Enclosed within the gold-plated canopy of the Boeing EA-18G Growler, Admiral Sullivan caught just a glimpse of the huge "WELCOME HOME" words painted on the runway of Whidbey Island's Naval Air Station before the pilot rolled his jet tightly to the left and entered the pattern. Tucked away at the north end of the island, just 30 miles northwest of Seattle, Ault Field's long runway and precise radar approach allowed the high-speed landing without delay. The final shutting down of the shrieking pair of engines, was followed by the pristine silence of an island previously known primarily for its peaceful Indian inhabitants.

The flight from Oahu had them screaming across the Pacific Ocean at speeds over 800 miles per hour, with one air tanker refueling, as the admiral had watched the sky slowly darken and the surface of the ocean, forty thousand feet below, transformed into a nearly-black surface. The pilot, who looked to Sullivan like a kid entering his senior year of high school, was a veteran of more than a hundred carrier landings and carried a demeanor throughout the flight suggesting everything up in the air was pretty much like a gigantic video game, to be enjoyed to the fullest—a contrast to the focused intensity of the admiral who sat silently in the back seat of the aircraft. His name was Rich, the pilot had announced about half-way through the flight, Lieutenant Rich Dungan, sir, he had said, happy to be at your service and hoping this will be a comfortable flight.

Captain Adam Parker, the commanding officer of the Whidbey Island Naval Air Station, walked briskly across the tarmac to welcome the admiral. A lean man with intense dark eyes and pilot crow's feet lines radiating out to his temples from thousands of hours of Naval Aviation sunlight, Parker was used to sudden arrivals of flag officers, but usually there was at least a day or two advance notice. The urgent encrypted message from Pearl Harbor earlier that day had taken him by surprise, but by the time the Whidbey Island air controllers called him about the arriving Growler, he was ready for the visit. As Parker's tall frame stood at near attention next to the aircraft, Sullivan lifted two bags filled with computer equipment from the back seat cockpit and climbed down the side of the plane. An enlisted man quickly grabbed the bags as the two men exchanged salutes and turned to walk toward the hangar.

"Welcome to the Rock, admiral," Parker said. "You had a good flight, I trust?"

"Excellent, Adam, thank you. Spend enough years in submarines and you forget how quickly you can cross the planet, even with an air tanker refueling. I appreciate your help with this."

"You're welcome, admiral, your residence at the flag officers' housing, a couple minutes' walk down the road, is ready for you. You are welcome to join my wife and me for a late-evening dinner, if that would fit into your schedule. Tomorrow, your driver will be ready at 0600 hours to get you off the island or to wherever else you need to travel. By the way, I'm sorry to hear about that submarine incident out of Pearl—any success in tracking it down?"

"Working on it, Adam, working on it." Sullivan said tightly as he scrutinized the captain.

"I understand," Parker said quickly.

“And, thank you for the kind dinner invitation…my workload unfortunately precludes the visit. Will my quarters have at least three high-speed gigabit per second level encrypted ports for the necessary computer links? ”

“Yes, sir, the office in your house is filled with state-of-the-art electronics, including the updated secure and encrypted Wi-Fi communication systems and a couple of dedicated servers,” Parker said as he guided his visitor toward a small white house a couple hundred yards from the hangar. “The refrigerator is well-stocked with plenty of food and drink—please enjoy whatever you’d like. Mary Ann sends her regards to you, and you should feel free to contact me at any time if you have any needs.” He looked at the admiral. “Do you know when you will be launching back to Pearl, sir?”

“It depends on how things go tomorrow in Seattle,” Sullivan said. “I don’t want to screw up your schedule, but I expect it could be at any time in the next two days.” He turned and pointed at the Growler jet pilot walking toward the front door of the hangar. “Would you keep this man and his aircraft, on ready-standby for the return flight?”

“No problem, sir, Dungan is one of the best pilots in the Navy, consider it done.”

The next morning, at 0645 hours, a gray Navy car holding Admiral Sullivan in the back seat entered the outskirts of the upscale community of Medina, near Seattle, as a sign flashed by indicating that the car’s license plate had just been recorded and would be “held by the police for 60 days whether or not any crime was committed.”

“Families in the Medina area are probably worth billions,” the young sailor driving the car observed, looking at the enormous homes surrounding them.

“I don’t know about billions but I would guess tens of millions at least,” Sullivan responded as he watched Lake Washington pass by in the distance. He knew that various mansions in the area belonged to the founder and CEO of Amazon, the co-founder of Microsoft, and many other reclusive families of power. Medina had been set aside, long ago, to house the people in Washington who control other people, he thought. People like Randolph Blackwell….

At the admiral’s direction, the sailor driver moved them down 76th Avenue NE, past tennis courts and multiple brick driveways, under massive trees, finally arriving at an expansive ten-foot tall decorative iron gate blocking a large driveway that led to a home concealed from the street.

"Pull up here," Sullivan said to his driver who angled the car close to a rectangular call-box with a single button. The admiral rolled down his window, reached out, and pushed the button.

After several distant repeated ringing sounds, a female Hispanic voice said, "Yes? Who is there, please?"

"Good morning," Sullivan said in a friendly voice. "I am Admiral Sullivan, United States Navy, and I have information about Peter and Caroline Blackwell regarding their absence this past week."

There was a ten second pause before the voice replied, "You know about Mr. and Mrs. Blackwell?"

"I do know a great deal about them, may I come in to bring your family up to date?"

"Yes, of course," the voice said. "When the gate opens, please drive up to the front entrance."

After a high-pitched beeping sound, the huge gates began to swing open as Sullivan rolled up his window and growled to the driver, "Get us in there, now."

The housekeeper, a middle-aged and slightly portly woman named Rosa, walked out the front door as the car stopped in front of the house. She greeted the admiral as the driver waited in the car, and she escorted him through massive front doors to a palatial living room, inviting him to be seated on a golden sofa.

"Would you like some coffee, admiral?" she asked and quickly added, "Miss Blackwell will be down in a moment."

"Yes, thank you," Sullivan said. "A cup of coffee would be perfect." He looked closely at the woman. "Miss Blackwell is…?"

"Oh, I'm sorry, I thought you knew. Sally Blackwell is Peter's sister, visiting here from Beverly Hills. When Peter and Caroline didn't return on time, she flew up yesterday to help out with the horses. I think those NSA people have gone to Los Angeles to look for her, said they needed to talk with everybody."

"Yes, the horses, of course. I would like my coffee black, if you please."

Sally Blackwell was an elegant-appearing woman about forty years of age, Sullivan guessed, and as she descended the circular staircase toward the living room, her red hair showed some disarray suggesting to Sullivan that the woman had recently been asleep. She wore a tight cashmere turtle-neck sweater over dark slacks that covered her legs all the way to the slippers on her feet. Although she wore no makeup, her face was smooth and flawless and she carried herself with a look of refined elegance.

"Welcome, Admiral Sullivan," she said as she walked up to Sullivan and put out her hand to greet him. "We were not expecting you but I hope you have some information about my brother and my sister-in-law?"

"Very nice to meet you, Miss Blackwell…"

"Oh…please. Call me Sally," she said with a look of mock admonishment.

"Sally it is," Sullivan said, taking her hand and smiling. "And, you may call me Sully. Yes, we've been receiving information about your brother, and we know about where they were before we lost communications…"

"In the Philippines, of course, they were looking forward to that little diving expedition for weeks. It is where they went *after that*, is what we'd all like to know. They were supposed to do more scuba diving somewhere else after that. But, not a word. Not a single word, not from either one of them. We are all very concerned. They should have returned yesterday morning, and now everybody's getting worried. Have you heard anything from them, and why, exactly, is the United States Navy involved? Is it because Caroline's father is a Navy man?"

"Yes, of course, and her father, Commander Moore, must be worried too…. We'll know more when he gets back into port." Sullivan briefly looked away from her gaze.

"Well, if he *was* back in port, I would expect some kind of communication if he's heard from her, to ease our concern. We haven't seen him since the wedding, and that was a couple of years ago."

"He is a very busy man…"

"Yes, on a submarine, if I remember right. Didn't a submarine just get stolen? He wasn't on *that* one, was he? I saw something about it in the news last night and the press wouldn't say who is onboard."

"The Navy investigators are working overtime to get the answers." Sullivan smiled again reassuringly. "Also, Commander

Moore has been out to sea a great deal, and it's not easy to call from under the ocean."

"Well, I would think not," she said energetically. "Please be sure to have him call when he returns. What's his name, again?"

"Commander Gary Moore."

"Ah, yes, I remember him, from the wedding. He's sort of a powerhouse-looking kind of man, and he dresses just like you, all Navy white and very impressive." She smiled, showing perfect white teeth.

"I'll pass on the message about the call, Sally. Do you recall their itinerary after Manila? You said something about a couple of scuba diving places?"

"They were going to Puerto Galera and Nablag, world-class diving destinations. Of course, Rosa didn't have that information two or three days ago when the NSA characters came by. They were very rude to Rosa, by the way. Where else would they go, certainly not to Bali or Indonesia, not with all the problems in those countries! There is a little island off the east coast of China…what was its name?" The woman rolled her eyes upward and thumped on her left cheek with her index finger. "Sana, Sanda, ah…Sanya, that's it. Supposed to be really beautiful."

Sullivan leaned forward and looked directly into Sally's eyes. "Have you heard anything from Mombo?" he asked.

"From Mombo? Of course not, why the hell would the chef call? Maybe if they had food poisoning or they were running out of food."

Sullivan sat back and smiled. "Did Mombo also work as their guide or was he just the full-time cook?"

Sally stared at Sullivan like he was very nearly the stupidest man in the world. "The cook? Mombo is not the 'cook,' he is the full-time *chef*!"

"I understand that…but he does cook for them, right?"

"I don't think you *exactly* understand, admiral. Mombo is a world-renown gourmet chef, and yes, on their boat, *The Sweet Caroline*, he does prepare the meals for them. Peter keeps the yacht in some of the most pristine harbors in the world. They fly into Manila, they sail to various islands, they dive and look at fish and reefs, and then they cruise back to Manila and fly home in our jet. I would suspect it is a kind of a micro-honeymoon for both of them, although I wouldn't know for sure." She raised her eyebrows and smiled like she knew a secret.

"When they didn't show up, we called the harbormaster in Manila," she continued. "The boat either never arrived back, or if they returned, they never registered like they always do. And if they returned, they would fly back here, but they never flew back. Does that make any sense? Nobody knows where the boat is. It is not like Peter to not let us know his plans, and his father is…well, I don't know about his father. He and I don't exactly have the greatest relationship. So here we are, wondering what to do next."

"Are there any other relatives we can talk to, other than his parents?" Sullivan asked. "Maybe another sister or a brother?"

"Nope, none. Peter and I grew up under the iron fist of our father, Randolph Blackwell—do not *ever* call him Randy if you value your life." She looked irritated and added, "Not that I have to worry about it since he won't even talk to me."

"Your father doesn't talk to you?"

"Not a word, not for about eight years now. Probably too busy grooming Peter for his future CEO position. If you can find Randolph in that Seattle Columbia Street castle, and if he will talk to you, *which I doubt*, perhaps you could ask him if he knows where the Golden Boy has gone."

After a moment of awkward silence, Sullivan scrutinized the woman closely. "Okay," he said. "I'm sorry about your family." He looked down at his coffee cup for a moment then looked at Sally again. "What I am going to ask now," he said, "is vitally important. Has anybody from that part of the world called here, talked with Rosa perhaps, or with you?"

Sally's eyes widened imperceptibly. "What do you mean by that?" she asked.

"I just wondered…."

"You mean somebody from the Philippines might call here *other than* Peter? Somebody *other than* Mombo? Now you're starting to scare me, admiral."

"Don't be alarmed, I'm just wondering. It's always possible somebody might call, but there's no reason for concern. I was just thinking if somebody called who might have seen them, somebody who heard their plans. Somebody who saw them tie up somewhere else in one of the diving places. Things like that."

"No, nobody called, at least not since I've been here. The answer is no." She turned and looked at Rosa. "Right, Rosa? Nobody called?"

Rosa shook her head emphatically. "No, ma'am" she said. "Nobody called, nobody at all. Makes me very worried. I wish *somebody* would call."

"Okay," Sullivan said. "Thank you, both of you. You have been most helpful." He pulled a couple of business cards from his shirt pocket and handed them to the women. "This is my direct cell number, you can call me at any time day or night if you hear anything at all." He smiled at the women. "Thank you for the coffee and for your hospitality. May I please have your contact numbers, also?"

USS *Monterey*, Pacific Ocean

At 0554 hours, as the early rays of the rising sun began to light up the peaks of the Yushan mountain range, rising 7,000 feet above Taiwan 150 miles to the north, the *Monterey* reached the expanding segments of the South China Sea. Captain Moore had ordered the submarine back up to periscope depth for a quick scan of the surrounding world as he and Chief Berry savored the horizon around them. With a look of pleasure at the vision of stark white snow on the mountain tops, Captain Moore finally dropped the port periscope and ordered the ship back down to 500 feet and altered her course to the south. As Wilson pushed forward on the control wheel and turned to the new bearing, Moore felt a moment of pleasure...we are on final approach for the waters off Palawan, he thought. We are approaching Caroline.

At the captain's order, Chief Berry hit the hydraulic lever to lower the starboard periscope and turned to watch Wilson ease the boat down.

"Sweet peace, and down we go," he mumbled under his breath. "Captain," he said, turning to Moore. "Permission to be relieved of the watch?"

"Permission granted, chief, I have the Con," Moore said. "Good job, go get some shut-eye. We'll continue our course down the west coast of the Philippines until we approach Palawan. We'll have about 18 hours to prepare."

"Thank you, captain," Berry said as he turned and stumbled his way toward the chiefs' berthing area.

It had not been a bad night, Moore reflected as the *Monterey* leveled out and accelerated into the South China Sea. There had always been the ever-present risk of being detected by whichever navy was monitoring every vessel passing through Balintang Channel, a monitoring with intent to kill, he knew. The search by the rest of the world had to be intense, he was certain of that from the array of NSA downloads. Submerging now was at least an opportunity to use the best weapon a submarine possesses—stealth and the ability to remain relatively invisible to anybody seeking her destruction.

Four hours later, after Chief Berry returned to take over the Officer of the Deck watch in the Control Center, Moore decided to make a quick inspection tour through the submarine before getting some badly-needed sleep himself. The Maneuvering Room in the engine room was, as always, hot and noisy from the thundering turbines and reduction gears nearby although powerful air conditioning systems lowered the temperature around the watchstanders by several degrees. The three nukes had set their rotation schedule for individual relief and sleep between monitoring the engine room equipment and the electrical system as well as the nuclear reactor control panels. Manny Munroe's large bulk was propped in front of the reactor control panel, next to a fidgety Jules Baxter, his hair was greasy and a stubble of a beard now covered the lower half of his face. There were plastic hearing protectors protruded over the ears of both men, quieting the continuous roar of machinery.

"I think we're making history, sir," Munroe hollered, turning his chair to face the captain. "First time on nuclear submarines that a machinist mate ran the nuclear reactor. Rickover must be doing rotations in his grave...."

"Robinson is nearby, right?" Moore asked, looking around for the reactor operator.

"Yes, sir, zonked out on the other side of the panel."

Baxter rotated his chair around to face the captain. "I'm watching him like a hawk, sir," he said, nodding at the machinist. "No telling what he might do with his wrench if a meter flicks in the wrong direction."

"I'd *fix it*, that's what I'd do," Munroe said with a huge grin. "Actually, Robby can be here in about three seconds. He told me to watch for any alterations in the meters and to call him if *anything* changes."

"Great..." Moore said. The Navy's Board of Review and the JAG[20] attorneys could hang a captain only once, he thought grimly.

Munroe pointed at the power meter at the top of his panel.

"The bad news is that 94 percent power is all we can get," he shouted. "Robby has tweaked everything. I may just be a machinist mate, but it seems we're just beginning to run a bit low on uranium, sir."

"Thank you, Munroe, we'll be okay," Moore said. "We'll get better mileage on the return trip. How is the repaired piping in the auxiliary seawater system holding up?"

Munroe flashed a big grin and gave a quick thumbs up. "Perfect, sir, at 500 feet, no leaks. However, would not want to stress it at test depth. There have been no piping x-rays and there are no guarantees."

Moving forward from the engine room, Moore found Bodine deeply asleep in the Crew's Berthing area, resting before relieving Wilson at the helm later in the morning, and he discovered Amanda hard at work preparing breakfast for whoever in the crew might be developing an appetite. Her long blonde hair was pulled tightly in a ponytail and she appeared comfortable in her dark blue boomer suit.

"Gonna have eggs and hashed browns ready for you, captain," she said, pointing at the food laid out across the galley. "Couldn't find any milk, for cereal, none. Is somebody hiding it somewhere?"

"Couldn't find any cows for the past two months...."

"Well, that's silly," she said, flipping a couple of eggs. "Over-easy?" she asked, smiling at the captain.

"Perfect, and I am really hungry, Amanda, thank you," he said. "If you could put something, anything, on a plate, I'll take it to my stateroom in a few minutes."

Amanda smiled. "I'll do you one better and *deliver* it to your stateroom. Ten minutes okay?"

"Excellent," Moore answered as he headed up to the forward torpedo compartment.

At first it looked as if the three SEALs had abandoned their model of the *Cho Ying Atlas*, meticulously displayed on a large flat board. There was a model of a submarine, of the mother ship, and models of small rescue boats scattered across the board. At the corner of the board were the architectural renderings of the freighter, showing the schematics of the different compartments that had been downloaded from the Internet. Probably gone to sleep, Moore thought, and then he heard the sounds of their calisthenics, on the other side of a barrier of torpedoes. Thor Chainsaw was quietly counting their cadence as the three SEALs grunted through their pull-ups, repeatedly lifting themselves up to a beam in the overhead, their muscles bulging, their skin shining with the sweat of the effort. They wore black T-shirts, drenched in sweat, and green-camouflaged pants, partly concealing their standard-issue boots.

Chainsaw nodded to the captain and said to his men, "Five more, two hundred forty-five, and six, seven, eight, nine, two hundred fifty, stand down, take a break." He turned to Moore and smiled a greeting. "Just staying tuned-up," he said, wiping the sweat from his forehead.

"Good," Moore said. "You need to be ready, although it appears you guys never sleep. How is your equipment? Do you have everything you need?"

"Yes, sir, we're in good shape." He studied the captain's face. "Do we have an ETA?"

"We do, Chainsaw, we'll be running full speed down the eastern Philippine archipelago today and tonight, and by tomorrow morning at precisely 0300 hours, we should be in position, about two klicks[21] from the *Cho Ying Atlas*. As you know, there is a one-eighth moon that night, and so we should have darkness on our side."

"Is she still in the same position?"

"Last look, yes, along with the skiffs, five of them now, tied up alongside. Nothing in the Internet news about the *Sweet Caroline* hijacking."

"Do we stay submerged as we approach that mother-thing?"

"Right, then come up to periscope depth as we move within striking distance of the ship. We'll stay submerged, at periscope depth, and you'll egress from the boat's airlock chamber, up to the DDS and then conduct the rescue operation. You will have exactly thirty minutes after reaching the *Cho Ying Atlas* before returning to our boat at 0500 hours. We broach the surface, you arrive with the hostage or hostages…"

"Including your daughter, sir."

Moore hesitated, his concentration disrupted. "Yes," he finally said, "including Caroline. We dive and we're gone before they can launch their skiffs, before they can pull out whatever firepower they may have, and before the sun rises."

"The weather?"

"Latest forecast is four-foot swell from the southwest, light and moderate wind at ten knots from the west, no precipitation predicted."

"No cloud cover, captain?"

"None. Typhoon Banco is a thousand miles to the east, moving away toward Japan, not a problem for us." He looked closely at the large man, studying his eyes, and finally asking, "Do you have any idea where the hostages would be held on the ship? It is almost a thousand feet long."

"That thing is bigger than the fucking Titanic. The difference is that almost all of the ship is chemical or oil storage and they sure as hell aren't putting any hostages or anybody else into those compartments. At least, I hope not. From the schematics," he pointed at the model, "there are four cabins on the D and E decks, three with a side view and one with a forward view only, which is on the D deck. The E deck holds the officers' rec room, where we expect the electronics, computers, and communications equipment will be kept. The B deck holds the citadel, we think. We'll be using the ladder up the port side of the bridge, but the challenge will be the area of the main deck, where the crew's mess is located, on the starboard side…we expect the pirates, or terrorists or whatever they are, will be housed there, but we don't know how many there are."

"And we also don't know how many hostages there might be," Moore said.

"Yes, sir, although from the last six weeks' hijacking news, it would seem there won't be more than five or six people—we'll bring them back, down the rope ladders, into our three inflatables, along with whatever intel we can gather."

"The *Cho Ying Atlas* had twelve crew members aboard when she was hijacked, the pirates killed several of them, threw them overboard. They only kept the officers…."

"The ones for whom they might command a ransom."

The sentence hung in the air as both men avoided eye contact. Moore had studied each day's news reports since they left Pearl Harbor, looking for any information about any ransom demands, anything to suggest that Peter Blackwell's company or family had received any claims made for his return. The thought, buried down deep in his mind and continuously suppressed from arising to his consciousness, was that if there had been a ransom demand, it would only be for Peter Blackwell. There simply was no financial reason for Caroline to be included in any ransom, and by that reasoning, there was no purpose for her to still be alive.

The captain shook his head, forcing the thought out of his mind. He looked back at the SEAL and said, "I would guess there are probably six or seven hostages, while somebody in Palawan, or on the *Cho Ying Atlas*, negotiates with the companies or families."

"There's no way to know the numbers," Chainsaw said, but we'll get her, sir. "If she's anywhere in the vicinity of those sons-of-bitches, we'll get her for you."

"Thank you, Chainsaw," Moore said, "and when you have done that…."

He was interrupted in mid-sentence by the concussion sound of a detonation, exploding in the ocean, causing all of the SEALs to simultaneously jump as Moore raced out of the compartment back to the control center. He found Berry hovering over Bodine's shoulders, looking at the gauges with an alarmed expression.

"Single detonation, captain," Doc Wheat called out from the sonar room at the side of the control center. "No screws, no ships in the vicinity."

"Maybe an ASW chopper in the air launching a sounding grenade, captain?" Chief Berry asked. "I've slowed us to two knots, silent operation, sir."

"Good," Moore said, "Take us down to seven hundred."

"Make our depth seven hundred feet," Berry ordered, immediately thinking about the repaired pipe in the lower level engine room.

"Seven hundred, aye, aye, chief," Bodine announced as he pushed forward on his control wheel.

"Gotta weak spot in that auxiliary seawater piping, captain," Berry said, watching the depth gauge slowly change to the greater depth.

"I know that's a risk we'll have to take," Moore replied, looking up into the Control Center overhead as if he could envision the source of the noise. Amongst the maze of wires and pipes coursing through the boat above their heads, a pair of light bulbs shined brightly down on the men. Moore looked at the machinery, his eyes locking in on the light bulb for a brief moment when a flash of certainty crossed his face. He turned away from the control center, climbed down the ladder to the crew's galley where he found Amanda crying and Wilson standing next to her, looking furious.

"Captain," Wilson said, "it's my fault for trying to teach her to operate the damn thing."

Amanda reached out and struck the man on his shoulder. "It's *not* your fault, Fred, it's *my* fault."

"The garbage ejector?" Moore asked. "What did you put into the garbage ejector?"

"I *told* her to keep light bulbs out of the ejector," Wilson said. "I told her…"

"Captain, I did it," Amanda said. "Fred showed me how to use the ejector, how to load the garbage weights, how to lock out the secondary door and how to eject." She looked at Wilson and wiped away her tears. "He told me no light bulbs, something about explosions or implosions or something, he *told* me, but I didn't see the damn thing. It was hidden under the garbage."

"Now you might have told the whole world where we are, Amanda," Wilson said. "It doesn't take much more than that kind of mistake to sink a ship."

"Amanda," Moore said, putting a hand on her shoulder, "I would guess that, you have learned…"

"I'm really sorry captain," she said, looking up at the man. "It will absolutely never happen again, and captain, I did fix your breakfast…"

She walked over to the galley and handed him the food tray with a metal covering over a plate filled with eggs, bacon, and hashed brown potatoes. As he thanked her and took his breakfast plate, the captain glanced at Wilson and said, "Would you bring a pot of coffee up to my stateroom, Wilson?"

"Yes, sir," Wilson said, walking into the galley to retrieve a pot of fresh coffee. With Wilson following behind, Moore climbed the stairs to the control center. As he passed Berry, he quietly ordered the Chief of the Boat to bring the *Monterey* back up to a safer depth, then he and Wilson continued forward to the wardroom area where he entered his stateroom. Wilson placed the pot on the table next to his desk and turned to leave.

"I'm sorry about Amanda…" he began, abruptly stopping as he felt the steel-like grip of the captain on his arm.

"Wilson?" Moore said, "Do you remember that time in the East China Sea, when we were near test depth, when we were rigged for silent operations, under the active and passive Chinese sonar systems during their fleet exercises last year?"

Wilson's face immediately flushed as he said, "I do remember that, captain."

"There was a wrench that fell from that torpedoman's hand, making a significant noise, even loud enough for me to hear in the control center."

Wilson looked down, his voice becoming a whisper. "Yes, sir, I do remember every single second of that."

"I thought you might remember that day, Wilson," Moore said, releasing his grip, "and now we will let *both* of these events go, won't we?"

Ten minutes later, Captain Gary Moore finished his breakfast and felt the familiar aching of fatigue spreading through his body. He had been awake all night, standing at the periscope station next to Berry as the chief darted in and out of the sonar room. To finally clear the Luzon Strait and the waters south of Taiwan and to dive deep beneath the ocean was, to every submariner on the *Monterey*, a return to the peaceful environment of concealment, the *native environment* for the boat.

Moore glanced at his picture of Caroline and his wife Meredith at the park, the time of happiness that had long ago receded to such a distant time and yet returned regularly and repeatedly in his mind. As he reached over to turn off the light above the small desk, a knock came to his stateroom door.

"Captain?" the familiar voice of Doc Wheat called from behind the door. "Could I have a moment?"

Moore opened the door and motioned for the hospital corpsman to take a seat next to the table in the cramped stateroom.

"Are you okay, Wheat?" the captain asked. "Who's on-watch at the sonar station now?"

"Wilson is covering it for a few minutes.... Everything is quiet out there, for now at least. I just wanted to ask you a couple of questions. When we talked on the pier, before the *Monterey* departed on this mission, I told you I'd follow you anywhere."

"You did, Doc, and thank you again. You said you wanted to come along on what you called the "Mystery Mission."

"Yes, sir," he said, his gaze averted for a moment. "I did say that, after I noted four or five guys depart O'Malley's Bar suddenly, right after you had that telephone call."

Moore said quietly, "You wanted to be a part of the action, whatever it was."

Wheat hesitated, looking down at his feet before finally looking the captain directly in the eye. "That is correct, sir, and I was curious to find out where everybody was going, especially since nobody would talk. And so, here I am, but with just one question. When this mission is over, I need to ask you, is my career totally screwed?"

"Wheat, you...."

"I mean when we get back, assuming we survive this thing, assuming the Chinese don't sink our asses, assuming the American Navy doesn't...."

"Wheat," Moore said, his voice becoming emphatic. "Nobody can fault you for following orders. On the pier, I said 'Let's get on the boat,' and you said, 'Yes, sir.' You are a submariner, you follow orders, and your thinking is focused on what you can do to help save lives in the upcoming action." He paused and looked directly at the corpsman. "I know the loss of those two SEALs is in your mind, Doc, but there was nothing you could have done for either of them, nothing."

"That's what's bugging me...they were dead by the time Chainsaw and Frog got their bodies back on the boat, there was nothing..."

"We need your skills Doc, and I'll tell you, after you leave the Navy...and you will leave the Navy after this mission...your future is clear, hell, you may even get a medal if we're successful. You have always wanted to be a doctor. If a good med school was looking for the best of the best, you would be a home run for them. You are going to apply to medical school, Doc. In fact, I'm going to *kick* your lazy ass into medical school. The profession *needs* people like you."

"And so, if we pull this off, that's where I go?"

"Unless you *want* to stay in the Navy, hell, the Navy may even recruit you into the military medical school. You already got a degree, Biology, right?

"Yes, sir."

"Okay, God knows, you already have more practical experience than most medical doctors, you'd be a great doctor. Forget the loss of the SEALs, Doc, there was nothing you could have been done for the two SEALs. Right now, my daughter Caroline is waiting. And, there is her husband, there are potentially other hostages, any or all of them may be wounded, you will have plenty of important work to do." Moore smiled. "You likely will save lives."

"Thank you, sir, that sounds like a great plan."

"Good, now get focused on what's coming. Have you prepared your medications, are your trauma kits ready, hemostasis systems ready? Have you talked with our SEALs, do you know what they might need in their rescue effort, in their own med kits? If you become focused on your job, Wheat, if you excel and help the medical side of this mission, everything else will fall into place. Amanda has said she wants to be a nurse, have you prepared her for the potential medical consequences from hostage starvation, malnutrition, gunshot injuries, hypothermia, scurvy, worms, and every other God-blessed thing that can happen to human beings who have been captured and moved into harm's way?"

"Yes, sir, I've thought about most of those things. I've inventoried my medical supplies, I'm getting ready for anything…"

"Good," Moore said, standing up. "Go find Amanda and take her under your wing. She's also feeling a bit down right now…."

"The light bulb in the garbage…"

"Right. Find her, don't mention light bulbs, don't mention garbage, work with her and be ready—we have less than twenty-four hours before the rescue begins. When this is done, I promise you, water will seek its level and you…and everyone else on the boat…will be fine. You may not see it now, but what is about to happen is unprecedented…."

"Yes, sir," Wheat said, turning to move out the door with renewed energy. "Thank you, sir. We will be ready. Also, captain, in case you might have forgotten, I have *three* daughters."

"Hell, I know about your three daughters, Doc, two of them are in high school, right? And, you should know that it is relevant," Moore said with a small smile, "that I have only the one daughter. When we have her back, this will be over and done, and we'll head back for you to see your daughters. We'll never have to do this again, no more daughters to find after this one. Now, get to work, we have a mission to accomplish."

Moore closed the stateroom door and sat down again. He rubbed his eyes, pushing away the aching fatigue enveloping him. He looked at the hidden packet of letters, now retrieved from the tight space between the mattress and the bulkhead. He reached out for them, then he pulled his hand away. It was the next letter, the one sent at the end of high school that had profoundly stayed with him over the past several years. He knew he shouldn't read it again, but it added to his *need* to find Caroline.

He wondered briefly if he was becoming crazy, if he might need the straight jacket he knew Wheat had stored in the back of his medicine locker. He turned out the overhead stateroom light and lay back on his rack, adjusting his pillow, and finally turned on the tiny reading light. His hand reached into the dark and he pulled out the letter. He found his own hands had developed a fine tremor as he opened it. He placed the single page in front of the light and he began to read.

Hi Daddy,

This won't be a long letter, on this day of graduating from high school, just a note to thank you for what you have done for me and to let you know how proud I am of you. It's not just your paying the Princeton tuition, and thank you again for that, it's for allowing me to rise to the highest level I can reach with the independence that my life without you, and without Mom, has created. Out there, invisible under the ocean, you have become the captain of your ship, and that brings me great pride, but now I am going to become the captain of my ship—the ship of life that I'm embarking upon during my future years in college and beyond. While the other students are preparing for college, and I am sure, are struggling with the trauma of departing their parents for a distant school, I have no such struggle—I am independent, I am captain material, and you have made this happen. While Aunt Marcy has taken care of the living details and has been sweet as ever, you have loved me, as Mom loved me, and this love from both of you is with me every day. Although I have known one or two guy friends in high school, the boys have had high standards and have been very high in quality, kind of like the men you would want on that submarine of yours. They have also respected my independence—nobody has found me to be vulnerable and for that, you should be very proud, especially since you are responsible. They are perhaps tired of my bragging about you, commanding a submarine with such unbelievable power, but you understand that this has been persuasive in keeping me safe.

And so, Daddy, you have prepared me for life, I love you, I will forever love you, and it is my hope that I will always make you as proud of me as I will always be of you.

Love,

Caroline

Chapter 11

Seattle, Washington

From the back seat of his Navy car, Admiral Samuel Sullivan knew it was going to be a very long and miserable day, a *Seattle* kind of day.

The weather was becoming cold and windy-wet, a shivering contrast to the balmy days in Hawaii. Agents from the NSA had already talked with everybody they could find who had even the remotest connection to the Blackwell family, everybody except the hard-to-find elegant and ostracized sister from Beverly Hills. Now, there was an ever-lengthening string of unhappy people, *the interviewed ones*, stretching from Seattle to the plush neighborhoods of the lavish Medina district. If the agents' reports to COMPACFLT were to be believed, all of those interrogations and briefings had, so far, gathered nothing of value about the missing submarine.

Sullivan looked out the side window from the back of the sedan as the driver accelerated through the increasing morning traffic across the Hadley Memorial Bridge in the direction of Seattle. For a moment, Sullivan thought he could see the snowy peak of Mount Rainer's towering precipice before it quickly became obscured by the darkening clouds from the violent cold front sweeping down from Canada. Now, we're going to get rain, a miserable dreary *Seattle* rain, he thought, that would add to the fun of pushing through the crowded streets of the downtown business district seeking answers that may not even be available.

"You know where International Cyber Systems is located, right?" he asked the sailor in the driver's seat.

"I do, admiral, right off the Northbound Five, ETA about ten minutes," he said with confidence.

"Very well, let's hustle over there."

"Yes, sir."

Sullivan looked out the window again. Now, there is that cantankerous curmudgeon billionaire Randolph Blackwell to deal with…the father of Peter Blackwell and his sister, Sally, the holder of the family fortune, the man at the top served by the Board, by the

Chairman of the Board, by the army of secretaries, accountants and attorneys. The man with the money. The guy everybody bows to.

Sullivan pulled out his cell phone and punched in Brenda Walker's number in Hawaii. Her voice answered on the fourth ring, sleepy and irritated.

"Walker here," she snapped.

"This is Sullivan, Brenda, I know it's early, very sorry to keep waking you, but I need your help."

There was a pause and she finally responded, "Good morning, sir, still in Seattle?"

"Affirmative, I need you to send me some data."

"What do you need?"

"The electronic line, ASAP, send me that long cell phone/localization line you've got that tracks the position of Mombo's call."

"The LEO satellite connection line across India, the ocean, and the Philippines?

"Right, I need the *precise* coordinates of that Low Earth Orbit satellite line from Mombo's call; you said it crossed the South China Sea. I believe Moore is heading for a point of intersection on that line."

"Yes, sir, we've got it down at COMSUBPAC."

"I need it as soon as possible."

"Yes, sir," Brenda answered. "I can launch it on the encrypted line from Pearl in about a half hour…"

"Good, thank you. At least you'll beat the morning traffic."

The International Cyber Systems glass and steel building on Columbia Street was surrounded by the hustle of early morning Seattle traffic as the business district began to recover from four days of Thanksgiving. The dark gray Ford screeched to a halt in front of the expansive glass doors and Admiral Sullivan bolted from the car. His telephone calls had already been stonewalled at every level of the corporation, on the emergency line, on the back lines, the inside lines, and even from the receptionist to the upper levels of executive management. Call after call was placed on prolonged holds that were never again answered. Sullivan had reviewed the company portfolios meticulously, scanning the individual photographs on their website. The single color picture of the Board of Directors showed a gathering of serious business-like men and women seated and standing behind a long wooden desk. A white-bearded thin man was seated in the prominent center position in a larger chair.

The message of the picture was clear that the founder and CEO, Randolph Blackwell, was the man in charge.

Yet, he had become secretive and reclusive, almost like a ghost. The Chairman of the Board, an executive-looking type in the Board picture, with just the right amount of requisite gray around his ears, stood with the other members of the Board, his gavel precisely positioned on a small block in front of him like a trophy. His name was Dominic Mathews, the legend below the picture said. He was the chairman and he was the man whose executive secretary would not even admit that anybody knew a man named Randolph Blackwell.

Make a call requesting an appointment with Mr. Mathews, a call from an admiral in the United States Navy? "Does he know you, sir? No? One moment, please," was the answer. The caller was abruptly put on hold, without benefit of music, a hold that never ended. A polite request for an appointment with Mr. Blackwell resulted in a flat response that "We are unable to fulfill this request at this time." At what time *would* such a request be fulfilled? "I'm sorry sir, not in the foreseeable future," was the automatic response.

Sullivan's attaché, Brenda Walker was rebuffed on repeated calls, and subsequently, a verbal venting from her to the admiral himself resulted in a frenzy of research to find leverage…what government contracts ICSI possessed, what IRS records they had, and how their company business model could allow a Federal monetary persuasion to be exerted? Three separate calls to the Securities Exchange Commission were made, looking for investigations, malfeasance either real or created, none was found. The sum of that effort was not just unproductive, it was a flat zero. The message from International Cyber Systems to the government was clear, this was an independent non-government linked company, generating billions for their investors through the sale of advanced software systems throughout the world, and they yield to no one. Especially no one in the Federal government.

Sullivan pushed open the glass doors at the entrance, walked past two guards who looked like steroid-abusing linebackers for the Seattle Seahawks, and moved up to a large reception counter that spanned the central lobby. A large Black man with intense eyes and a cold face, about 40 years of age, Sullivan estimated, stood behind the reception desk and stared at the admiral as he approached.

"Good morning, sir," he said in a surprisingly deep voice as he studied the man and the uniform. "I presume you are Admiral Samuel Sullivan from Hawaii? You had notified us that you were coming?"

"I am Admiral Sullivan, I did send notification, and I need you to deliver a message to Randolph Blackwell," Sullivan said, leaning over the counter and staring straight into the man's dark eyes.

"Let me have your message, sir, and I'll pass it on to management."

Sullivan narrowed his eyes and felt his heart pounding as he said, "Inform Mr. Blackwell that his son Peter is likely to be tortured and killed in the very near future if he and I don't talk this morning."

Five minutes later, Sullivan dropped into the leather chair across from the empty desk of Dominic Mathews. The room, surrounded by glass looking out over an expansive stormy panorama of Seattle, was absolutely silent after Margarita Lindsey, the sinewy frozen executive secretary, pulled up a straight-back chair without a word and sat down in the corner of the room. The coldness of the woman was further underscored by her complete silence, not a welcome, not an offer of coffee, and nothing about the man he was about to meet. Ten minutes of hostile stillness later, the door abruptly opened and Dominic Mathews walked across the spacious room, crossed in front of the admiral without comment and seated himself at the other side of the massive desk.

"You've moved one step further than the NSA, admiral," Mathews' booming voice roared, "and what in hell are you doing implying to our staff that you know *anything* about the life of Mr. Blackwell's son?"

Sullivan immediately jumped to his feet, taking Mathews by surprise as Margarita Lindsey visibly flinched in her chair. "Peter Blackwell and his wife have been on their yacht, *The Sweet Caroline*," he said. "Are you aware of that little fact?"

"Go on."

"Their scuba adventure became interrupted, and he and his wife are now gone, Mr. Mathews, are you aware of that?"

Mathews swallowed hard. "The family of this company's CEO is a private matter, admiral, and..."

Sullivan slammed his hand down on the chairman's desk. "What is not a private matter is that this country has just lost a nuclear submarine."

Mathews' eyes widened as he hesitated. "*What are you talking about?*"

Sullivan leaned over the desk. "What I am talking about is that your company's CEO's son married a woman whose father is the commanding officer of a nuclear submarine. This exact same fully armed nuclear submarine is now missing. Does this seem to be a bit more than a coincidence and a hell of a lot more than a private matter?"

"Okay, admiral, I am sorry about your missing submarine. How does that have anything to do with this company?"

"Mr. Mathews, I presume you are an intelligent man. This country is missing a submarine, and its absence is directly related to Peter Blackwell's recent disappearance. The United States Navy is looking for it, the Japanese are looking for it, the goddamn Chinese are looking for it, the whole fucking world is looking for it, and the CEO of this company is the only man who can tell us what has happened. This information is critical to putting the brakes on an emerging risk of a goddamn World War III."

The two men stared at each other for a moment before Sullivan took a deep breath and sat down. Mathews looked straight into the admiral's eyes and he softly said, "Thank you for your visit, admiral, and I appreciate your concerns. However, this is a private company and if you need to know anything more about our operations, please return with a subpoena."

He reached over to his telephone, pressed a button and nearly instantaneously two oversized security officers suddenly appeared at the door as Margarita Lindsey quickly stood and glared at Sullivan.

"These gentlemen and I will escort you to the exit, admiral," she said, "please follow me."

Sullivan began walking toward the door then turned to face Mathews again. "Let me talk with Randolph Blackwell," he hollered. "We need to know how much time we have before it's too late."

Mathews ignored him as he began to study several papers on his desk.

"Just let me talk with him," Sullivan pleaded. "We are running out of time!"

With the two security guards at his side and Lindsey leading the way, Admiral Sullivan was escorted to the elevator, down to the main lobby and to the front door of the building. As the guards opened the door, Margarita Lindsey turned to Sullivan and held out her hand as she said, "It was a pleasure meeting you, admiral."

Sullivan looked into the woman's cold eyes and said nothing as he shook her hand, realizing only as the security guard opened the door ahead of him that she had handed him a little folded scrap of paper. He plunged his hands into his pockets and stormed out the front door. Spotting his car down the street with the driver still inside and waiting, Sullivan opened the back door, climbed in and slammed the door shut.

As the Navy sedan pulled out onto Columbia Street, the admiral ordered the driver to take them back to Whidbey Island as he sat back and very carefully opened the note from the cold executive secretary at ICSI.

USS *Monterey*, Pacific Ocean

Fred Wilson and Amanda Peterson stood in the corner of the *Monterey's* bow compartment, quietly watching the three SEALs review the coordination of their impending rescue effort. Chainsaw, towering over the other two men, did most of the talking, Silverback and Frog watching him closely and nodding from time to time as each part of their attack was reviewed. A brilliant light had been positioned over their model of the mother ship, bathing the tiny structure with white light.

"We are launching the rescue in six hours," Chainsaw said, the pointer in his powerful right hand pointing at the target ship. "Remember, we are not trying to kill the bastards, this is a *rescue* mission. As I've said, other than my quick search of the computer room, we do not split up on the ship. We stay together, with Frog covering our six, Silverback watching the overhead and laterals, and I'll clear the path in front of us."

"Glad you're a big guy, dude," Frog said.

"Lots of cover to hide behind," Silverback added with a smile.

"Great, thanks, guys," Chainsaw said, looking at the two men. "Okay. We want to get in, we want to gather the hostages, and we want to get out, quietly and quickly. The *Atlas* is anchored both fore and aft but we'll be boarding on the stern where there hopefully won't be any watchstanders—it will be just like we did on the *Gravely*. This will be the most vulnerable part of the mission. We will be exposed to whatever crap they may throw at us. We don't know how many of them are on the ship, we don't know for sure where the hostages are kept, and since the ship was taken, the citadel safe room has almost certainly been compromised. We don't know how many hostages there are, we don't know what weapons the hostiles have, and we don't have any idea how many guards might be posted around their hostage-container room."

Frog sat up straight and said, "I just *love* the mystery of it all!"

Silverback grimaced as he waved his left hand to talk. "I may be wrong, Chainsaw, but if we start this little briefing with what we *do* know, our plan will be easier to discuss."

Chainsaw looked at the men for a moment, took a deep breath, and continued. "What we *do* know, is that it will be dark, the moon is a waxing crescent barely 10% visible, with about three hours before sunrise from the moment of launch. We are expecting a state 2 sea with about a four knot wind out of the east. The dolphins will stay in the *Monterey*. Since our own underwater approach inside the SDV[22] will be fully submerged at 20 feet, we'll move briskly toward the *Atlas*. During our approach to the tanker, the *Monterey* will remain submerged, behind us, but we'll be in radio contact with Captain Moore and Chief Berry throughout the mission. Our three IBS rafts won't be inflated until we're secured to the *Atlas* stern anchor chain."

Amanda leaned over to Wilson and whispered, "What's IBS mean? Like, Irritable Bowel Syndrome?" She smiled.

Chainsaw paused and looked across the compartment. "Inflatable Boat, Small...."

Amanda immediately smiled self-consciously and said, "Thank you, Chainsaw, sorry."

Wilson whispered in her ear, "I knew that," as Chainsaw continued.

"After securing our SDV to the anchor chain and inflating the two IBS rubber boats, we'll launch our TAILS[23] from the boats onto the ship and then climb the ladder to gain access..."

Silverback paused, looked at Amanda and smiled. "TAILS as in Tactical Air Initiated Launch System," he said.

Wilson whispered under his breath, "I didn't know that."

Chainsaw continued, his voice rising. "If everybody is finished talking, maybe we can get through this. After the approach onto the stern of the *Cho Ying Atlas*, launching our rope ladders as far away as possible from both the port and starboard side of the A deck where the officer's and crew's mess is located, the *Monterey* will stay submerged until we return with the hostages. At that point, we'll move in and find the hostages. As we head back, the skipper will then surface enough to bring them onboard. We may be in a rush to get them into the sub if any of the hostiles are coming after us. All three of us will provide cover fire, and for this part, we'll use our MP-7's and the Nightforce scopes. At that point, the crew gathers the hostages as they make it down the ladder, we follow behind, we shut the control room hatch, and we're outta there."

The compartment became quiet as they thought about the challenges before them. "Any questions?" Chainsaw finally asked.

"Any changes about how much time we have on the ship?" Frog asked quietly.

"The timetable is mandatory, Frog. We have exactly twenty minutes to find the hostages, to free them, and to get them down the rope ladder. At twenty minutes and one second, whether we find or free any hostages, we are gone, and I mean gone, out of there. Anything more than that exponentially increases the risk of none of us making it back. Those waters are crawling with pirate skiffs. That is an absolute time limit, and I think it's enough time to get them out."

"Right," Silverback said, "depending on how many pirate sons-of-bitches are guarding them.

"You are correct, Silverback," Chainsaw said, "and so we do to the pirate sons-of-bitches what we have to do."

"Kill the fuckers, rescue the hostages, and hopefully, the captain's daughter will be among them," Amanda said, turning to leave the compartment as the three SEALs stared at her departing figure.

"We are hoping…" Chainsaw said quietly as he carefully laid his wooden pointer across the table, just on the far side of the *Cho Ying Atlas.*

International Cyber Systems, Inc., Seattle

In Seattle, the top floor of the towering glass structure holding the offices of ICSI was dark with the exception of the light shining from under the door at the far end of the central corridor. The overhead corridor lights were off, the elevator was locked to the public, the message was clear that none of the ICSI staff was to enter this part of the building. The voices within the locked room were muffled by the most advanced sound silencing system in the United States. Thirty yards down the passageway, a light popped on above an electronically-isolated elevator with a faint noise. The door slid open into the darkened area and a pair of security guards walked out and strolled down the aisle, each with a hand casually resting on a Glock 19 pistol. They carefully inspected the lighted conference room and finally walked down the corridor to look outside through the wall of glass at the world surrounding the building.

The panorama of Seattle buildings in front of them was obscured by the dark clouds and the swirling hail slamming into the structure and bouncing off the glass. There was no sound from the storm, nor was there any noise from the conference room behind them. The guards commented to each other of the remarkable silence, here at the top of one of the most prominent buildings in Seattle, almost like being within a tomb one of them said before they wandered back into the elevator and descended to continue their patrolling guardianship of ICSI.

From within the conference room, seated at the end of the long polished table, Randolph Blackwell hunched over the speaker phone while Margarita Lindsey sat next to him, writing furiously on her SolidTek electronic note pad as the recording machine next to the CEO blinked its cold blue light.

"The stock has been sold, Mr. Khalid," Blackwell said into the telephone, "the money is ready to transfer from our company to Zurich, and I expect my son and his wife to be placed on the first aircraft out of Palawan. Are you familiar with the Philippine and United Airline schedules of aircraft departing the Puerto Princesa International Airport on Palawan?"

"Mr. Blackwell!" the British voice roared out of the speaker, "I am a resident of Palawan, and I am well aware of the airlines operating out of our airport. However, since I am in the possession of your son and your daughter-in-law, why are *you* making demands?"

"This is a business arrangement, Mr. Khalid, and if you are unable to handle the details, put somebody on who can," Blackwell said, his deep voice devoid of emotion. He reached over and hit the hold button as Lindsey watched her boss.

"Give him a sense of 100 million dollars vanishing," Blackwell said as Lindsey silently nodded.

Several seconds later, Blackwell hit the hold button again and said, "Did we just lose our connection or are you still there?"

"I'm still here, goddamn it, and you know it. Let's get on with this, Mr. Blackwell. Have you notified the police, the NSA, *anybody*?"

"Nobody but you and me, Mr. Khalid, this is a private transaction. As I have told you, prior to the transfer of our company's money, I need you to provide me with proof of life of Peter and Caroline Blackwell as well as their current state of viability. That means I will need to interact with them by video link, they will each describe their condition, they will each confirm they are uninjured, and then, and *only* then, will a transfer of ninety million occur."

"Blackwell. You are about to sign your son's death certificate. The ransom is one hundred million and you know it."

"When they are on the aircraft and my sources confirm the plane is cleared for departure, the final ten million will enter your account, Mr. Khalid. If you then interfere with their take-off from Puerto Princesa, you will never live to spend any of it, that is my promise to you, sir."

"Okay. Okay!" the British voice said furiously. "However, if you change one more…"

Blackwell leaned forward, his white beard not more than an inch from the telephone. "Our money is ready," he growled, "I am now waiting for the proof of life."

"I know what you are waiting for, Blackwell. Give me four hours, and I will give you one goddamn minute to discuss matters of health with Peter and Caroline Blackwell. You will then initiate the transfer of ninety million or you will watch them both become immediately deceased in a most unpleasant manner."

Margarita Lindsey looked into the reddened eyes of the white-haired CEO, his lined face showing the strain of the past four days.

Her gaze returned to her electronic notepad where she logged the information that documented the precise timetable spelled out by Guleed Khalid into her computer.

After ten seconds of silence, Blackwell finally spoke. "Okay, Khalid, we are agreed," he said, reaching out to hover his finger directly over the disconnect button on the front of the telephone. "If I even think I detect any harm has come to these two people, my company's money will never leave the city of Seattle."

His finger dropped to the telephone and he broke the connection. The two of them sat for a moment in the silent room before Blackwell turned to Lindsey and flashed a quick smile that almost looked like a grimace. "Ten million to insure they at least get on the plane, it was worth a try," he said.

"You pushed it to the edge, sir, but there is really no way to guarantee their safety. No matter how much money they get."

The CEO took a deep breath and the lines of his face seemed to harden. "You are correct. They will kill them, Ms. Lindsey," he said. "They have killed others after ransoms have been paid. This man in particular has killed many others; he favors beheading, he is a barbarian. Once they have our treasure he will most likely kill them both, but they have, on occasion, spared some hostages and so it is worth the effort. If they put them on the plane, they may take them off the plane and that will be the end, but we can always be hopeful."

"That is about all we can do at this point," she said quietly.

He looked at her and briefly touched her arm with his gnarled hand. "It has been a long day, Ms. Lindsey," he said with a quiet voice filled with aching fatigue. "It has been a very long day. I will see you in three and a half hours and we will send them some money."

"Yes, sir," Margarita said, her thin frame rising from the chair. "One more thing, Mr. Blackwell. There is an admiral in the United States Navy who has wanted to talk with you about your son…."

"I know about Admiral Sullivan, Mathews and I have talked. And I know about the United States Navy not even offering to help find Peter…and Caroline, no offer to help *any* hostage ever held by these creatures. Admiral Sullivan knows more than he should and yet there has been no offer from him on behalf of American citizens captured abroad, nothing. They do not really care about this." He reached down to the table and turned off the recording machine.

He began walking to the door, turning at the last moment to tell his executive secretary. "Admiral Sullivan and his Navy can do nothing for us, and I have nothing to say to him."

Whidbey Island, Washington

In the small wooden house on Oriskany Avenue, not more than five hundred yards from the hangar at Ault Field on Whidbey Island, Admiral Samuel Sullivan carefully placed his coffee cup on the side of his desk and clutched the mouse controlling his computer. As the rain pounded on the roof, Sullivan looked around him to insure no leakages from the ancient ceiling allowed water to drop on the array of computers stacked across the back of his desk. The encrypted images had flowed through the high-speed Internet links into his portfolio of Cisco blade and rack servers and onto the screens from the Intel processor in a rapid-fire succession, each scrutinized for relevance and printed if deemed potentially valuable. The stacks of papers were then further scrutinized for actionable potential, with nearly two-thirds of the pages then being shredded in the massive Security Level 6 Datastroyer, each page immediately being reduced into more than 40,000 random-sized pieces, creating an expanding mound of dust that God himself could not decipher.

Sullivan rubbed his eyes and stared at the remaining stack of paper. All of this intelligence was seemingly infiltrated with massive amounts of stupidity.

The search mission to find the vanished submarine or to even uncover a reasonable clue as to why it had disappeared was, so far, amounting to a spectacular failure. The Navy had all but given up the search at the Strait of Magellan off the South American archipelago of Tierra del Fuego, where the snow and the winds howling across the sea state 6[24] had made thousands of sailors' lives miserable for the past week. Most of the beleaguered ships in those waters had already retreated to the Falkland Islands, seeking a calm water refuge with their British allies. The oceans off North and South Korea, as well as Japan, were too vast to allow a reasonable search pattern but the ongoing order of the day to each U.S. Navy vessel in the area was to "remain vigilant."

"Remain vigilant, aye, aye," the admiral muttered quietly, sarcasm dripping from his voice.

The NSA and the CIA had been very busy. They had interviewed at least 400 people, at last count, including "relatives of the commanding officer's daughter" without any measurable intelligence forthcoming. They had interviewed the commanding officer's deceased wife's relatives and found no individuals having any history of subversive intent; to the contrary, they found that the late Meredith Moore's family was uniquely patriotic and supportive of the *Monterey's* commanding officer "no matter what he has done." They had also interviewed the top executives with Iridium Global Network regarding the single telephone call from Mombo, resulting in their finally discovering the long electronic line, stretching across a third of India and across the globe into the Philippines. Useless. They searched for any history of Mombo calls to Captain Moore during the months or years before and found no evidence of contact. They had interviewed their human resources throughout India and had found at least 648 Mombos at last count and still counting…no Mombo had yet been interviewed but potential links between any Mombo and Commander Gary Moore were still being researched.

There were at least four memoranda regarding the commanding officer's daughter Caroline, who had graduated *magna cum laude* from Princeton prior to a whirlwind marriage to a man of great wealth. No history of association with enemies of the state had been uncovered. The NSA had established that the couple was traveling to remote destinations around the world in a serendipitous honeymoon-like manner and had been visiting at least nine countries during the month before the submarine disappearance. They had studied the seventeen reported piracy acts in the waters off the Gulf of Aden, the South China Sea, and the Arabian Sea as well as the Malacca Strait during the previous three weeks and had found nothing remarkable beyond the name "Caroline" attached to one of the reported boat hijackings in a Japanese freighter report…an association that had been dismissed as spurious.

Neither the NSA nor the CIA had interviewed Sally Blackwell, the vanishing sister of Peter Blackwell from Beverly Hills, California, and nobody in the family had mentioned that the woman even existed beyond noting she was "another" relative who enjoyed taking care of horses.

The tentacles of every element of the United States intelligence community had spread out across hundreds of locations to interview people remotely linked with the crew of the *Monterey*. No pattern of subversion had yet been identified. They had interviewed the three SEALs who had *not* gone on the hijack mission, and other than being extremely angry about the preceding Indonesia debacle, there was no knowledge about why the three other SEALs had disappeared aboard the *Monterey*. They had spoken with the families of the reactor operator, Brian Robinson, and the machinist mate, Manny Munroe, and everybody seemed shocked that these men could possibly be a part of such a thing. They were always such "nice guys" everybody said; even Munroe's family, who did note their son had a record of fighting, drinking, and carousing, as well as having been busted in rank to a third-class petty officer, revered the captain and said he was a true patriot of the Navy. Everybody was in agreement that these were very good sailors, and why they would do anything like this was a mystery. They quickly located Claudia Baxter, *or, to be more correct, she found them*, and the interview with the wife of the electrician, Jules Baxter, had been shortened by her repeated and aggressive demand that she be paid "survivor's benefits" immediately since her husband was now "gone forever."

They had aggressively and repeatedly interviewed Ashia Jamila, Amanda Peterson's college roommate, and were in the process of interviewing her family members via their operatives in Iran to seek out subversive linkages. At last report, Ms. Jamila began to experience a "nervous breakdown" from the badgering nature of the interviews and had thereafter lawyered-up and refused to cooperate. Throughout this entire process, the NSA stressed in their voluminous reports that the presence of a Muslim roommate in the same dorm as the woman who had then *coincidentally* established a torrid sexual relationship with a nuclear submariner, and who had then *coincidentally* come aboard the very submarine that *immediately thereafter* disappeared into the vast Pacific Ocean was all problematic. If not problematic, it was at least highly suspicious. The NSA was in the process of dissecting every piece of information within the computers of both women, looking for suspicious e-mails, Jihad propaganda, Internet linkages, mosque associations, and anything else to confirm their complicity with the hijacking of an American submarine. They found nothing.

Sullivan grabbed the remaining stack of pages from the side of his desk and jammed them into the Datastroyer, mumbling, "Mombo combo bullshit" under his breath as the internal pile of dust grew another ten per cent.

Without warning, the computer printer suddenly came to life. The Mombo telephone data from his dedicated Brenda Walker appeared on the paper, the Mombo of chef fame, the Mombo whose telephone call had generated a long electronic line from India into the ocean. Sullivan leaned forward to study the coordinates, immediately wondering why the NSA had not published the information. The coordinates of a Mombo telephone call, he thought, were almost certainly deemed irrelevant by the NSA perspective until some of the Mombos in India could be found and interviewed. The NSA must have asked themselves, Sullivan thought, what would a bunch of telephone coordinates stretching a few thousand miles across ocean and land have to do with the organized hijacking of an American nuclear submarine from Pearl Harbor? He studied the numbers, each stating the potential positions of the Mombo telephone call as the two satellites had moved across the sky.

Feeling a sense of excitement he had not felt since he had departed Hawaii, Sullivan quickly moved the mouse clutched in his right hand, bringing Google Earth to the screen. Using a ruler, he carefully created a line across the screen following precisely the coordinates of the telephone call. He then found the Philippines and Manila, and drew a second line, a north-south line to represent *The Sweet Caroline's* potential path across the ocean. Where the lines crossed had to be the precise point of origin of the cell phone call to Gary Moore that night, the call from his daughter on Mombo's telephone, the call of distress leading to the most audacious theft of government property in the history of the United States Navy.

Sullivan scribbled down the coordinates of the intersection point and the ocean around the precise point of the call. He reached for his cup of black coffee and took a quick sip as he studied the scattering of islands to the south of Manila. He now knew exactly where out in the ocean the call had originated, but he did not know what had happened to the captain's daughter and her husband *after* the call. Mombo was not in India, Mombo had to have been on the boat, and Mombo was likely dead. But there was no evidence of any ransom and there was no information about a timetable to allow the *Monterey* to intervene.

And, most worrisome of all, there was no evidence that anybody else was still alive.

His eyes lifted to the waters south of the intersect point, to the western coast of Palawan, to Borneo, Brunei, and to the Sulu Sea. He took another sip of coffee as his eyes came to rest on Palawan. As he reached for the telephone sitting on the edge of his desk, he picked up again the small piece of paper handed to him by Margarita Lindsey, the cold woman who would say nothing to him, the woman with the thin body and the hard eyes who wrote she wanted to meet with him at precisely 1230 hours that afternoon, down the Waterford Trail near the Arboretum Foundation Building, just east of Seattle.

Chapter 12

USS *Monterey*, Pacific Ocean

Captain Gary Moore looked again at the clock on the desk in his stateroom.

0300 hours, early morning in the dark ocean above, one hour remaining. The *Monterey* cruised quietly at four knots, remaining 300 feet beneath the surface, like a lion creeping up on its prey in the dark of night, the captain thought, the anchored prey of the oiler *Cho Ying Atlas*, now just eight miles away.

The submarine was filled with adrenaline, Moore could feel it in the air, and he could feel it in himself as he reviewed, for the hundredth time, the battle plan in his stateroom. It was a cold tingle that seemed to move through his body like an electrical wave, energizing his mind, creating a hyper-alertness that moved the world around him into a slow-motion arena of action allowing an enhanced anticipation of events before they occurred. The SEALs had practiced their routine, over and over again, they had exercised, and they had checked their equipment, all fulfilling the pattern that had been drilled into their psyche from the first day of training in Coronado, California.

He looked at the clock again, the second hand monotonously counting down the diminishing time before the final assault.

The *Monterey's* transit down the west coast of the Philippine archipelago, at high-speed and at around eight hundred feet below the surface, had been nearly uneventful and had allowed everybody, from Amanda and Wilson in the forward torpedo room to the nukes in the engine room, to catch up on sleep while moving into a routine that became increasingly efficient. Robby had done everything he could to streamline the efficiency of the reactor but the consumption of power was taking its toll—down to 89% at last look, enough to do the job but increasingly less available power to the propulsion turbines for any emergencies.

Doc Wheat had taken Amanda under his medical wing; both of them had laid out their emergency medical supplies, and Wheat had run her through a series of lectures about blood pressures, bleeding, sepsis, and fractures that would have impressed any medical school instructor. Chief Berry had caught up on his sleep and looked alert and ready for action. Billy Bodine stayed on the helm for eighteen hours at a time, divided into segments with the help of Wilson, discovering that if he regularly scanned the instruments across the panel while playing mind games like recalling every single sexual detail about every single girl he had ever met in high school, he could stay remarkably alert.

Moore looked back at the frayed envelope containing the letters, still tucked in the tight wedge-space between the mattress and the bulkhead. They had served as a catharsis of sorts, his mind sorting out his feelings, his guilt, his depression, his regrets, and the love he had for his daughter. His mind had become clear, helped by the adrenaline now pounding through his brain, and he had finally settled the biggest question that had dominated his thoughts during the past several years. When all was said and done, it was Caroline who had answered the question for him, and it was Caroline who had put him at ease, who had told him that he had made the right choice. During the years since his wife's death, when he was out to sea and never there for Caroline's major events in life, it paradoxically was his *absence* that brought her such eventual maturity and success. For it was not an absence borne of neglect, she knew that and had made it clear to him, it was an absence caused by his commitment to success that stirred her own development.

She became successful not just because of her own brains and energy, but also because of watching her father's dedication to duty and country, his years patrolling beneath the sea, eventually moving to the command position of one of the most complex pieces of nuclear-powered machinery ever created by the human race. Caroline had given him the answer to the question that had plagued him over and over again: Should he have stayed in San Diego, doing whatever shore duty the needs of the service dictated, doing a desk job in the Navy but being home to watch out for her every night, or should he do what he had done, what he was trained to do? Most importantly, since the wrong choice would bring a lifetime of regret, *and was irreversible*, his mind had been tortured by the worry about what kind of a daughter would he then have, since there would never be a chance to go back and do it differently.

Now more than ever, it was time to bring Caroline and her husband home.

Captain Moore walked out of his stateroom to the control center where Chief Berry hovered over Bodine at the helm.

"Chief what is the distance from the *Atlas*?" he asked.

"SINS[25] has us eight klicks out, sir, we are steady at four knots, 300 feet," Berry said, absently touching the black-knob lever that actuated periscope hydraulics.

"Slow to three knots and bring us up to periscope depth," Moore ordered crisply.

"Three knots, periscope depth, aye, aye, captain," Berry said. "Helm make your depth sixty-five feet, do not broach, for God's sake, do not broach."

As Bodine answered, Berry grabbed the 7 MC microphone communicating with the engine room. "Engine room, control, slow to three knots, do not cavitate, repeat, do not cavitate."

"Down to three knots, do not cavitate, engine room aye, aye," answered Manny Munroe over the loudspeaker.

Captain Moore watched the depth gauge unwind and at eighty feet, he ordered, "Up periscope, starboard only, medium wavelength infrared detection. Let's take a look and see what's waiting for us out there."

Whidbey Island, Washington

Without bothering to open his umbrella in the roaring rainstorm, Admiral Sullivan ran to the waiting gray Ford, opened the back door, and jumped in.

"Seattle Arboretum, now, as fast as you can get us there," he ordered the sailor in the front seat.

"Yes, sir," the man responded, tossing his magazine onto the other side of the car as he started the engine and accelerated the car in the direction of Ault Field's main gate. "ETA probably a half hour with the rain and noon traffic, sir," he added after a moment of thought.

"Hustle it, sailor, we need to be there in twenty-five minutes."

"Yes, sir," he said as their car raced past the Marine guards and the Prowler jet mounted on display at the front gate. "I can call for an escort, admiral, to get us there in maybe ten minutes if needed. We could get a chopper if the weather hadn't closed in on us."

"We can't come in there in a chopper or with sirens, just get us there as fast as possible," Sullivan said, removing his light coat and mentally thanking Martha for packing one change of civilian clothes. The dark blue slacks and plaid sport shirt would have gone better at a golf game in Hawaii than in a weather system of hail and freezing rain in Seattle.

The car swerved as the driver accelerated in the direction of Burlington and Interstate 5. The note had been handwritten, with a female script, hurriedly and secretly, and had specified the location, the time, and the need for the admiral to wear no uniform. The instructions were cryptic and specific. At the parking lot, he would walk *alone* down Park Trail to the Arboretum Waterfront Trail where she would meet him along the pathway. The woman clearly did not trust telephones or any other electronic means of contact, and the note left no information about how to reach her if there was a problem with her instructions. The final instruction was to shred the note, to leave no trace of her communication with him.

Eighteen minutes of rain and traffic later, the car screeched to a halt at the north corner of the Arboretum parking lot, the sailor set the parking brake and turned around to face the admiral.

"We're here, sir," he said, a youthful smile lighting his face with the pride of his accomplishment. "Arboretum. Less than twenty minutes."

"Sailor, what's your name?"

"Garrett, sir, Jack Garrett." The smile faded.

"Garrett, you've done a great job. Now, I'm going to give you a specific order that I want you to follow precisely."

"Yes, sir."

"Do not let anybody into this car while I'm gone. Keep the doors locked. Talk with nobody. Do you understand?"

"I understand that, yes, sir."

"Next, I want you to mark the current time and in precisely forty-five minutes, if I'm not back to the car, I want you to call 911 for a 'man down on the Waterfront Trail.'"

"You want me to call 911?"

"Garrett, do I need to repeat anything to you?"

"No, sir, got it, 911 if you're not back in forty-five minutes."

"Correct. Finally, if I do not return I want you to call Admiral Stephen Kent's office directly at CINPACFLT at this number. Tell him to access my computer at Whidbey for the linear intersection point."

He handed a card to the man who immediately jammed it into his shirt pocket and said, "CINPACFLT? Linear intersection, yes, sir." His face became pale as he looked at the admiral for more directions.

"That's it, that's all," Sullivan said, grabbing his umbrella, opening the back door and rapidly disappearing down the trail into the driving rain.

The rain was not going to stop for another twelve hours, the NOAA[26] forecast had said that morning and as Sullivan zipped his rain coat and pulled the umbrella closer to his head, he began searching the path ahead for the woman. Visibility was obscured to about one hundred yards and he walked briskly while looking beyond the 520 Tollway overpass. The trail extended another quarter mile beyond the highway toward the waters of Union Bay off Lake Washington, and if the woman didn't show, there would be nowhere else to go. The roaring of rain drowned out the sounds of cars passing overhead as he crossed through the small tunnel to enter the final few hundred feet to the water's edge. There were no people on the trail—it passed quickly through his mind that only lunatics and admirals from Hawaii would be walking down the Arboretum Waterfront Trail as dark clouds closed in and the water and ice poured down from the clouds. He smiled ruefully. Lunatics, admirals, and a wiry executive secretary from the biggest software company in the country.

At the moment he began to regret not bringing a weapon with him, a harsh voice called out from off the trail, a female voice calling, "Admiral Sullivan."

He turned toward the sound and spotted her, camouflaged among the trees and bushes, a tall thin figure with a heavy dark raincoat and a black umbrella held closely to her head.

"Over here," she ordered, more than requested, as Sullivan left the path and crossed the grass toward her.

"Ms. Lindsey," he said as he moved closer, "why are we here?" He studied her face, streaked with rain that had passed around the umbrella, her stringy dark hair sagging down across her forehead. The top of her coat was soaked and he thought he could detect that she was shivering. Her bright eyes stared straight at him so hard that he felt a chill down into his bones.

"Yes, admiral," she said, "I apologize for weather. It would have been much easier to meet you in a restaurant or wherever you're staying. You should know that I am taking an enormous risk, meeting you while working for a company that is world-renown for security. I have a brief lunch break and so we have only a moment. There are ICSI guards everywhere, watching everything."

"To protect corporate secrets, it would seem."

"Of course. But now, what I have, what Randolph Blackwell is concealing, involves innocent lives, people who do not deserve to die but who will very likely not survive. Furthermore, the consequences of anybody knowing of this meeting would get me summarily fired from Cyber Systems. Do you understand what I am saying?"

"Do you understand that an admiral of the United States Navy with a top-secret clearance does in fact understand the meaning of secret? Tell me why we're here."

"First. Are you carrying any recording devices?"

"I am not, and I must ask the same question of you."

"No, sir, I am not. When we finish this conversation, it will not have occurred, is that understood?"

"Of course, Ms. Lindsey." Sullivan smiled. "Now, before this rainstorm turns into a monsoon and before we both freeze to death, could you proceed with our meeting that is not occurring?"

"The captain of your stolen submarine, this Commander Gary Moore, has a daughter, Caroline."

"I know about the daughter…."

"And she is married to a man whose family is one of the richest in the country. To a man whose father is the CEO of International Cyber Systems, my boss…."

"ICSI, right, Randolph Blackwell, I know, and as you know, I tried to talk with him a couple of hours ago."

"You may give up on that idea. He won't see you and he's currently trying to save his son's life."

"We can order him to see me."

Her eyes widened with surprise. "Oh *really*, admiral? I promise you that won't work. I repeat, the man is busy himself trying to save Peter Blackwell's life. If you start any kind of court bullshit order, there will be an army of attorneys that can create stone walls faster than your Navy bulldozers can remove them. You may also become responsible for his son's execution."

Sullivan studied the harsh lines creating a mosaic across the woman's face. "Okay," he said, becoming impatient. "So, we'll hold the order for now. Let's get on with this."

Lindsey sounded almost breathless as the words rushed out. "This daughter Caroline and her husband, Peter Blackwell are being held ransom for the sum of one hundred million dollars."

A moment of silence passed and Sullivan finally asked, his voice a whisper, "There is a chance they're still alive? Where is the captain? Every navy in the world has spent most of the past week..."

"We do not know where your captain is, and we do not know where your submarine is, but we do know that, if the police or the press get any word of this ransom, the hostages will be immediately killed."

"Who is doing the negotiating?"

"It is not a negotiation, admiral. It is a demand from the pirates, the terrorists, for money. Randolph Blackwell is ready to give it to them. The company stock has been sold during the past 24-hours, the money is in a transfer account ready to be sent to Zurich."

"I'll ask you again, Ms. Lindsey, who is demanding this money?"

"There is a leader there who has handled everything. He is apparently like the Godfather of the pirates, on Palawan Island in the Philippines, one malicious son-of-a bitch known as Guleed Khalid. The man is smart, he is ruthless, and I assure you, he is uncompromising. He has made his demand from somewhere near Puerto Princesa on Palawan Island and now he wants his money."

Sullivan gripped his umbrella so hard that his hand began to ache. "Jesus Christ," he said quietly, "how much time is there before the money is transferred?"

"One more thing, admiral. Randolph Blackwell may seem cold and tough, and he is plenty of that, but he has a good heart and soul, and he did forge an agreement that Caroline be included in any ransom pay-off. Khalid has agreed to confirm the life and health of *both* of them before the money is transferred."

"Khalid agreed to that? The ransom is for *both* of them?"

"He did and it is. The problem is that once the ransom is paid, the lives of Peter and Caroline will be worth nothing and Khalid is not a man of honor."

"Okay..." Sullivan paused, studying the woman's harsh features closely. "Why are you doing this? You are taking a terrible risk if this gets out, why? I would just like to know, with the amount of money involved and the magnitude of the secrecy mandated, why are you now stepping forward?"

"Alright," she said, startling Sullivan with the intensity. "Admiral, you are talking to an Army brat. Do you have any idea what that means? Fourteen years of my life, from base to base, *I know what it feels like*. I know what it is like to have a father off in Vietnam, gone from our home throughout most of my childhood and teenage years. I know how it feels to move from one high school to another, to lose friends and struggle to make new friends." She looked closely at Sullivan, and he thought he could just see a suggestion of tearing in her eyes. "*Admiral, I know what it feels like to be Caroline*!"

The two people stood face to face in silence, the rain pouring off their umbrellas, the darkness of the Arboretum forest closing in around them.

"Okay, exactly, how much time do we have, Margarita?" Sullivan asked again, his voice gentle. "How much time before the ransom is paid?"

Lindsey looked down at her watch and then riveted her eyes back on the admiral's face. "The ransom has already been gathered by Mr. Blackwell, taken from the company in a legal stock transaction, and will be transferred to Guleed Khalid's bank account in Zurich in a little under three and a half hours."

Petty Officer first class Jack Garrett, drumming his fingers idly on the Ford's steering wheel, could hear the admiral before he could see him.

"Start the engine!" Sullivan yelled from a hundred yards down the trail, "Start it now!"

Garrett immediately fired up the Ford as Admiral Sullivan's running figure appeared out of the rain. The admiral's umbrella had been folded and tucked under his arm as he ran toward the car and jumped into the back seat.

"Whidbey Island," Sullivan yelled. "Now! Go! Go! Go!" he shouted as he pulled out his cell phone. "911, this is Admiral Samuel Sullivan." he said into the device. "Pulling out of Lake Washington Boulevard at the Arboretum onto the 520 West. I need police escort to Whidbey, now." He paused and added, "Yes. This is a life and death emergency—Admiral Kent of the U.S. Navy has cleared this, we need an escort immediately." He listened again and gushed out, "We are in a late model United States Navy black Ford, license number…"

Sullivan paused and immediately Garrett hollered, NAV 327.

"November, Alpha, Victor 327," Sullivan said as Garrett pulled out of the Arboretum and onto 520 West. Another moment passed and he said, "Yes, ma'am, thank you ma'am, I'll stay on the line."

Garrett gunned the engine and accelerated into the crowded northbound lanes of Interstate 5. Within thirty seconds, two police cars raced up the emergency lane with sirens blaring and red lights flashing.

"Yes. Your guys have us, tell 'em they're right with us now," Sullivan said into the telephone, adding, "Correct, Whidbey Island."

At the moment the Washington State patrol cars swerved into position in front of and behind Sullivan's car his telephone began to ring, the screen announcing Admiral Kent, calling from Hawaii. Sullivan hit the buttons on the phone, switching away from the police frequency, and heard the familiar voice booming out of the device.

"Sullivan, what the fuck is going on, are you still in Seattle?"

Sullivan tightened his seatbelt as Garrett followed the lead trooper into and out of the emergency lanes, swerving around the traffic in the rain.

"Admiral, we're running out of time!" Sullivan shouted into the telephone.

"What in the holy hell is happening, Sully?" Kent's voice crackled.

"The captain of the *Monterey* is trying to save his daughter. He's going to the west coast of Palawan Island in the Philippines."

"Jesus Christ, you might have let me know that without calling in the state militia. I just got a call on our hot line from Chief Hal Ramser at the Washington State Patrol headquarters in Olympia, says you're declaring a fucking national emergency. He's now calling Homeland Security, the Investigative Services Bureau, and he's going to call the NSA."

"Stop him, Stephen! If the networks go live with this, they'll kill the hostages. It's a goddamn ransom going down. If it goes public, they're gonna kill his daughter and her husband!"

"Who's on the other side?"

"One hundred million dollars is transferring within the next three hours to Palawan pirates, to some kingpin son-of-a-bitch named Guleed Khalid for the daughter and her husband's safe return. I don't think the captain knows about the ransom—we just need to radio the *Monterey*...."

"Where the hell is the money going?"

"There's got to be a pirate ship out there somewhere. I got the coordinates, at least the approximate position. I plotted the line, from the Mombo call and from Peter Blackwell's course across the Arabian Sea. His father's a CEO and rich as hell..."

"I don't need all the details, Sully, just give me the coordinates—we'll get there and try to get them to surface. How much time do we have?" Kent asked again.

"I'll have the location to you in about five minutes, Steve. We are running out of time. Do we have any resources in the area? If the ransom is paid, they may spare their lives..."

"Holy shit!" Kent's voice blasted out of the telephone. "The goddamn pirates have already killed hostages this past year, and half of them were executed *after* the payoff. The bastard Khalid was responsible for most of the deaths, he likes to behead his victims. He's a coldhearted son-of-a-bitch. The remnants of our Seventh Fleet are more than two hundred miles away, conducting the Operation Cobra Gold exercise in the middle of the South China Sea...."

USS *Monterey*, Pacific Ocean

At exactly four kilometers northwest of the *Cho Ying Atlas'* last recorded position, the port periscope of the *USS Monterey* slowly rose above the glassy night waters as Captain Gary Moore peered through the night-vision enhanced lens. Berry and Wheat had conducted an extensive passive sonar search of the surrounding waters as they approached the area and the only detectable noise was a distant sound of high-speed screws churning the water several miles away. Without activating the submarine's active sonar, there was no way to be certain that silent objects were not lying on the surface until a visual scan could be completed.

"One tanker, thirty degrees off the starboard bow, about three point five klicks," Moore said, rapidly rotating the periscope handles a full 360 degrees.

"Come right thirty degrees," Berry commanded from the starboard periscope as Moore completed his sweep.

"Right, thirty degrees, aye, aye," Bodine answered from the diving station, turning his control wheel to the right. "Steady at three knots, sixty-five feet."

"No other visible targets," Moore said to the chief petty officer. "Bring up your 'scope."

"Roger…" Berry said, hitting the black knob at his side of the periscope station, actuating the hydraulics to accelerate the starboard periscope out of the water.

The two men stood side-by-side, peering through their periscopes at the outline of the ship, barely visible across the dark water, her silhouette clearly that of an anchored chemical ship, exactly as the NSA downloaded information had portrayed. There was almost no moonlight and the only visible light was from a couple of bright white bulbs near the front of the *Atlas* bridge that shimmered in the infrared display from the starboard periscope.

"Nothing but light bulbs on infrared scan," Berry said.

"Roger that, nobody on-deck that I can see," Moore said, clicking the handle on the side of the periscope to increase magnification, scanning for any infrared evidence of human life.

"Nope, maybe some of those fuckers do sleep at three in the morning."

"Let's slow us down some more, chief, we're getting close enough."

"Aye, aye, sir," Berry said, his eyes brightening with excitement as he gave the order to slow to two knots. "Another quarter mile, we'll lock into place. Let's get ready to wake up some people in the citadel."

In the middle of the *Monterey*, just behind the spaces used for the control center, the three SEALs inventoried their weapons, prepared their equipment, pulled their SCUBA masks over their faces and opened the watertight hatch leading to the transfer chamber. Two minutes later, the chamber was flooded with seawater and the SEALs floated up to the hangar space above them. Breathing from their tanks, they climbed into the minisub, Frog in the back seat, Silverback in the copilot's seat, and Chainsaw in the pilot's seat. Chainsaw lifted his head as the captain's voice crackled out of the submerged loudspeaker in the overhead. "Cleared for op, ETD[27] five minutes, ready the SDV."

Having rehearsed the rescue mission over and over during the previous week, the three men had spent the final day and night filling the SDV minisub with every weapon they could think of. Chainsaw's favorite firearm was the M79 grenade launcher and his Sig Sauer P226 pistol, with the MP7A submachine gun backup—all three of them close at hand attached to his body in one way or another. He could wipe out gatherings of enemies at a distance or at close range for any final shots that might be necessary. He had to admit, although he would never say it to anybody but himself, that the monster-barreled M79 grenade launcher, the "pirate gun thumper" of his inventory, made him feel like superman…so long as the other weapons, with their rapid-firing capability, were always within reach.

Chainsaw answered the captain through the microphone in his diving mask.

"Copy, cleared for op, ETD five minutes," Chainsaw said tersely.

From the pilot's position, Chainsaw reached down to the control stick between his legs and placed his feet on the two pedals that allowed directional control of the minisub, similar to rudder pedals in an airplane. Not a word was said to his copilot as he began flipping switches, activating the battery-driven electronics on the screen in front of him. Chainsaw heard the sliding canopy over their head slam shut as Silverback reached up and locked down their forward canopy. He clicked the microphone and spoke through his diving mask to the men inside the submarine control center.

"SEAL team inside the SDV, operational and ready to depart," he said, his speech slightly garbled over the loudspeaker in the *Monterey's* control center where Captain Moore and Chief Berry stood. To prevent any detection of the minisub by listening sonar on the *Cho Ying Atlas*, there would be no communication between the SDV and the *Monterey*. With all the weapons and all the fighting skills held by each SEAL, their collective best weapon continued to be the absolute secrecy of their approach to the *Atlas*.

Whidbey Island, Washington

The black Ford screeched to a halt in the driving rain in front of Admiral Sullivan's house on Whidbey Island. Sullivan checked his telephone again for any calls or messages and then he rapidly punched in a string of numbers.

"Hello, Adam?" he asked, putting the telephone to his ear as the commanding officer of the Whidbey Naval Air Station came on the line. "Yes, that is correct, this is Sully, and we're in the car in front of the house right now. I am activating a *Response Code Green, Combative with Contagion,* need SP's[28] here, immediately, and I want an ambulance. Red lights, siren, the whole show."

Garrett turned around in the front seat and looked at Sullivan. "Sir? Is there a medical emergency?"

"It's a contagion, captain," Sullivan said into the telephone, ignoring his driver. "We will need complete isolation during the incubation period."

"What disease are we talking about?" crackled from the telephone into Sullivan's ear.

"Drug resistant, aerosol spread, biological warfare, Class C, probable Hantavirus or Nipah. Have your men come here in full Hazmat Suits."

"Yes, sir," the voice crackled back. "They're on their way. We train for this all the time."

Garrett's eyes widened and he began hyperventilating. "Sir, with this virus and all," he asked, staring at the admiral, "why aren't you wearing a mask?"

"I have immunity, sailor," Sullivan said. "You need to remain in the car, right here until the support vehicles arrive. You will be sequestered for a couple of days at the base medical center, and I will be inserting a commendation into your service record. Is that understood?"

"Yes, sir," the sailor answered respectfully. "Thank you for the commendation. And, I presume that I will be talking to nobody about anything during the time I am presumably contagious and isolated, is that correct, sir?"

"Correct," Sullivan hollered as he bolted out the back door and raced to the house while two paramedics and four Shore Patrol officers in Hazmat Suits, surrounded the black Navy car in front of his house. The admiral picked up the encrypted telephone and thirty seconds later, Admiral Stephen Kent, the Hawaiian-based commanding officer of the Navy's Pacific fleet, possessed the precise coordinates of the hijacking in the South China Sea.

Chapter 13

USS *Monterey*, Pacific Ocean

In the control center of the submarine, Captain Moore glanced away from his periscope at the bearded face of Chief Berry. "I'll take the conn,[29] chief," he said, "we're ready to go."

"Yes, sir," Berry said, his eyes remaining glued to the periscope eyepiece. "The DDS chamber is flooded, SEALs ready in the minisub, standing by to open the shelter hangar door."

"Roger that," Moore said, glancing toward Bodine sitting in front of his airplane-like controls. "All stop."

"All stop," Bodine said, reaching over to the enunciator communicating with the engine room. A moment later, he called out, "Engine room answering all stop."

"Very well," Moore said. "Open the hangar door."

With the distant sound of hydraulics, twenty feet below the surface of the ocean, the huge hangar door slowly swung open to expose the minisub to the open sea. No one heard the exit of the three SEALs as their submarine quietly glided out of the DDS hangar for the black open water, its tiny screws propelling it in the direction of the *Cho Ying Atlas*. Inside the SDV, the three SEALs could see nothing outside. There was no moonlight to illuminate the surface, the water was completely black, and the glowing lights on the panels in front of Chainsaw and Silverback provided their only illumination. Chainsaw moved his stick slightly up and down to hold their depth at twenty feet, his toes lightly touching the rudder pedals to hold their course in the GPS-guided direction toward the *Cho Ying Atlas*. Having practiced this exact procedure more than a hundred times, and at least thirty times during previous similar operations, none of the men said a word to each other. There was no sound except their breathing through their SCUBA masks and the rhythmic hum of the SDV electric motor propelling them through the sea.

It took exactly fourteen minutes for the SDV minisub to reach the oiler, her screws moving slowly, her passive sonar homing in on the ever-increasing scraping noise of the ship's anchor chain rubbing against the side of the tanker. When the sonar showed imminent contact with the chain, Silverback reached down to the control by his right leg and pulled, immediately ejecting two packets filled with equipment—they shot straight up to the surface, and within a few seconds, two IBS rubber boats inflated automatically and floated next to the surfacing SDV minisub.

The SEALs quickly slid back their canopies after the top of the minisub broke the surface of the water. The towering black shape of the *Cho Ying Atlas* was not more than ten yards away as both Chainsaw and Silverback reached forward and quickly secured the minisub to the ship's stern anchor chain. Behind the men, Frog pulled the tow rope holding the rubber rafts, bringing them alongside the SDV.

Without a word, as the SDV bobbed on the surface next to the huge anchor chain stretching down from five stories above them, the three men quietly removed their masks and tanks, attached their weapons to their gun belts, and slung the heavier weapons over their shoulders, finally cinching the straps tight against their chests. Frog reached over to the neatly-stacked pile of devices and weapons next to his seat and pulled out the TAIL device. He carefully leaned back in the minisub, and expertly fired the single shot of nearly-silent compressed air, watching as the two-pound titanium grappling hook carried 100 feet of Kevlar line and its attached rubber-coated titanium grappling hook over the railing of the ship where it tightly latched. The men waited quietly for a moment, listening…all remained quiet aboard the tanker.

In less than a minute, all three SEALs climbed the rope ladder and arrived at the dark A level of the tanker, rapidly moving to the port side as they had rehearsed. They hugged the steel wall for a moment, then moved quickly in single file down the decking toward the bow of the ship in the direction of the citadel, exactly according to plan. The safe-room of the ship, had been shown on the ship's plans to be in the amidships area, the center of the ship on the B level. Their heads swiveled around as they silently progressed along the deck, each man hyper-alert for any signs of activity on the dark passageways around them. As they approached the area of the bridge, Chainsaw looked up at the decks above them. Three levels up, on the E deck, was the operations center, complete with computer banks. Silverback's expertise would be to collect, in less than five minutes, all of the Intel he could find as soon as the hostages were located and their removal assured.

Silverback's side-operation had generated more discussion than any other part of the mission and the discussion had been intense back on the *Monterey*. The biggest problem with the E deck was that the officer's recreation room was immediately next to the computer room, increasing the risk of discovery. Chief Berry had even tossed in his opinion as he wandered through the boat one day, advice which they completely ignored, as SEALs are routinely inclined to do. After another two days of discussion amongst themselves, they finally decided it would be appropriate for Silverback to give it a try if the safety of the hostages was not compromised.

The tanker ship continued to remain silent, almost like she was deserted, and the three SEALs quietly moved up the port ladder to the B level. Although the citadel should have protected the crew, it was clear from the satellite recording of mother ship operations that the pirates had breached the room and now were using the room to house their hostages while they bartered their lives to whomever in the world would pay the highest price. The standard "all-safe" transmission of crew members locked in a citadel never came from the *Atlas*, and it remained unknown why the crew had not been able to lock themselves away from the pirates.

Moving in the opposite direction down the side of B deck toward the stern of the ship and the area of the citadel, they froze as Chainsaw held up his hand. A fuzzy-headed bearded man wearing a dark tee-shirt was holding a 9 mm Kashtan machine gun as he leaned back on his chair near an open door. The SEALs studied him closely and quickly realized that the man was sound asleep.

Five seconds later, without a sound, the guard was dead, his neck broken in two places.

The three SEALs quickly moved through the dark open door where Frog almost tripped over the mattress of a portly bearded man who was also sound asleep. At that instant, another man in a chair on the opposite side of the room turned on a light and tried to stand up, lifting an assault rifle half way up from his lap. Two silenced shots to his head blew him off his chair and up against the bulkhead where he crumpled to the decking in a pool of expanding blood. The entire floor of the citadel was covered with mattresses and a group of waking men, each quickly scanned for weapons by the SEALs. Silverback jumped across a mattress to turn off the light as Frog called out, "Stay quiet!" as he held his finger to his lips. "Does anybody speak English?" A dim light from above a toilet at the far corner of the room cast shadows across the floor, lighting up the men as they tried to stand.

"The crew of the *Cho Ying Atlas* is from China," a rotund man spoke from his mattress at the far side of the room. "Except for the Master[30], they speak Chinese. I am Mombo, I was working on a yacht named *Sweet Caroline,* and I am from India. Two others here are also from India."

"Are there any other guards on this deck?" Chainsaw asked the man as Silverback stepped back outside the citadel, scanning the deck, his weapon held ready in front of him.

"My name is Alex Wong, I am the Master of the *Cho Ying Atlas*," an older Chinese man with weary eyes said. "Two guards make rounds every fifteen minutes."

"When did they last come by?" Frog fired back.

"I don't know, I was asleep" he said. "Have you come to rescue us? How did you get here without anybody seeing you? There must be twenty guards on the upper decks."

"Where is Caroline Blackwell?"

"The woman from *The Sweet Caroline*?" Mombo asked. "She and her husband, the owner Peter Blackwell, were taken away yesterday, they're gone. There are only ten men here."

"*Jesus fucking Christ,*" Frog muttered with exasperation, quickly looking outside the door to scan for guards.

"Gone *where*?" Chainsaw fired back. "Where have they taken them?"

"I don't know where they took them and neither does anybody else," Mombo said. "Also, I don't know why they didn't take me too since I was on the same yacht. They just hauled them out of here yesterday. We thought they were going to kill them…"

"Are they okay, were they injured?" Chainsaw growled.

"Just bruised up pretty bad, but otherwise okay," Mombo said. "They slapped Mrs. Blackwell around every chance they got…she was pretty feisty and they didn't like that."

Two quick muffled shots from the door silenced the man as Silverback stepped back inside the door. "Two guys on patrol, down, we better get going," he said quickly.

"Are there any other hostages onboard?" Chainsaw asked the man.

The ship's master stood up and announced, "We are the only hostages on this ship, right here in this compartment. We're the only ones."

"Okay, move," Chainsaw said, "move quietly and follow me."

As the hostages began grabbing various bags and personal items, Chainsaw said, "Drop everything. You don't have time, and we don't have room, out the door, now."

Silverback abruptly left the group again and began climbing stairs up to the E level. The hostages crowded out the door, following Frog forward, and down the ladder to the A level as Chainsaw followed behind, rapidly looking around for anybody approaching from above or behind. One minute later, as the group rushed across the deck toward the stern of the ship, they heard the sounds of men shouting on the upper decks. Reaching the top of the rope ladder leading down to the water, Frog rapidly descended in front of them, stepped onto the SDV minisub and reached up to help each man into the rubber boats.

"Get in, hurry, hurry!" he ordered the men climbing down the ladder. He could see Chainsaw, still on the tanker at the top of the ladder, guarding their exit, looking back and forth for any signs of pursuers. There was no sign of Silverback. Frog loaded the two boats, a total of five men in each raft, all of them clutching the topside grab lines and the inboard handles.

He looked up the ladder again where he saw Chainsaw lift his MP7A submachine gun to fire off a burst at somebody. Silverback immediately appeared, and while yelling in Arabic, ordered a wiry dark-haired man down the ladder, the SEAL's pistol waving in the direction of the man's head. As Silverback climbed down behind him, Chainsaw slung the strap of his gun over his shoulder and followed the two men down to the minisub.

"Got him in the computer room, he's from Palawan, running the Intel operation, put him in the back seat." Silverback told Frog, who quickly directed the man into one of the two back seats of the minisub as he took a seat at the copilot's position.

The hostages tightly clutched the lines attached to the inside of their rubber boats as Silverback strapped himself into the other back seat of the miniature submarine next to the prisoner. He continued to wave his Sig Sauer P226 handgun in the prisoner's general direction. He told the man to sit down and don't move while

Chainsaw climbed into the pilot's seat and cut the line holding the boat to the ladder. As the SDV electric motor began to rotate the screws, Frog tightened the rope towing the two boats behind the minisub.

"They're all waking up back there, we gotta move out, now," Silverback hollered at Chainsaw, scanning the area of the *Atlas* railing as the SDV drifted away from the anchor chain and began to accelerate across the dark ocean. The two loaded rubber boats, pulled by the small submarine's connecting lines, rotated around, following the SDV as the small armada began a transit back across the water toward the *Monterey*. The wind and wave action moved them back and forth as they trailed behind the minisub.

Two minutes later, at the instant Chainsaw's radio crackled a question from Captain Moore, they could hear the sounds of gunfire as the water next to them began splashing from the impact of incoming rounds from a gathering of men leaning against the railings at the side of the *Cho Ying Atlas*.

"Do you have Caroline?" the captain's voice called, almost pleading for the right answer. "Is she on the raft with you?"

"Negative, captain," Chainsaw grimly answered. "Caroline and her husband were taken from the citadel. We have ten hostages and one prisoner, and Silverback has some Intel. Captain, we're taking small arms fire from the terrorists."

"Roger that," Moore's voice answered without a trace of sentiment. It was crisp, it was military, and it was followed by the next question. "Are there any hostages remaining on the mother ship?"

"Negative, captain, just a ship filled with fucking pirates and they're firing at us." The minisub suddenly rocked from the impact of two shots that hit the back of the vessel.

"Roger that."

Five seconds later, Captain Moore's voice crackled again over Chainsaw's radio. "Confirm again, no hostages left on the ship."

"There are no hostages left," Chainsaw's voice broadcast into the control center.

"Your distance from the *Monterey?*" the captain hollered into the microphone.

"About one klick, captain. We don't have a visual, heading to Sector 14 GPS."

"Roger," Moore hollered back from the *Monterey's* periscope station. "All ahead one third," he ordered to Bodine, immediately confirmed.

Chief Berry backed away from his periscope in shock, looking at Moore. "Captain. Our guys are still…"

"Prepare the Mark 48's," Moore ordered to the forward torpedo room. "Flood the tubes, open the outer doors, standby for four shots, running depth eight feet."

In the bow compartment of the *Monterey*, Wilson bolted out of his chair like he had been shot and began racing toward the inner torpedo tube doors, hollering at Amanda for help.

"Come right five degrees," Moore ordered to the helm as he peered into the port periscope. He clicked a button on the handle of the 'scope and locked in the heading to the *Cho Ying Atlas*. "Hold the heading, 097 degrees," he ordered Bodine.

"Aye, aye, captain," Bodine said.

"Firing solution complete," Berry said as he raced back from the fire control panel. "Tubes are flooded, three of four outer doors are open!"

Captain Moore reached over his head and grabbed the microphone again. "Wilson, stand by…stand by!"

"Aye, aye, sir, tubes loaded and ready, except the fourth tube's door…" Wilson's excited voice broadcast into the control room from the overhead speakers. In the background, before Wilson released his microphone switch, everyone could hear Amanda's voice calling, "Fourth torpedo tube outer door is open, Fred."

"Torpedoes ready to fire!" Wilson hollered.

Half a mile east of the submerged *Monterey*, inside the minisub splashing on the surface of the dark ocean, Chainsaw and the other SEALs ducked low in their seats as rows of tracer rounds raced through the night air over their heads and into the water around them. Silverback, from his copilot seat of the minisub, slid his canopy back slightly and lifted his head to look back at the ship where flashes of gunfire lit up the deck. He immediately slammed the canopy shut and ducked as low as possible. Next to Frog, the *Cho Ying Atlas* captive screamed endlessly in a foreign language as the two rubber boats behind them snaked back and forth against the line holding them to the minisub. Chainsaw watched his computer display carefully, guiding the three vessels in the direction of the last known position of the *Monterey*.

The minisub's display showed they were about a quarter mile from the submarine's previous position when he looked up and spotted a white flare fired by the pirates, lighting up the waters around them.

"Holy shit!" Chainsaw hollered at exactly the instant he spotted four furious florescent streams of churning bubbles under the ocean, moving in the direction of the *Cho Ying Atlas*. His eyes widened as he watched the trails of contra-rotating propellers, accelerating four Mark-48 ADCAP torpedoes, straight through the water at more than fifty knots. The torpedoes were almost directly below them, their wires unwinding back to the *Monterey* for guidance, their active sonar systems acquiring and locking on the oil tanker.

Within ten seconds, as two more brilliant flares accelerated up into the night sky, the South China Sea lit up with four thunderous and nearly simultaneous explosions.

The two rubber IBS boats and the SDV minisub rocked violently from the detonations behind them, followed immediately by a thunderous secondary detonation from residual oil stored in the tanker. The shock wave forced the hostages to tightly grip the rope handles on the side of their boats as they nearly capsized. All tracer rounds abruptly stopped as the massive hull of the *Cho Ying Atlas* folded neatly in half and rapidly sank. As the SEALs searched the dark ocean surface, the black shape of the *Monterey* abruptly surfaced, not more than fifty yards from the flotilla. Within three minutes, all hostages were on the submarine deck and being led down the forward hatch, as Silverback led his prisoner behind the group.

After Frog and Chainsaw placed their SCUBA masks back over their faces, and the *Monterey* slowly submerged back down to periscope depth, Chainsaw guided the minisub beneath the surface where he smoothly accelerated back into the *Monterey's* hangar. They locked the minisub on the decking of the hangar and actuated the hydraulics to shut the hangar door.

Two minutes later, the three men dropped down into the submarine's pressurized escape chamber, pumped it dry, and finally they ripped off their masks and climbed through the watertight doors and out of the chamber.

"Where's that Goddamn screaming Islamic jihadist Palawan son-of-a-bitch?" Frog immediately hollered as he ripped off his SCUBA mask and looked around for the man.

"He's right there," Wilson said, pointing to the far side of the passageway where the man sat on a chair, his hands secured behind his back. "He only speaks Palawan dialect. Silverback knows the dialect—he needs to ask him some questions."

The watertight door slammed closed behind them as Captain Moore walked up to the two SEALs. His face was grim, his eyes were narrowed, and speaking in a quiet voice, he asked, "Where is Caroline?"

"Sir, they took her, just yesterday, away from the ship with her husband," Chainsaw said. "Somebody named Mombo had been on the yacht, we got him, sir. It would seem likely that she could still be alive."

The men walked across the compartment where Silverback nodded at the captain and pointed at the wiry captive, now sitting quietly and staring at the men with open hostility. "This slime ball was in the computer room of the *Atlas*," he said. "We think he may know something."

"His language?" Moore asked as he crossed his arms and gazed at the captive.

Silverback brightened. "It's a variant of the Palawano language," he said, "spoken on Palawan, one of three dialects, Kalamian or Banggi, or…"

Moore waved his hand. "It's okay…"

"It's a bastard to learn," the SEAL said, "but I know the dialects. The guy's name is Faarax Shirdoon, and that's all he'll say."

Moore scrutinized the prisoner. The man was skinny, his bones jutting out, his eyes darting back and forth, looking at the array of submarine equipment around him, taking it all in, looking like he was trying to figure out what everything did. He wore a tattered white tee-shirt, filthy pants, and an old pair of sandals clung to his feet. Everything was still wet; his black hair was a thick mat across his head and his stubble of a beard created an appearance of abject homelessness.

"Has he said anything else, anything valuable?" the captain asked Silverback after five minutes of Silverback's rapid exchange in the Palawano dialect.

"Like, anything about Caroline? No, sir, just that he doesn't know what we're talking about. He said his job was to do some computer work for the captain of the *Atlas* until those pirates terrorized him." Silverback glared at the man and fired off another rapid sentence in Palawano; the prisoner immediately became agitated and began yelling in his native tongue. After a minute of gesturing and hollering, the man finally stopped talking and defiantly glared at everyone.

Silverback looked at the captain. "He essentially told us to go to hell and that he isn't going to tell us anything about anybody. I think he also said to go fuck ourselves, but I'm not sure about the translation. I personally think he's scared to death. I could wave my gun at him, if you think that would help."

"Okay," Moore said, "that's a consideration. Put a jacket on him, give him some food, and take him to the torpedo room. Let him know he has twenty minutes to tell me where my daughter and her husband were taken or he may soon be joining his friends in hell. He does know we sank his ship, right?"

"Oh, yes, sir, he knows…he had a front row seat."

Moore turned to leave. "The thought of that may help us get him to talk. Berry and I are going to the computer station, we'll dig through the reams of Intel you brought back, nice work, and thank you."

"Yes, sir," Silverback said, turning to gather his prisoner for the short walk to the bow of the submarine.

Pearl Harbor, COMPACFLT Headquarters

Admiral Stephen Kent stood in front of the huge flat screen display lighting up behind him. Most of the chairs were empty, with about only fifteen men and women present, all in uniform with ranks ranging from captain to admiral. There was no press, there were no civilians, and the entire room was uncharacteristically silent as everybody waited for the COMPACFLT admiral to speak. The commander of the Pacific Fleet held a laser pointer in his hand and stood patiently, waiting for the guards at the doors to step outside into the balmy Hawaiian air and to close the doors behind them.

Kent began to speak into the microphones attached to his podium, his voice harsh and staccato-like as he fired out his sentences.

"I do not need to tell anybody in this room that this is a top secret, code-word only briefing about the recent hijacking of the nuclear submarine USS *Monterey* from Pearl Harbor by Commander Gary Moore and eleven other individuals. We have with us, by computer link with Washington, the President of the United States, the Vice President, the Secretary of the Navy, and the Chairman of the Joint Chiefs of Staff. Admiral Samuel Sullivan is also conferenced in from Whidbey Island where he has been working these past couple of days to clarify the reason or reasons behind this hijacking by the submarine's commanding officer. Admiral Sullivan has recently successfully identified a possible cause for this action, that of a rescue mission by the captain to save his daughter, who with her husband, is being held captive in the area of the Palawan Island in the Philippines. This is at the eastern border of the South China Sea."

Kent glanced at one of the microphones in front of his podium and spoke into the communication system. "Admiral Sullivan, we have a good link here? What is the information that led you to obtain the coordinates?"

Immediately, Sullivan's voice boomed out of the loudspeakers from Whidbey Island, outlining his search. As the screen behind flashed a huge and grainy black and white photograph of Khalid, he said, "First, some background. This man is Guleed Khalid, one of the most notorious leaders of pirate activity from the shores of the South China Sea to the Strait of Malacca. He is currently holding Caroline Blackwell, and her husband Peter, at an unknown location. It is not known if they are still alive. He is linked with the growing Muslim extremism problem in Southern Mindanao on the eastern border of the Sulu Sea and has merged with the ISIS operation expanding in that area. They recently killed a number of Filipino soldiers in battles there, and they just beheaded a ransomed Canadian citizen. They intersect with civilians either to spread terror or to exact ransom demands to fund their operations.

"We know they were held on a mother ship tanker called the *Cho Ying Atlas.* There is no record of the citadel on this ship ever becoming activated, and it is likely the crew was not successful in isolating themselves from the pirates. It is not known how valuable

Captain Gary Moore's daughter is to the pirates, but from a classified source, her husband is currently under a ransom demand for one hundred million dollars by Guleed Khalid."

"Sully, great work, let me intervene here," Kent said, turning to the captain operating the display computer system and said, "Captain, would you go to the NSA download of current time on the *Cho Ying Atlas*?"

Pointing his laser at the dark screen, Kent spoke. "This shot was recorded half hour ago, and as you can see, it was still night in that area; it was about zero three hundred hours." Kent turned to the captain again. "Move it up to fifteen minutes ago," he ordered.

The screen moved jerkily for a few seconds until pinpoints of light appeared, stretching out from a central point across the screen. "There is a battle going on here," he said. "This is small arms fire from the *Cho Ying Atlas*, firing at a presumed attacking force that has entered the area. This may have been a SEAL force from the *Monterey*." Kent turned to watch the screen, when the entire display suddenly lit up with a silent blinding flash followed by secondary explosive flashes, the white light rapidly becoming extinguished and the screen returning to darkness. Several gasps of shock from the audience filled the room.

"Captain," Kent said to the computer operator, "give us a slow-motion on that explosion again."

"Yes, sir," the captain's voice called out from his position near the front of the room. The screen again lit up with the tracer rounds flying across the entire screen in slow motion for about thirty seconds, followed by the incandescent light of two flares. Suddenly, a single flash began to enlarge at the front of the ship, joined rapidly by a second and then a third and fourth as a massive fireball became united and the ship disappeared into blackness.

Kent turned off his laser and activated the overhead lights. He looked around the room at the seated members of the military, nobody saying a word.

"Ladies and gentlemen," Kent said, you have just seen the detonation of four torpedoes from the USS *Monterey*, and you have seen the end of the *Cho Ying Atlas*. We now know precisely where our submarine is..."

"Admiral?" a voice called out from the audience. Kent pointed at an admiral sitting in the front row. "Go ahead, Harris," he said.

Admiral Zehner stood up and faced the audience. "Vice Admiral Harris Zehner speaking," he said, "wondering if you or anybody else has any idea why Captain Moore would torpedo the mother ship holding his daughter and presumably the other hostages including the ship's crew. This does not appear to be a rational act."

"This torpedo attack does not appear to be the action of a rational man," Kent said. "However, we must assume one of *two* possible scenarios. Either Captain Moore has become irrational, and that seems unlikely considering he has spent the past week evading detection by every navy in the world, or the hostages, including his daughter, have been rescued or have been removed from the ship. This raises the additional question, if his daughter has been removed from the ship, where is she? While I have at least twenty investigators working to determine that, I also have the entire Seventh Fleet steaming across the South China Sea in the direction of Palawan Island. These ships are currently 250 miles west of the *Cho Ying Atlas* previous position before she was torpedoed. On that note, I would like to remind all of you that, while the *Monterey* has expended four of her Mark 48 torpedoes, she has more than twenty torpedoes remaining and twelve Tomahawk missiles which can be launched submerged through her VLS[31] at damn near any target in the world."

He paused for a moment, waiting to let his words sink in. He then leaned forward, speaking into a larger microphone at the corner of the podium.

"Mr. President," he said, "As you have seen, sir, we have just confirmed an American submarine has torpedoed a captured foreign national vessel inside the twelve nautical mile international boundary of the Philippine Islands. It is possible, sir, that this hostile act may be considered part of our sanctioned collaborative war with the Philippine Navy against international terrorism."

The President's voice blasted into the room from Washington D.C. "The problem, gentlemen, is that diplomatic channels have confirmed that nobody in the entire Philippine government has any knowledge about a mother ship or an American submarine launching a torpedo attack in their territorial waters. We have three Navy ships tied up in the Manila harbor right now and there are about one hundred Philippine warships scattered throughout their islands. The president of the Philippine Islands, Isko Fermin, will be tuning in to the upcoming news conference but I will call him before we go live."

The President continued, his voice rising and echoing off the walls of the room. "Admiral Kent, as this captain and this submarine are potentially bringing us into a state of war with the nation of the Philippine Islands, what do you recommend I tell Mr. Fermin?"

Kent leaned closer to his microphone. "You may tell Mr. Fermin that this captain of this submarine has just eliminated a pocket of radical terrorists that had just attacked and captured an American vessel on the open seas!"

USS *Monterey*, Pacific Ocean

Doc Wheat and Amanda converted the amidships auxiliary space to an impromptu medical bay, stacking piles of gauze, sutures, antiseptics, and medical supplies across the flat top of a CO_2 scrubber.[32] Struggling and straining and cursing, the corpsman lugged in his small refrigerator filled with antibiotics and clunked it on the deck between the racks. Most of the hostages lay in the various bunk beds previously used by the men who had filled the submarine. Apart from anxieties, ravenous hunger, and some skin tears, they were in relatively good shape. The ship's Master, Alex Wong, told the story of the *Cho Ying Atlas* hijacking and of his inability to get the entire crew into the citadel before the pirates were aboard. A crewman had held the door open a moment too long for one more Chinese machinists to seek safety after scrambling up several levels from the engine room. The pirates had killed the machinist and other crew members and had forced their way into the room before anybody could secure the citadel and deactivate the engines.

Wong reported almost like a confessional, with this one exception, the crew had followed all the other mandates of the BMP, including the Vessel Movement Registration Form and the regular Daily Reports. The information from the *Cho Ying Atlas* had been gathered and disseminated by the Piracy Reporting Centre in Malaysia. It was all to no avail…the closing of the citadel door was delayed seconds too long. So, during the past week, Wong recounted to Commander Moore and Chief Berry, the pirates brought three more hostages aboard, using the mother ship headquarters for negotiations to gather ransom from anybody with money.

Doc Wheat brought the master of the *Cho Ying Atlas* into the control center and up to the periscope station. Captain Moore turned to face the man. The master's uniform was torn and stained with sweat. He had one shoe missing and his gray beard was matted and twisted.

"I wanted to tell you something, captain," Wong said quietly. "Caroline was your daughter, sir?"

"Caroline *is* my daughter, Mr. Wong," Moore said forcefully.

"Sorry, sir. You should be very proud of her. She was the toughest one of us all, but they made her pay for it. Her husband did what they asked, he followed their orders, but *Caroline*? She resisted every step of the way. She interrupted and created problems for them continuously, she was an inspiration to all of us. I thought they were going to kill her." He shook his head and looked down at his remaining decrepit shoe. "Remarkable, it is amazing that they did not," he added softly.

"Where do you think they took them?" Moore asked, his voice tightly controlled. "Caroline and her husband, do you have any idea? Where did they go?"

Alex Wong lifted his eyes and looked directly at Moore. "They wouldn't tell us, captain, they wouldn't say a word. They told her husband that he was the most valuable person in the room, then they just took the two of them away. And they left Mombo. They may have been expecting some kind of battle; before your SEALs killed the two guards, they had brought more ammunition clips to them. But they told us nothing."

Captain Moore and Chief Berry returned to the control center and stood on the periscope station above the ballast control panel where they watched Bodine guide the *Monterey* through the water at three knots. The helmsman kept his eyes glued to the depth meter, holding the submarine steady at the ordered speed, two hundred feet beneath the surface of the South China Sea. The periscopes had been retracted into the submarine, the door of the DDS hangar was closed, the hatches had been shut tight, the hostages from the *Cho Ying Atlas* were alive and beginning to heal, and the nuclear reactor's highest power level was now 84% and continuing to drop.

Bodine glanced at the two men standing behind his seat and immediately turned his eyes back to the depth gauge, making miniscule corrections with his control wheel to hold them steady at the assigned depth. Nobody said anything, but the captain knew everybody, from the nukes to the torpedoman, would welcome his simple order at this time…the order to make their heading 00º, directly back to the Balintang Channel and home.

They had failed to find her, Caroline was gone, her husband was gone, and nobody seemed to know where.

Captain Moore and Chief Berry gazed silently across the control center, neither man wanting to say anything. Resting his hand lightly on the steel support surrounding the periscope station, Moore's mind raced ahead. The men throughout the submarine were waiting for instructions and a decision had to be made. They had already destroyed whatever career they might have had, they were increasingly at risk of becoming stranded by the nuclear reactor's core depletion, and they remained at risk from an incoming weapon from virtually any country's military arsenal. He was a rogue captain, they all knew that from the beginning, they had joined together to create a rogue crew now cruising within a steel enclosure that had become a rogue submarine—they all were doing nothing less than what was evolving into an illegal unsanctioned black op attack straight into hell. Their location was now known to the entire universe—you can't put four torpedoes into a massive ship like the *Cho Ying Atlas* without every satellite in the sky taking note. And yet, there was still a tiny crack in the challenges that had increasingly surrounded them, a faint gleam of light and hope shimmering through.

Caroline had been alive yesterday. *Caroline had been alive yesterday.* And if ransom was the game, there was a chance she was still alive.

Moore felt himself breathing faster as a sheen of sweat covered his forehead and his fists clenched against the steel railing. At that moment, the captain slowly turned to Chief Berry, he pressed his fist against the thick pipe of the starboard periscope and spoke with a deep but barely audible voice.

"Let's go see what our captive has to say about Caroline."

They could hear Silverback before they closed the watertight door and they found him facing Faarax Shirdoon in the torpedo room. The captive was standing against the torpedo tube door, his hair still wet, his hands tightly secured with PlastiCuffs behind his back. Silverback stood two feet in front of the man and was speaking in Palawano, intently, forcefully, his voice rising as Shirdoon listened. As Silverback finished his sentence, Shirdoon shook his head, speaking back to the SEAL in his rapid dialect. They went back and forth again, Silverback speaking, Shirdoon shaking his head and saying something in Palawano again, while Silverback spoke again, interrupting the man. A final word was said by Shirdoon as Silverback pulled out his Sig Sauer P226 pistol and delivered the first round into the chamber as Shirdoon' s eyes widened in fear.

Moore and Berry stood behind Silverback, watching the exchange and saying nothing.

That was the moment Amanda wandered into the torpedo room with Wilson and leaned up against a Mark 48 torpedo to listen to the incomprehensible back-and-forth dialogue. After watching for a few seconds, she leaned toward Wilson and asked, "He's not going to *shoot him*, is he?"

Wilson smiled and shook his head.

"Do you think he knows where Caroline and her husband were taken?" she asked.

Wilson looked at the prisoner for a moment and finally said, his voice hushed, "I am sure he knows. Silverback found him in the communications center of the *Cho Ying Atlas*, the guy was involved with the brains of the mother ship operation. Silverback is just ratcheting up the interrogation with his pistol."

Five minutes later, as the exchange between the prisoner and Silverback became heated, Captain Moore finally interrupted and said, "Okay, we're running out of time, where are we with this?"

Silverback stopped talking, looked at the pirate with penetrating disgust, jammed his pistol back into his holster, and then turned to the captain. "He is not talking, captain, but I think he knows everything. I pulled the guy right off his computer chair in the operations room of the tanker, he *has* to know where they took her. If you give us a green light, and clear this civilian out of here, we should know exactly what he knows in the next half hour."

Captain Moore glared at the prisoner. "We'll come back to him," he said, turning to leave the bow compartment. "Chainsaw, Silverback, chief, we're going to have a conference. Let's go, they'll be closing in on us in another hour or so. We are going to finish dissecting the computer intelligence. There has to be some information there." He looked at Wilson and added, "Call me if he says anything."

Securing the prisoner to the torpedo tube hydraulic piping, the four men walked out of the compartment. Fred Wilson stood in front of Shirdoon, arms crossed in front of his chest, glaring at the man before finally turning away and sitting down in disgust. Amanda's eyes narrowed as she sat at the corner of the compartment, watching Shirdoon closely. She sat up straighter as she observed that the man had developed a faint smile, like a victory smile she thought, almost a smirk while he looked back at her.

They locked eyes for a few seconds before she suddenly stood up and screamed, "Fred! Open the fucking torpedo door NOW!"

Wilson jumped straight up as Shirdoon jerked on his plastic cuffs in terror.

"I can't do that," Wilson said. "I can't just open the inner door!"

"You can! For God's sake, the skipper's trying to find his daughter! This slime ball has the key! Do it now, Fred, or I'll do it for you!"

"He knows English, Fred, look at him!" she screamed again. "He knows everything we're saying! Open the inner door of the torpedo tube, we're going to flush him out of here like you showed me, like a garbage ejection!"

"Jesus Christ, Amanda! He'll be pulverized into shark food!"

"Fred! We need to launch him right back to his fucking Allah and we need to do it NOW!"

"No! Don't do it!" Shirdoon gasped.

"Where's Caroline, you bastard?" Wilson shouted into the prisoner's face. "Tell us where they took her!"

"Khalid will kill me if I say *anything*!" Shirdoon screamed, his voice a shrill sound with a heavy Filipino accent. "He will track me! He will find me and do much worse things than you could ever do..."

"I'll free his hands, you throw him in!" Amanda said.

"Shark food, he's on his way!" Wilson said as he flung the #1 Torpedo Tube door wide open, stepping back as residual sea water splashed onto the decking. Amanda cut the restraints as Wilson grabbed the prisoner and launched him head-first into the steel container. They slammed the door shut, and in the distance, they could hear the frantic squealing of the prisoner.

"Bleed in just a little sea water equalizer, Fred," Amanda said. "Just a little…"

Wilson smiled as he turned a round green metal knob, creating a faint hissing sound. The screaming within the tube became louder and shriller.

"The captain would kill us if he knew…" Wilson began.

"Now! Open the door!" Amanda said as Wilson unlatched the door and grabbed the prisoner's legs, dragging him back out of the tube and throwing him down on the deck.

"Fred!" Amanda screamed. "We forgot to launch him! Put him back in and do it again with more pressure!"

"I'll talk!" Shirdoon screamed, coughing and spitting out saliva and sea water. "I'll tell you…"

They stood him up in front of the other torpedo tubes as Amanda moved directly in front of his face. "What do you want to tell us, Shirdoon? What?"

He jerked back his head in terror. "I'll tell you *everything*! Tell the captain that his daughter kept fighting. Khalid slapped her, many times. He taped her mouth shut, he tied her tightly, and he finally took both of them to the black fortress."

"What black fortress?" Wilson fired back.

"The fortress at the water, on Boayan! It's an ancient stone fortress, impenetrable, with thick walls and many antennas!"

Amanda grabbed the man's hair and turned his head to face her directly. "What are they transmitting?"

The prisoner's eyes opened wide with fear. "I don't know, Guleed won't tell us! They transmit, and then the hostages are both gone! Forever, I am sure of that!"

Amanda turned and looked at Wilson. "Handcuff him again, Fred," she said softly. "Please? And then we're going to take a high-speed trip to the captain's conference room for a little chat with the boys."

Two minutes later, the conference room door flew open as Fred Wilson launched a thoroughly drenched Filipino prisoner across the room in front of the gathered men, while Amanda stood back and smiled.

"Our prisoner has decided to tell us where they have taken Caroline and her husband," Wilson said. "He has suddenly remembered that he is able to speak perfect English and he would like to tell us everything!

Chapter 14

USS *Monterey*, Pacific Ocean

Fifteen minutes later, the rapid-fire interrogation of Shirdoon in the officer's wardroom was over.

Silverback turned to the captain as the prisoner finally stopped talking, and said, "That's it…."

Shirdoon had spit out the details, including the ransom to be finalized in a waterside fortress, all controlled by Guleed Khalid on the island of Boayan a few miles from where the *Cho Ying Atlas* had been anchored. It is a 6-sided hexagonal fortress, he had choked and gasped, a nasty looking structure, three stories tall, right on the shore of the harbor. And, the thin man added with a dark fear filling his eyes as he glanced at Amanda, "Everybody on Palawan knows Khalid as 'Big Mouth,' and nobody trusts him. He is a very mean man. He is supposed to be retiring soon, after he collects this ransom." He looked at the captain as a toothy smile emerged. "Maybe you could retire him sooner, captain?"

"Thank you, Mr. Shirdoon," Moore said, his voice tightly controlled. "The interrogation is over. Take him back to the bow compartment, secure him to the piping—he's either going to America or he's going to the bottom of the sea with all of us. And, in the next hour, we will expedite the retirement of Khalid."

"There have got to be mines around the fortress, captain," Chief Berry said quietly as Amanda and Fred Wilson escorted the prisoner from the compartment. "Right there on the coast, a minefield for their defense, possibly with some kind of radar system."

"Actually, that's no problem, captain," Silverback said. "Taser and Domino will be happy to take out the mines, that's why we brought the dolphins. If there's radar, they won't see the minisub."

Moore looked grim. "Give the dolphins the good news and let's finish the job" he said. "The window before sunrise is now very small."

"Yes, sir, sunrise is at 0545 hours," Silverback said, looking at his watch. "We're good to go, captain, and in fact, we're feeling a bit overdue for a successful shore op. If needed, Frog will have the dolphins ready to clear a Q-Route[33] path through any mines, and we'll go in immediately thereafter. The C-4 bananas[34] will open us a direct path. We'll set them to 0430 hours, they will go off all at once, and we'll be there immediately thereafter...."

"Soon as the charges go off, they'll know we're coming," Berry said.

"Right, but at 0430 hours, it will take them at least a half hour to figure out the mines they laid didn't just go off by themselves, especially when they look out and see nothing but black water. It will be too dark and our minisub will be submerged. They really won't know what hit them until it's too late."

"Your lives, hell, all of *our* lives, will be depending on that," Moore said quietly.

"Yes, sir," Silverback said. "Captain, we will get your daughter and her husband, and we will kill them." Silverback paused and looked directly at the commanding officer. "Also, captain, this thing with your daughter, has become very personal...to all of us."

"Okay, we're going," Moore said as he stood up, his mind struggling to block the possibilities and probabilities. "Thank you, Silverback. Get the dolphins ready, get your weapons ready. Berry will make the calculations, and I will set the course."

Twenty minutes later, Moore and Berry finished gathering everything they could find about Boayan and the small harbor. Through their periscopes, the two men could see the faint outline of the tower protruding above the shoreline. A cluster of antennas and receiver dishes covered its roof. They downed their 'scopes and met the SEALs in front of the hatch leading to the escape chamber and their beloved minisub. The three men stood in their wetsuits, masks in their hands and oxygen tanks strapped to their backs, tactical vests bulging with waterproof ammunition clips and handguns, their favorite assault rifles strapped to their shoulders, waiting patiently for the final clearance as they had done on so many missions before. The dolphins remained waiting in their DDS hangar beds, restless and ready to be released into the sea to begin their mission.

"Gentlemen," Moore said to the SEALs, "Good luck and Godspeed. Do you have any questions?" he asked.

Chainsaw straightened up to his full height and smiled as he said, "We'll get her sir."

Moore nodded and said, "Thank you."

The SEALs quickly climbed into the escape chamber, placed the scuba masks over their faces and sealed the watertight door behind them. Three minutes later, the submerged minisub and a remarkably frisky Taser and Domino moved out of the DDS hangar to the surface of the night waters as the SEALs surfaced above the *Monterey* and their black rubber boat inflated behind the minisub.

Silverback lifted a bag filled with banana explosives and Frog loaded a bag filled with frozen herring into the rubber boat, both men pulled the advanced night vision goggles over their eyes. Silverback energized the small hummer motor and accelerated the rubber boat away from the minisub and toward the Boayan shore as the two dolphins darted back and forth in a serpentine pattern ahead of the boat. Behind them, Chainsaw sat in the pilot's seat of the minisub, closely watching his instruments as the small vessel carefully followed the raft progressing toward the harbor.

A quarter mile from the harbor opening, Domino suddenly popped up in the ocean, swam up to the side of the rubber boat, and rapidly wagged his head to indicate a mine was ahead of them.

"Gimme one of those Y-B's," Frog whispered to Silverback, who promptly tossed him a rounded "Yellow Banana" tube filled with the C-4 plastic explosives. He carefully set the timer and inserted the device into the harness around Domino's body. The dolphin immediately accelerated away from the rubber boat, and one minute later, it was attached to the bottom of the cable securing the first mine to the ocean rocks below. Once the banana was secured to the cable, Frog knew, it would float up to the underside of the mine as the timer precisely counted the seconds before exploding. Before Frog could look around for Taser, the dolphin appeared at the other side of the boat and moved his head to indicate another mine was between their boat and the shoreline. Thirty seconds later, with the Y-B attached to his harness, he was gone, moving quickly to attach the device to that mine's cable.

For the next twenty minutes, Frog worked with the two dolphins, grabbing more yellow bananas, setting more timers, dropping more reward herrings into their mouths, and marking the coordinates on the GPS computer screen to generate the anticipated Q-route to shore. Finally, Domino arrived at the side of the boat and moved his head in the opposite direction, indicating the path was now clear.

"No more?" Frog asked, waving his arms in the direction of shore. Domino waved his head again in the opposite direction. He challenged the dolphin three more times and with the third negative response, the biggest piece of squid Frog could find in his fish bag went promptly into the dolphin's mouth. At exactly that instant, Taser arrived at the other side of the boat and waggled his head, indicating a good Q-route had been created.

"That's it," Frog said to Silverback who immediately powered the boat in the direction of the *Monterey* while Frog entered the GPS coordinates into the computer. Five minutes later, after the dolphins swam back into their holding chambers within the submarine's DDS hangar, the two SEALs joined Chainsaw in the minisub.

"Now, we can make some noise" Chainsaw said as they tightened their SCUBA masks across their faces and pulled the canopies shut over their heads. They submerged the SDV and accelerated away from the *Monterey*, finally entering a holding pattern off the coast, a pattern far away from the pending explosions.

Chapter 15

Boayan Island, Philippines

Caroline Blackwell felt like she was going to smother to death before the morning sun arrived.

She had been secured with PlastiCuffs to a steel chair on the darkened top floor of the Boayan fortress and a wide strip of duct tape sealed her mouth. She struggled to breathe through her nose, holding her breath from time to time, as she strained to hear the conversations in the room below them. They were deep voices, intense voices, speaking another language, and she tried to sense their actions before another visit by the guttural monster who delighted in hitting her face. She felt the tightening of her airways, reacting to the moist night air flowing from the ocean through the open stone windows, and she could hear a distant wheeze from the depths of her lungs. Since Peter had been better behaved, his reward was being secured to his own chair at the other side of the room without tape across his mouth. Both hostages wore dirty dark green clothes presumably salvaged from some other piracy activity.

"I think something is about to happen," Peter hissed to his wife, receiving a quick nod in reply. "I think there are more of them down there—they might be making some arrangements to let us go. Maybe the ransom has been paid, maybe it has something to do with that explosion we heard coming from the ocean."

Caroline nodded again quickly although it seemed unlikely to her that freedom was going to be any part of her future. Her husband was always so innocently optimistic, that was one of the things she loved about him, such that under the worst of circumstances, *and right now had to be among the absolute worst of circumstances,* he still saw elements of hope and rescue. They had been kept in the nearly-empty top room of the stone structure for the past several hours, fed small portions of humus-tainted corn washed down with water that regularly gagged Peter. The stone-enclosed chamber appeared to be the most isolated and protected floor of the ancient structure. There was a guard with a frightening automatic weapon in his grip sitting just outside the door as ragged-looking men who always seemed to be semi-stoned entered the room from time to time to check on the two hostages.

Then, there was the top pirate, the one Caroline identified as the son-of-a-bitch at the very top. Every half hour or so throughout the past couple of hours, he would walk into the hexagonal room. She had labeled the man Fuzzball, for his matted collection of kinky dark hair. His name was Khalid, he had said, he was the tall one, the one with a frighteningly large mouth, the bad breath and the rotten teeth that she had heard was a sign of chronic meth addiction. He had been the leader of the yacht hijacking, he had given the orders to everybody on the *Cho Ying Atlas*, and finally he had directed the move to this cold stone fortress. He was the man in charge.

He was also the man most savage to the two prisoners.

Khalid, the fuzzy-headed monster of a man wanted to kill them both, she was sure of it ever since he had hustled them off the tanker. She could see it in his eyes, she could *feel* it every time he walked into the room. He broadcast a cold killing instinct, the kind she imagined that would be without a human reaction to the most heinous damage he could create for his victims. He would dispatch her purely for the pleasure of killing her, a pleasure that would be more important than power, leverage, or money. And, for Caroline, Fuzzball had a chill in his gaze that stared more than looked, eyes that seemed continuously twitching from smoking shabu[35], and showed no hint of human self-awareness or sensitivities. He was clearly the most powerful man in this tower filled with shabu-puffing men, each seeming to have meth-mouths filled with rotting teeth. His violence as a routine means of communication included, in the beginning, a powerful blow with one of his huge hands to her face every time he was displeased with her answers to his inquiries. His displeasure occurred regularly, always followed by another blow, routinely delivered immediately after he shouted something in Palawano followed by a diatribe of British-accented English.

The walls of the room were composed of large gray stone bricks that looked to Caroline like they were at least a thousand years old. The room was about the size, she estimated, of a single-car garage. In the center of each segment of the hexagon, a two-foot square opening in the stone functioned as a window. The guards would make a circle around the perimeter of the room, holding their assault rifles across their chests and talking rapidly in Palawano to each other as they guarded the openings. Every visit or two, Fuzzball would turn to his captives, rip the tape from her mouth, and shout questions in a clipped British accent. If answers were not immediately provided, or if she answered with the venom that raged from within, another violent slap left the painful stinging residue.

Fuzzball and the other pirates were increasingly nervous, that was becoming obvious to Caroline, and she felt a rising anxiety about their immediate future. They had killed everybody else on their yacht, except Mombo, and since her husband's life was obviously the primary prize, her own life could not be very valuable to these men. During the sudden and surprising transit from the mother-ship to the shore, they had repeatedly molested her while forcing Peter to watch, taking delight in his distress as they repeatedly reached into her blouse, finally ripping her blouse and bra from her and laughing as her husband cursed and yelled from the other side of the transporting skiff that pounded across the ocean to deliver them to the fortress.

It was a form of torture, she knew, not only to herself, but to her husband as well, a demeaning torture that emphasized the men's power and control over their victims.

As they had approached the harbor, they tossed her a green denim shirt, snickering and talking amongst themselves before presenting the captives to Fuzzball for inspection and marching them up the three stories to their prison on the top floor. Although she was certain she would be raped by these creatures, once Fuzzball was on the scene, there was no further molesting, just the repeated slaps as she rejected every question about her family and her fortune with a responding insolence that enraged the man.

But, now, as the night seemed to go on forever, it became more vicious, more intense, especially after the creature in charge rushed into the room and immediately slammed his hand across the side of her face.

"Do you feel that?" Khalid asked with a furious voice, taking pleasure at her pain. He hit her again, and ripped off her tape as he yelled, "Do you feel that, Caroline?"

The sting of his hand's impact seemed to penetrate deep into her tissues, a sharp pain that only slowly dissipated. In spite of her husband's pleading for her to stop her resistance, she continued to battle him with screams and insults until he finally taped her mouth shut again and wrapped additional bands of tape around her ankles to the point of painful immobility.

He finally pulled her head back, his sweaty hand grasping her hair, and he stared straight into her face as he hollered, "Today, you are going to die!"

For the first time since they were captured, the man caught a satisfying first look of terror in Caroline's eyes. "You sink my ship, I end your life," he screamed at her, the message delivered with sputum flying from the oversized mouth not more than four inches from her face. Caroline stared at the man, feeling a deepening fear that these comments, this rage that had been delivered for no apparent reason had somehow been provoked beyond her fiery resistance. As the man yelled at her and slapped her again, Peter hollered from across the room to leave her alone, a command immediately rewarded with the same Palawano curse and slap across his bearded face before Fuzzball spun around and walked out the door, his entourage of goons again leaving them in silence.

"I wonder what *that* was all about," Peter said from his chair, the right side of his face reddening from the blow. "Their ship was sunk? What does *that* mean?"

I am probably going to die, Caroline thought as she thought about the hostages, Mombo and the others remaining on the ship. She looked beyond her husband's chair, out the window and into the black of night. There will be no children in the years ahead, no life in Seattle with Peter, no helping the man ascend into the leadership of his family's company. Her husband was the one person of value to these men in this fortress, they had made that clear, and if there was a ransom, it would be paid for his release, not for her no matter how much he pleaded on her behalf. And, once he was released, should he not be killed after the payment, she would then not be there with him for the years ahead…she would never be there with him again. Who would he then find to take on as a wife when he returned to Seattle, she mulled, what woman would then share his love and bear his children?

She felt the deep pain from inside as she knew that the good man strapped to the chair across the room could easily find a woman who could have his children, and yet he would *never* find a woman who loved him as much as she did. For the first time since their capture, she felt the sting of tears and a crushing sense of hopelessness.

The call to her father, without a word coming back beyond his happy answer and his fearful inquiry, had not helped. She took a deep breath and let it out slowly. At least he was not still out to sea for that call, at least he was able to answer. But, he could not help her because he was not in a position to help. He loved her, she knew that. He had told her that so many times over the years as his reputation in the Navy was regularly enhanced by his demonstrated capabilities. If he could bring anybody in the Navy's command structure to help, the structure that could order men and ships in fleets across the oceans of the world, he would by God try to make it happen. He might have tried, making frantic calls to the government in the middle of the night on that terrible night of her capture.

But he was not in charge of the Navy, he had no power over the armed forces. In the background, *like a piece of history that sealed her fate*, there was the loss of dedicated men, what was it, fifteen men, twenty men, lost the last time the United States military tried to intervene in the hell-hole of Mogadishu with their Blackhawk helicopters. That would never happen again, she knew that, not with that history, no matter what her father told the admirals who rested comfortably in their Hawaiian homes, the admirals surrounded by orchids, blue skies and security, their families safe, their daughters without molestation, violence or impending death.

Her mind began to cloud as she tried to concentrate. What was Fuzzball talking about? "You sink my ship…" he had said, the words spinning in her mind. But *they* sank *our* ship, or boat…. What are we all doing…sinking each other's ships? Let's sink our ships together, maybe, let's all try to do it at the same time? Her head dropped down and her eyes closed briefly before she sat upright again, forcing her sleep-deprived mind to make sense of it all. She looked out the dark window again at the dark sea and at the stars staring back at her, her mind savagely depleted of rest, trying to hold on to reality. Without warning, three bright LED[36] lights suddenly shined straight at her husband. She blinked, forcing her eyes to open and to focus, looking into the dark as a table with a camera was pointed directly at Peter's face while the powerful white glare illuminated his body.

Khalid and two of the guards were back.

"Blackwell!" she heard Fuzzball holler, "in thirty seconds, the camera is going to be turned on and if you give exactly the correct answer, you will live. Do you understand what I am saying?"

Peter Blackwell blinked at the harsh light, trying to turn away, a movement that immediately triggered the sound of a large-bore bullet being inserted into the chamber of an automatic weapon.

"I understand," he said quickly. "Who is behind the camera, who is looking at me?"

"Nobody right now," Fuzzball said. "Sit up straight!"

The guards spoke rapidly to each other in Palawano and one of Khalid's group reached out and carefully combed Peter's hair as another released the tape around his hands. The prisoner stretched out his arms and opened his hands, looking at his fingers in the light, his face like a child amazed that parts of his body still seemed to work. He put his arms over his head, stretching expansively, and at exactly the moment he dropped his arms back to his side, the red light at the top of the camera popped on and Randolph Blackwell's harsh voice filled the room.

"Khalid, I want to talk with him, right now."

"So talk," Guleed Khalid hollered back. "Here is your son, he is in good condition, go ahead and talk."

Peter Blackwell stopped moving, his eyes, his face, and his entire body frozen. He tilted his head to one side slightly and briefly closed his eyes before staring straight at the camera.

"Dad?" he asked weakly. "Dad, is that you?"

"Peter, have they harmed you?" his father asked, his unmistakably deep gravelly voice crackling over the rudimentary speaker.

"Dad, can you help us?"

"Peter, tell me they haven't hurt you," his voice commanded.

Peter Blackwell squinted against the lights. "I'm okay. I'm sorry that I took us…"

"Where is Caroline?" the deep voice demanded. "Mr. Khalid, where is Mrs. Blackwell?"

"Caroline Blackwell is fine," Khalid answered, motioning to the others to remove the tape from her mouth and the tape holding her wrists to the side of the chair. "We will show her to you in a moment. Any final words to Peter Blackwell?"

Before Randolph could speak, a thunderous series of explosions coming from the dark harbor shook the building, vibrating the camera and lights and stopping the dialogue. "Turn off the lights!" Khalid commanded, stepping around his captive's chair and rapidly moving to the window where the other pirates joined him, staring out into the night. They looked at the dim lights in the distance, marking the rock pilings of the breakwater and the boats in the harbor, searching for any signs of activity around the fortress. Beyond the area of the Boayan harbor, the black ocean was silent, stretching to the horizon without any light or sign of shipping activity. Speaking in Palawano and broken English, one of the pirates, an obese man with thick hair and pudgy face said, "Nothing out there that I can see."

"Sounded like some of the mines exploded," Khalid said, sticking his head out the opening and looking up and down the coast line.

"Couldn't be a boat," the terrorist answered behind him. "Anything hit by a mine would be up in flames or sending out distress flares."

"Besides," the fat man added, "boats aren't moving anywhere in the harbor at night."

"*Something* set the mines off," Khalid said, looking up and down the coast again. "Those were mines, sounded like five or six of them."

"More like about ten of them. Shall we take the prisoners inland to the Abu Sayyaf safe house?" the pirate asked.

Khalid said nothing for a moment, then finally turned and said, "It may have been a school of large fish, or something like that, triggering the mines. I don't see anything and we're running out of time."

"Blackwell!" Khalid hollered as he returned to his position near the prisoner's chair. "Are you still there?"

The voice roared out of the speakers. "I was ready to hang up and reverse the ninety million!" Randolph Blackwell's voice shouted. "You have turned off the lights, you have not shown me Caroline, and…"

"There was an event in the harbor, Mr. Blackwell," Khalid said. "Have you told anybody about our arrangement?"

"Nobody, Mr. Khalid!" the speaker roared. "We have an agreement and all you need for your goddamn ransom to be paid is to show me my son's wife. Where is Caroline?"

"Turn on the lights," Khalid said in Arabic, "and point them at the woman." He rotated the table holding the camera away from Peter Blackwell, moving it toward Caroline as the blinding lights flashed on again.

"Here she is," he said with his heavy British accent as he clipped her cuffs from her wrists. "Do you have any questions for her?"

The white LED glare lit up Caroline's bruised face. Her hands lifted up to her hair, pulling it to the back of her head as she looked straight at the camera. She rubbed her mouth where the tape had been and said, "I'm okay, Mr. Blackwell...."

"Jesus Christ, Khalid, what have you done to...." was all the crusty voice said before the three pirates turned at the sound of a body and a chair falling over just outside the open door of the room.

"*What the fuck was that*?" Khalid said in English, motioning to the others. "Go check it out," he hollered. The room was silent as the obese man stepped out the door, his assault weapon ready. Caroline peered through the doorway, her eyes widening as she saw his massive shape suddenly fly away from the door, his chest fragmenting as he disappeared with the sound of automatic weapons fire. An instant later, a round black canister hit the floor just inside the door, immediately followed by a thunderous concussion and a blinding flash that lit up the room. Two of the three lights immediately went out as both captives' chairs tilted backwards from the concussion. The camera flew off the table, struck the stone floor and broke open.

Caroline's head hit the floor as her chair fell back, stunning her as she tried to hear what had suddenly become a deafening cold silence from the concussion grenade. Flashes of gunfire immediately lit up the room from a strangely silent battle and five seconds later, a large injured man in a wetsuit hit the wall next to her, a collection of night vision lenses falling from his head with the impact. He dropped to the floor next to Caroline's left arm, his head bleeding from the blow and blood oozing from a bullet hole through the wetsuit covering his right thigh. Lying on her back, she stared at the man's unconscious face; he was young, about 25 years old she guessed, his eyes were closed, and except for very slow breathing, he did not move. His presence seemed strange to Caroline as she struggled to process who he was, why he was there, and why she was nearly deaf.

She turned her head slowly, *so painfully slowly*, to the right and she squeezed her eyes tightly shut, trying to stop a throbbing pounding sensation within her brain. She could hear the distant sound of her husband's voice screaming her name, the words barely audible, sounding like they were echoing down a long tunnel. She opened her eyes again and peered around her chair, trying to focus. One of the pirates lay on the floor in the grotesque positioning of the dead, but Fuzzball seemed to have simply disappeared.

In the distance, like from a faraway place on the floors below, she could *feel* as much as hear additional explosions and the rapid cracking sound of gunfire.

She turned her head to the left again, looking at the young man's eyes that began to open and close, and when she turned her head back again, she could now see Khalid in the dark at the far side of the room, on the floor by the door, slowly struggling to stand up behind Peter's chair. His back was against the wall as blood flowed from his left shoulder. He was holding his weapon, some kind of strange automatic rifle with a very long curved clip sticking out of the underside of the gun, clutching its strap as he turned and tried to get up. She strained to free herself from the chair but the cuffs around her ankles prevented all movement. As her eyes widened with shock she watched Khalid slide his back up against the wall, slowly straightening to his full height while struggling to lift his weapon to his chest.

She frantically looked back at the young man lying next to her, pleading with him, screaming at him for help, her voice sounding tinny and distant. As the pounding inside her head became unbearable, she saw a black pistol with numbers stamped on its barrel lying not more than a foot from the man's right hand. She clenched her teeth together and lunged out for it, stretching her left arm as far as possible, straining to touch its cold handle and finally grasping it. As she turned her head again, she could see Khalid now holding his weapon and lifting the barrel up as his left arm hung uselessly at his side.

She moved the pistol to her right hand, and with both hands gripping the gun's handle, her eyes blurry, her hair partially covering her eyes, she tried to focus on Fuzzball's chest. Everything seemed to be in slow-motion as she wondered briefly about the gun's safety, if it might be on or maybe off. In the next instant, she began squeezing the trigger as fast as she could, her index finger pulling over and over again.

The gun fired nearly silently, jerking up abruptly with each blinding flash as she screamed, "Do you feel that?" Her voice and the sound of the gun were strangely muted as she pumped a rapid staccato of ten shots directly into the man's chest, yelling after each shot, the bullets pinning him to the wall with the impact of the rounds. His gun dropped to the floor and he finally slid slowly down the wall, his mouth open as if in shock, his eyes staring straight at her, his body leaving a wide smear of blood on the stones behind him.

After the final round left the barrel, Caroline continued squeezing the trigger, over and over again until her hand finally cramped and locked into a spasm. With a blinding fury, as Fuzzball's body fell forward onto the floor and Caroline screamed, "Today, YOU die, you bastard!!"

Abruptly, a large hand, reaching from behind her head, closed around her own hand, and gently pulled the weapon away. The injured man was now behind her, water still dripping off his wetsuit and mixing with the blood from his leg wound. He said something to her that she couldn't hear, and she turned to look up at him and asked, "Who are you?"

His voice sounded faraway as he said, "You are coming with us, Caroline, can you walk?"

She stared at the man. "Who are you?" she asked again, her voice sounding distant. "How do you know my name?"

"U.S. Navy, SEALs, doing a special op. We have come to take you home." He looked at Peter Blackwell and added, "We have come to bring both of you home."

She blinked, her mind swirling as she tried to understand the impossible. "You are *Americans*?" she asked softly. "How did you get here? The Navy sent SEALs to rescue us?"

"Not the Navy, Caroline," he said, "your father."

She stared at the man with wide eyes, her mind clearing and racing to understand. Before he had the chance to answer, two more men in wetsuits, with optical devices attached to their heads and M4 assault rifles in their hands, rushed into the room. Nobody said a word as they rapidly rushed back and forth between the two prisoners, cutting away the tape holding their legs to the chairs. One of the SEALs pulled out a huge ACE dressing and wrapped it around the injured SEAL's leg, slowing the oozing of blood.

"How is your leg, any numbness?" one SEAL asked.

"No problem," the wounded man quickly answered as he adjusted the dressing. "My bone phone[37] is out from the flash bang, we have no communications."

Helping Caroline and Peter to their feet and removing their restraints, the men looked down at Khalid for a moment.

"Big Mouth, Guleed Khalid, confirmed dead," one of them said quickly before turning and helping the injured SEAL. Peter, Caroline, and the three SEALs rushed to the staircase where they saw the early gray change in the sky, the *light of the false dawn* as the five moved down the stone stairs toward the ground level. Scores of dead men were scattered about on the different floors, lying in the inert positions of the violently deceased. On the second floor, she caught a quick glimpse of a thickly bearded pirate lying flat on the stone floor, face down, his right hand moving rhythmically and randomly. In a flash of sudden movement, one of the SEALs shot the pirate three times, immediately stopping the rhythm and bringing his body to a rock-still silence.

"Jesus…" she whispered as they moved to the ground level, stepping over the scattering of rocks and sand, moving around three more bodies to an area where the marker of the SDV minisub was barely visible above the water. As they walked into the ocean, the SEALs' heads turned back and forth, night vision goggles in place, scanning up and down the waterfront for any signs of activity.

"Clear to the north," one of them said.

"Clear to the south," the smaller SEAL immediately answered.

"Frog, you're sitting up front with me," the larger SEAL said to the injured man. "Silverback, you're in the back with Caroline and Peter."

The larger SEAL looked at the two hostages. "With only four seats, it's going to be tight, very tight," he said. "You are both going to be in the back starboard seat, we will be submerged. You will both be wearing scuba gear, okay?"

"We're both scuba divers, *just get us out of here,*" Caroline said intensely as they stepped into the shallow water and pulled on their masks and breathing gear.

USS *Monterey*, Pacific Ocean

In the control room of the *Monterey*, Captain Moore and Chief Berry stood on the periscope station, their eyes tightly pressed against the rubber seals around the lens, night vision turned on, infrared sensitivity maximized, focus adjusted on the distant fortress. They had seen the flashes lighting up the tower's small square windows, they had seen more flashes of gunfire, and they finally saw a cluster of figures leaving the fortress, the white heat images of their bodies shimmering in the dark. The images finally moved down the beach toward the water, and disappeared into their SDV. The flashes of light from the fortress had been intense and blinding to the night vision devices, especially the brilliant flash of the concussion grenade on the top level. That was the moment when the communications with the SEALs had gone dead.

"Did you see how many there are?" Moore asked, turning his periscope up and down the coast to look for other heat sources.

"Negative, sir," Berry's raspy voice replied. "Even at 24x power, and with the infrared thermal imaging, I can't really tell if there's any more coming out than went in."

"We'll know soon enough," Moore said, focusing again on the SEALs getting into their SDV. "It looks like there's a little more body heat in the SDV."

"Hard to say, sir,"

"So we wait and we listen."

"Yes, sir," the chief petty officer growled, scanning the coast through his periscope. "And then, we get out of here…gonna need another two or three hundred feet of ocean before we can dive."

Moore glanced at his Chief of the Boat. "Get them aboard and we haul ass for the open sea."

Running a submarine on rocks in the pirate-infested waters of Palawan would have to be another court martial offense, the captain thought with some irony.

The *Monterey* was nearly submerged, her DDS hangar space fully underwater, the hangar door wide open as everybody on the submarine waited for the SDV arrival. Moore had guided his ship as close as he dared in the shallow waters, the threat of grounding a continuous concern. The top of the sail sat just above the water, the periscopes another twenty feet higher, and Bodine worked vigorously at the ballast control panel to maintain the equilibrium above the rocks below them on the ocean floor.

"SDV screws approaching!" Doc Wheat hollered from the sonar room.

The minisub was inbound and Captain Moore felt the flash of a chill running down his back. His jaw muscles tightened as he tried to focus on the periscope, scanning the waters between the *Monterey* and shore, the waters under which a miniature submarine controlled by three SEALs was approaching. The SEALs, he knew, were there to retrieve the hostages, not to assure their good health. Though Caroline had been strong in both mind and spirit, they may have broken her or maimed her in some permanent manner. As he found his thinking moving into the possible ways she could have irreversible injuries, or that a post-mortem evaluation may be approaching, he abruptly reached into the overhead area, grabbed the 7 MC microphone and put it close to his mouth.

"Engine room, switch main coolant pumps to high speed, prepare for emergency full speed ahead, continue to maintain battleshort protection," he announced. He turned to Bodine. "Helm, maintain thirty feet, prepare for high speed shallow transit." He turned back to his periscope where the black waters showed no sign of the SDV's submerged approach.

The engine room and Bodine acknowledged the orders from the captain; all they needed was to hear the clanking noise of contact between the SDV and the rail running the length of the DDS hangar. The SEALs were coming hot and fast, at top speed for the mini-submarine, the kind of speed that could deplete or burn out their SDV lithium batteries in record time, but the kind of speed in a short run could save lives and bring the fastest possible protection from within the *Monterey.* One clank, shut the DDS door, communicate, and everybody's on their way to sea.

"Captain!" Berry hollered from his starboard periscope. "I have weapon flashes from south of the fortress. They are firing in our direction, sir."

"Roger," Moore said crisply, rotating the periscope to the right, seeing flashes with intermittent tracer rounds skipping across the water. "Probably 50-calibers…range would be just a little over a mile."

"We're slightly more than that, sir," the chief said. "Sunrise in about 15 minutes, they can already see us."

"Right, and I can see them even without the night-vision scope…there's a collection gathering at the fortress, looks like they're going into the building."

He was interrupted by a distinct clang of steel against steel followed by a humming hydraulic sound as the hangar door closed. An instant later, a red light above the navigation table flickered and abruptly turned green.

"The SDV is in, captain, and the hangar is shut," Berry said. "I'll stay at the diving station with Bodine, sir, if you would like to go check it out."

Moore nodded. "Keep us off the bottom, chief, top of the sail out of the water for a mile or two. Do a quick sounding, and if we're greater than 500 feet, ease us down to periscope depth."

"Aye, aye, sir," the chief's crusty voice replied as he peered through the periscope at the shoreline. "Oh shit!" he exclaimed. "Infrared indicates they're launching boats. They're coming after us, only a mile away!"

Moore grabbed the 7 MC microphone again. "Engine room, control. Full speed ahead. Repeat full speed ahead." he commanded. He turned to Bodine and hollered, "Set course for the open sea!"

"Aye, aye, sir," Bodine answered as he turned the rudder hard for the escape.

As he briskly left the control center for the SEAL re-entry hatch, the captain heard the first sound of an errant shell, perhaps a projectile of some kind, he thought, skipping off the ocean and slamming into the *Monterey's* sail that was still protruding about twenty feet above the water. The submarine began to vibrate with the accelerating propulsion turbines as Munroe opened the throttles and Robby increased the reactor power to accelerate the *Monterey* away from the shoreline. The captain could almost *feel* the submarine's movement through the water, its speed slowed by the sail's resistance against the surface of the ocean. Of greater concern, Captain Moore knew, was the fact that they were now leaving a visible wake across the surface, removing all elements of submarine secrecy, a foaming trail of churning water, like a long white arrow, pointing directly at the *Monterey*'s protruding sail.

The captain walked briskly into the compartment holding the SEALs' transfer chamber and stood, waiting, Wilson on his left side, Amanda on his right, and Doc Wheat behind him. Nobody said a word and all was quiet as they listened to the sounds of the returning SDV crew within the pressure chamber. The captain could hear them as they glided down the ladder inside the tank, followed by the noise of the hatch shutting, the hissing of air vents and the flowing of water as the chamber drained its contents.

Moore waited, his mind a scramble of thoughts, the time moving in aching slow motion, as he knew with certainty that what happened next would define the years, the decades, *his entire life* ahead. He looked around at the others, all silent and waiting with him, and he focused his eyes on the round hatch door in front of him, the unknown fueling his imagination, stimulating the worst from the darkest nightmares, tinged with the hope that she might still be alive and that she had returned.

It was a certainty that, if she was not in the pressure chamber, if she was left behind in Palawan and far away in a prison cell or worse, there could never be any hope that life, his own life, could become meaningful again.

When the round hatch finally swung open revealing the grinning face of the huge SEAL, Chainsaw, Captain Gary Moore knew what awaited.

Chainsaw stepped aside and Caroline appeared before the captain, her eyes bright with excitement, her drenched hair hanging over a soaked denim shirt, remnants of tape residue still clinging to the bruised side of her face that was radiant with life. She stood in knee-deep water inside the chamber in front of the watertight door, saying nothing for a moment, just staring at her father as if she was struggling to comprehend it all. It was only when Moore saw the tears streaming down her face that she finally flashed her beautiful smile, ducked her head, and rapidly climbed through the watertight door.

"Daddy!" she said with a voice that was hoarse and much weaker than he remembered. She seemed to struggle to talk for a moment, and then she finally reached out and hugged her father as she tearfully blurted out, “Thank you! Thank you, Daddy, I never thought you could…I love you!”

“You are safe now…” Moore began, speaking gently to her as he hugged her tightly, his own tears flowing freely down his face.

“Oh…God,” she exclaimed, wiping tears from her eyes. “There was no hope. I was sure we would never get back, I thought I would never see you again, you’re always gone. They broke Mombo’s phone, and I never knew how much you heard when I called you.”

“I’ll never be gone again…we have Mombo with us, and the other hostages on that ship,” Moore said as he continued to hold her tightly. The others stood back and waited quietly.

“The only thing I need now is to get away as quickly as possible from this horrible part of the world,” she said, turning around toward the hatch. “Peter,” she called to the man waiting inside. She wiped her tears away again and motioned her husband to join them. “Come on,” she said as she helped him through the hatch, “our nightmare is over….”

As her disheveled husband climbed from the hatch and profusely thanked the captain, Chainsaw appeared at the hatch door again. “Captain, Frog has a through-and-through gunshot wound in his right thigh, no nerve or artery damage but Doc Wheat needs to clean it out and get him on antibiotics.”

Moore turned to Doc Wheat and stepped back from the hatch. “Doc, and Amanda, you both have a patient,” he said as the SEALs helped Frog through the hatch, a large and wet blood-soaked compression bandage around his thigh.

“This is no big deal, captain,” Frog said as the captain directed them to follow Wheat to the *Monterey’s* improvised sick bay area for treatment. “It was that bastard Big Mouth who did this,” Frog said, “only wish I had a chance to nail him before your daughter….”

“Dad?” Caroline interrupted, “You said you have the other hostages? And, since when does your submarine have women onboard?” She gestured toward Amanda who took a step backward, quickly shook her head, and smiled.

“She was a last-minute volunteer,” Moore said, smiling. “A *very helpful* volunteer. It’s the newest thing on submarines.”

Caroline crossed her arms over her chest. "You know, we wanted to fight when they attacked us. Mombo gave up, when we still had a chance to fight them off, he surrendered."

"I know, I heard his story. But, actually, he saved you, not only by stopping the killing before they got to you, but they were very likely going to kill you. Having his satellite phone on your boat allowed your call to get through to me. Without that call, we wouldn't have known where to look. Also, this Mombo guy reports that he is a chef, and he has already started preparing meals."

Amanda smiled. "Food from cans, Caroline, didn't know it could taste so good. He…"

They were suddenly interrupted by the sounds of incoming shells hitting the *Monterey*'s sail, the noise filling the submarine with a staccato vibration as the captain broke away from the group and rushed out of the compartment and back to the control center. Chief Berry was still peering through the starboard periscope, rotating it back and forth.

"There's a whole *fleet* of them coming out of the harbor in boats, sir, we're making nearly thirty knots but some of them are catching up."

The captain grabbed the microphone. "Engine room say reactor power."

"Full power is 72% captain," Robby's voice shot back. "We are rigged for 100% power but this is all we can get."

"Very well," Moore said, slowly returning the microphone to its holder. As long as the nuclear reactor could produce more than 60%, they would be okay, he thought, although full speed ahead was increasingly impossible. It was becoming more of a "partial speed ahead," with whatever power the reactor could still provide. Even with that, he thought, partial power from the nuclear reactor is vastly better than diesel power, especially when they could submerge. The diesel would add nothing to their speed and would lock them onto the surface or force them to continuously snorkel, an unacceptable consequence. At least one thing was certain, he thought, the pirates of Palawan have zero anti-submarine capability and a submerged submarine would accelerate them immediately out of harm's way.

"Bodine, fathometer report," he called out.

"One hundred twenty feet, sir," Bodine immediately answered.

"Can't dive," Berry said, looking away from his periscope. "If they hit the 'scopes or the snorkel, we're screwed, sir," he said, watching tracer rounds arcing out from their weapons in the direction of the *Monterey*.

Another sudden staccato of bullets hitting the sail created a deafening noise throughout the compartment. Moore caught a glimpse of Caroline standing in the corner of the control center, her fingers in her ears trying to block out the noise of the bullets' impact on the submarine's sail.

"We're stuck on the surface for another five minutes or so, sir," Berry said to Moore as they both watched the pirate boats gaining on them. "I've got the sail as far down as possible!"

The captain did a quick 360^{0} turn of his periscope, spotting numerous fishing boats scattered across the waters off the coast. He looked back at the coast line, switched to high power, and watched more men enter the fortress, their figures now easily seen in the rising sun. Some of the men were racing to the top floor with binoculars, scanning the waters off the coast as others moved in and out of the doors leading to the balcony of the building.

"Chief, light off UHF SATCOM system," the captain said, clutching a red microphone attached to the side railing of the periscope station.

Chief Berry glanced at the captain briefly, his mustache twitching nervously. Any SATCOM broadcast would reveal their position to the world, and yet at the same time, anybody looking at this particular area of the world already knew the submarine's exact location. He shrugged, jumped off the periscope platform, and darted into the *Monterey's* communication center.

Ten seconds later, from the radio room, Berry hollered, "UHF SATCOM operational, using the AN/BRA-34 antenna, captain."

Moore raised the microphone to his mouth, painfully aware of the unprecedented action about to occur. *Submarines don't broadcast radio messages while at sea, especially under battle conditions....* He glanced at Caroline, watching the action closely from the corner of the control room, he winced as additional incoming rounds from the pirate's boats hit the sail, and he finally squeezed the switch on the side of the microphone.

Whidbey Island, Washington

Admiral Samuel Sullivan had just poured his fourth cup of coffee that afternoon in the little house next to Whidbey Island Airfield when the tiny red light next to the third computer screen, the one on the far right, popped on. He bolted upright, grabbed the computer mouse and activated the screen, immediately staring at Admiral Stephen Kent's face. The man's eyes were bloodshot, Sullivan could see that with the high resolution picture, the clone of Chester Nimitz looked exhausted and clearly agitated.

"Sully. Are you with me?" Kent almost shouted.

Sullivan adjusted the microphone resting on the table at the base of the computer and immediately answered. "I am here, sir, I have been watching the emerging littoral[38] battlefield at the Boayan harbor, and…"

"What I need, Sully, is an immediate opinion on a classified radio transmission from that battlefield. Has the ransom been paid?"

"I am trying to find out, sir, last word was that the payment was imminent. We're serving up a subpoena for Randolph Blackwell at this moment to find out what he has done and what he is doing. The SEC is out of the loop for the ransom money since the stock was sold, Margarita Lindsey cannot be reached…"

"Goddammit, Sully, I don't care about all that crap. Listen to the message we've intercepted from the COMSAT link off the fucking *Monterey*."

"Go ahead, sir."

Sullivan sat back in his chair, watching the COMPACFLT admiral flip two switches on a computer base. There was silence for a few seconds, followed by a loud hissing noise, and finally Captain Gary Moore's voice roared out of the encrypted speaker system. The words were intense, they were crisp, and in the background, the sound of incoming shells hitting steel could be heard.

"*Monterey! Monterey! Hostages aboard, five klicks out, hostile fortress spotters in Boayan bay, no innocents! Sully, mobilize Sick Vibrators! Do it now!*"

"That's it," Kent said, "nothing else."

"Captain Moore is asking for help."

"*I know that!* What is he saying?"

"He doesn't want the 7th Fleet to sink him, sir, like from friendly fire! He has acknowledged the hostages. He's the target of that battlefield with spotters in the waterfront building."

"Wonderful, where the hell is he?"

"He's five klicks west of Palawan, probably straight out from the harbor to the South China Sea, too shallow for a submarine to dive."

"Great, got it. What are the fucking Sick Vibrators?"

"The Sikorsky Seahawks,[39] sir, Sick Vibrators is what we used to call them last year. They vibrate like hell when they're on the attack. Are there any outbound choppers from the carrier group?"

"Hell, yes, they're always out there during war game operations, got four of the MH-60R's out there in the air heading in that direction at full speed right now. That's why they call it a goddamn battle group."

"Sir, he is under fire, there are hostages aboard, and the pilots will need orders to engage…"

"Got it, Sully, they're fully armed and they will have orders to engage."

"The *Monterey's* sail has got to be visible above the waterline, if you could let the pilots know that, sir. Also, Captain Moore's message has just given us a green light on the fortress. It is hostile, admiral, there are no innocents in the tower, someone in the fortress is directing the attack on one of our submarines."

"I will let them know, Sully, and one last question."

"Yes, sir," Sullivan said.

"Why the hell is Moore running the *Monterey* in such shallow waters? The *Cho Ying Atlas* was miles out to sea. The poor bastard can't even dive."

USS *Monterey*, Pacific Ocean

Chief Berry and Captain Moore rotated their periscopes around the horizon and as they both simultaneously focused on the waters ahead of the *Monterey*, the only words from the chief was a loud, "Holy mother of sweet Jesus Christ…."

"Raise the BRA-34 communications mast—everyone needs to hear this. Four choppers coming in our direction, we just got help!" Moore said, adjusting his power on the periscope.

Berry's voice was unusually soft as he replied, "I just hope they're not coming after us."

For the next five minutes, the two men watched what amounted to an air show in the waters off the east coast of Palawan, beginning almost over the horizon but rapidly descending into the waters of the *Monterey*, as four Sikorsky MH-60R helicopters, each of them low to the water, closed in on the position of the submarine. Two miles away, the attack began, tracers from the 7.62mm and 50 caliber machine guns marching a splashing pattern across the water, skirting around the *Monterey* and directly intersecting the closest incoming pirate attackers, blowing up the boats with a mixture of engine parts, body parts, and fragmented skiff. The loudspeaker broadcast the pilots' tight battlefield commentary from the AN/BRA 34 mast into the *Monterey's* control center, immediately switched by Moore to every speaker in the submarine. Moore found himself gripping the handles of the periscope as the dialogue unfolded, a tight clenching kind of grip, his eyes beginning to sting from the sweat running down his forehead.

Tiger 23 flight inbound... Visual friendly[40]*, weapons free... Tiger 25, tally targets at my eleven o'clock, 2 klicks and closing, I have TAC lead... Tiger flight, racetrack attack, right pull... Tiger 25, commencing engagement, in heading 3-1-0... Tiger 26, in heading 3-0-5... Tiger 25, off right, safe, flares... Tiger 23, in heading 3-1-0... Tiger 26, off right, safe, flares... Break left! Break left! Tracers at your two o'clock!... Tiger flight, maintain standoff... Tiger 24, in heading 3-0-0... Tiger 24, off right, safe, flares... Tiger 24 is Winchester*[41]*...*

Tiger flight, Havoc 41... Havoc 41, Tiger flight, go ahead... Tiger flight, Havoc 41 is single F/A-18,[42] *15 miles out at Angels 20, 0+15 playtime, with a GBU-16 and a bent laser*[43]*... Are you designator capable?... Tiger flight copies, we are laser capable... Laser code 1688, priority target delta, three-story stand-alone structure located at grid GI 8756 2943, call capture... Searching.... Capture, laser-target line 2-7-0, 1688 set... Verify target... Three-story building, satellite dishes on the roof, one truck out front, truck oriented east... Target confirmed... Capture, tally... Havoc 41 will be in from the northeast, twenty seconds... Tiger 23 in position, laser-target line 2-7-0, 1688 set... Ten seconds... Roger, ten seconds... Havoc 41, in heading 2-3-0, one away... Laser* *on...Lasing...Lasing...Impact, terminate, target destroyed...Blackhawk down payback! Engagement complete, Tiger 23 has TAC lead, holster check*[44]*, report FARM-E*[45]*...*

Simultaneous with the final call from the F/A-18 jet, the stone fortress at the edge of the Boayan harbor disappeared in a massive explosion leaving a flat collection of sand, weapons, rocks and scattered body parts behind. Moore and Berry rotated their periscopes around repeatedly, watching the explosion followed by a cloud of dark smoke rising across the Palawan skyline. The waters around the submarine, stretching all the way to the shore behind them, became calm and peaceful. And most favorable was the total cessation of incoming shells and bullets striking the sail, allowing a welcome peace within the submarine.

They rotated the 'scopes again, and apart from a scattering of fishing boats in the waters ahead of them, nobody with any apparent hostile intent appeared to be in the area. At the moment Bodine reported the depth of the ocean to be 217 feet, Captain Moore turned to his chief.

"Dive. Dive," he ordered, "drop the 'scopes, take her down! Make your depth 100 feet."

"100 hundred feet, aye, aye, captain, Chief Berry answered as he grabbed the 1MC microphone. "Do you think our guys will come after us?" he asked the captain.

"Negative," Moore said softly. "We have hostages aboard and they know that. Set a course for Papa Hotel. We're going home."

Chapter 16

Guided Missile Cruiser USS *Stout*, Pacific Ocean

Five days later, in the nighttime warm waters of Hawaii, one hundred ten miles southwest of the island of Oahu, the guided missile cruiser USS *Stout* prepared to return to Pearl Harbor.

Commander Ralph Ginder's thin frame nervously paced the bridge of his ship. He gripped a coffee cup in his left hand and an Apple computer in his right hand as he prepared to order the cessation of the search for the submarine, *Monterey*. It had been a fruitless search, as it had been since the very beginning nearly two weeks before, and it hadn't mattered that he had their Towed Array system extending thousands of yards behind the *Stout* or that his sonarman was one of the best in the Navy. The *Monterey* had been like a ghost ship, a *fucking phantom* under the water, he thought, moving where it wanted with her full load of weapons, frustrating the Seahawk chopper, frustrating the entire *Stout* crew, and frustrating the officers charged with the responsibility of finding the son-of-a-bitch who liked to steal submarines.

There had recently been an operational top secret rumor, widely circulating through the Navy from "unnamed sources," that the submarine *Monterey* had surfaced far away, in the South China Sea during a classified 7th Fleet skirmish with pirates. There had even been a protest from the Philippine government about military actions off Palawan Island that did not include advance diplomatic notifications and that did not invite the Philippine military's participation. The rumors and protest were ridiculous, Ginder knew, because everybody, that is, *everybody with half an ounce of knowledge*, knew that submarines and pirates didn't have any reason to be interested in each other. Pirates can't capture a submarine and submarines can't torpedo a pirate boat.

Really.

Ginder took a sip of coffee and smiled, confident about this last piece of knowledge, *obvious to the most casual observer*. Just for fun, try asking any submarine skipper mingling with his group of irreverent socially awkward submarine officers who frequent bars on Hotel Street, ask him why he might even think about planting a Mark-

48 into the side of a 4-man pirate skiff. He sipped his coffee again and put his coffee cup down on the polished brass in front of him. Best thing, he concluded, was to just don't even try to be friends with the submariners—they were a different breed, they were a strange bunch, and they never mix well with the good and refined men of the surface Navy. They don't even like to talk with the men of surface ships, so often derisively called "skimmers" by the bubbleheads who lurk below.

His reverie was broken by the sudden announcement from his sonarman, "Contact. Bearing 327 degrees, approaching at…standby, standby, at seven knots. Screws are cavitating, sir."

Commander Ginder put down his coffee cup and keyed the microphone connecting with the sonar room. "Whatchagot, another Japanese fishing boat, maybe?"

"Can't say for sure, captain, could be," the sonarman said. "Diesel engine, twin screws. Bearing now 318 degrees."

"Very well, carry on," Ginder said, walking out of the cruiser's bridge to the outside watch station after a quick glance at his beloved AN/SPY-1 radar display, the high-volume, computer-guided system that could track over 100 targets simultaneously. *Such* a capable system, Ginder thought, and now all it has to do is find one little miserable blip on a clear night. The display showed no target and after two minutes of scrutiny at 318 degrees with his powerful night vision binoculars, he confirmed there were no targets in the area.

Five minutes later, when the Towed Array system confirmed what the sonarman had said and when at least forty of the crew looking off the port side of the *Stout* also confirmed, the target was determined to be a submerged submarine with its snorkel and periscopes just above the black water line, emitting bubbling diesel fumes through its submerged exhaust pipe. A small cloud of dark smoke fanned out behind the snorkel mast as the submarine slowly moved by the cruiser in the direction of Pearl Harbor.

"I think it's a submarine," Lieutenant Commander Brook Brinda said to his commanding officer.

Ginder glared at the executive officer as the surrounding enlisted men on the bridge tried to fade away from the two men.

"Thank you, Lieutenant," Ginder said sarcastically, "I'll be sure to credit you for that observation in your fitness report. Have you determined *what* submarine it might be?"

"No, sir, looks like a diesel submarine, maybe Chinese or Japanese…or something?" Brinda said quietly as he began to ponder alternative career pathways.

USS *Monterey*, Pacific Ocean

Inside the radio room of the USS *Monterey*, Chief Berry hunched over the receiver and scanned the frequencies for anything worthwhile among the ships that had gathered and now surrounded the submarine. He suddenly stiffened and called out to Captain Moore at the periscope station, his face pressed against the eyepieces of the port periscope.

"Captain, Pearl Harbor COMSUBPAC is coming in over the SIX[46]."

"Okay, chief," Moore said, "put them over the speaker." He reached up and grabbed the SATCOM microphone. At the helm, Billy Bodine sat up straight, listening carefully as he guided the submarine in the direction of the Pearl Harbor entrance.

Admiral Sullivan's voice boomed over the speaker into the control room. "Welcome home, Gary, and you are in one big world of hurt."

"Yes, sir, I know," Moore said into his microphone. "We'll get it sorted out."

"You are goddamn correct we will do that. Right now, you need to let us know your intentions. The *Monterey* is currently classified, to our Navy and to every other navy in the world, as a rogue submarine with hostile intent; your position was belatedly reported by the USS *Stout* and….

"Yes, sir, and right now, we're on our diesel at periscope depth and steaming next to the *Stout.* Also, Sully, a few other skimmer ships appear to be gathering around us."

"Correct. *As I was saying*, if you didn't have a couple of hostages aboard…"

"Twelve, admiral, we have twelve."

There was a moment of silence. "Twelve?" There was another pause while Sullivan digested that fact. "Our report was that you possibly had two hostages."

"Yes, sir, we have those two, plus all ten from that mother ship, the *Cho Ying Atlas*. We also have a prisoner, captured off the mother ship. Considering the risks to all these hostages, the submarine *Monterey* requests safe passage to the base."

Another long pause, followed by, "Roger, safe passage granted to the sub base. However, there is an armada of people, starting with the President on down, who are lining up a very, *very* long list of infractions covering almost the entire UCMJ.[47] I won't lay out the details right now but suffice to say the JAG team is preparing your noose at this very moment."

For the first time, Captain Moore noticed Caroline standing in the corner of the control center, quietly watching her father.

"And furthermore," Sullivan's voice continued over the speaker, "considering your years of service to your country, I've put in a good word to Admiral Kent over at COMPACFLT. You are in desperate need of good will, Gary. If he continues to be amenable, which I doubt, you will not be stopped and arrested in the waters outside Pearl."

"I understand, thank you, sir. We've been snorkeling on the diesel for two days, Sully, we're almost out of food, our sail is damaged from hostile fire, and maximum reactor power is 32%. We'll be surfacing momentarily. I would appreciate it if the *Stout* didn't fire on us, sir." Moore rotated the periscope to the starboard flank of his submarine, clicked it to high-power, and stared into the glowering eyes of Ginder, his face lit up on the bridge, his skinny frame leaning over the port lookout station of the *Stout*. The smallest hint of a smile began to form on Moore's face.

"Roger that," Sullivan said again. "I'll tell Ginder to back off. Maybe he can do *that* right. Do you have any wounded aboard?"

"Petty Officer Olsen," Moore answered, "one of our SEALs was shot and will need some attention, although it is a non-critical leg wound and is healing."

"We'll have the medical team ready for you and the hostages. We'll have an interrogation team for the prisoner. I would guess he is a Guantanamo candidate."

"That seems probable and thank you, sir."

Moore turned to Chief Berry, watching him through the radio room open door. "Chief, shut down the radio," he ordered, "and take us up."

Within two minutes, every ship in the waters around Pearl Harbor received the direct order from COMPACFLT to take no hostile action against the submarine surfacing in the nighttime waters off Oahu. Stand down, the cryptic message from Admiral Kent said, with additional orders to provide unrestricted passage of the USS *Monterey* to the Pearl Harbor Submarine Base.

By the time the *Monterey* reached the outer shelf of Oahu's shoreline, she was plowing through a rising black surface swell with no less than five Navy ships around her and one Seahawk chopper directly above. The helicopter hovered directly over the top of the submarine's battered sail, its position locked by Doppler and gyroscopic computer controls at precisely 500 feet. Its Hoverlight and auxiliary searchlights glared accusingly down at the *Monterey*, the chopper's fifty caliber machine guns and Hellfire air-to-surface missiles primed and ready. Four armed members of the helicopter crew, attached to the helicopter frame with cable harnesses, leaned out through the open door and looked straight down at the submarine captain and his lookout standing in the cockpit of the sail as the black shape slowly rumbled in the direction of Oahu. The commanding officers of each surface ship, fully aware of the previous *humiliating* escape after the most extensive ASW[48] effort in history, kept their hair-trigger attention on the *Monterey*, ready to unleash nearly unlimited firepower should there be any deviation from a precise path to the Pearl Harbor entrance.

Twenty-five minutes later, as the *Monterey*'s diesel pushed the submarine across the dark waters of Pearl Harbor, two heavily armed escort boats pulled alongside and the surface vessels backed away. Berry took over the helm controls and Captain Moore and Bodine, standing side-by-side in the cockpit at the top of the sail, watched the surrounding lights of Pearl Harbor move by.

Moore pointed in the direction of the lights at Ford Island, on the port side of the submarine. "Know what that little cluster of lights is over there?" he asked Bodine, his voice rising above the thumping sounds of the helicopter above them.

Bodine turned his binoculars and looked past the moored battleship USS *Missouri*. "I don't know, sir.... Is that part of that museum, or housing for officers or something?" He turned to look at the captain.

"Partly right, Bodine. Actually, those lights belong to the Navy brig."

"Oh…" Bodine said, refocusing his binoculars on the building. "That's nice. The brig. Not far from the sub base…."

"1.6 miles, a quick drive."

Bodine paused, then turned to look at Moore again. He said nothing for several more seconds, and finally smiled as he said, "It was worth it, sir."

Chapter 17

Pearl Harbor Submarine Pier, USS *Monterey*

The instant the brow and heavy lines connected the boat with the pier under the pulsating roar of the Sikorsky MH-60R Seahawk Helicopter hovering 500 feet above the *Monterey,* its powerful LED spotlight pointing straight down, a surge of authoritative humanity moved onto the deck of the submarine. Agents from the Naval Criminal Investigative Service, the Federal Bureau of Investigation, the Central Intelligence Agency, and the National Security Agency, all of them in suits and most of them carrying briefcases, streamed in from the dock, their faces reflecting the importance of the agenda before them. Doc Wheat and Wilson rushed back and forth across the deck, securing the lines connecting the submarine with the pier, wrapping the final forward line around the boat's cleat before surrendering to the agents. From the inside of the cockpit at the top of the sail, standing nearly 25 feet above the submarine deck, Captain Gary Moore and Petty Officer Billy Bodine watched the flood of humanity below them and glanced at each other without a word. Before the hatches could be opened, Moore reached under the cockpit steel overhang and picked up the operational 1MC microphone connecting to the interior of the submarine.

"Attention all hands, and attention all civilians aboard the *Monterey*, this is the captain speaking. We are now secured at the pier, Amanda and Frog prepare the dolphins for a morning transfer to shore, reactor operator, shut down what is left of the reactor, engine room, shut down the diesel, control center and torpedo room personnel secure all equipment. All civilians will gather in the control center for processing and for transfer to the medical clinic. A final word of thanks to all of you who have sailed to the South China Sea and back with me, it has been my pleasure to serve with you to complete a job well done by all hands. I encourage everybody to cooperate with the agencies charged with the acquisition of our good submarine, *Monterey*."

He quietly placed the microphone back in its holder, and after Bodine saluted the captain and disappeared down the interior ladder toward the main deck, a female voice echoed up from the depths of the sail.

"Daddy?" she asked. "May I come up?"

"Caroline?" he called down the dark hatch leading to the submarine. "They're going to want you to go with them, honey."

She climbed the long ladder to reach the upper deck of the sail's cockpit and studied the eyes of her father under the brilliant shimmering light of the helicopter. He looked back at her and smiled. "Are you okay?" he asked.

"I am just fine…" she said, reaching up to place a couple of fingers across his lips. "Don't say anything! Please don't say anything. Peter is going up to the topside deck but I just want to be with you for a little while longer."

She looked over the edge of the cockpit, down into the dark at the swarming of civilians and military police moving onto the submarine, then she turned back to him. Her eyes burned into his as she remained silent before finally hugging him tightly and whispering, "Thank you, daddy, I love you, and words can never say..."

"Captain Moore?" a high-pitched man's voice abruptly called up from the depths of the sail. "Agent Anderson, NSA, would you please step down to the topside deck? We would like to talk with you, sir."

"I'll be seeing you later, honey," Moore said to his daughter as he gave her a quick kiss on her cheek. "I love you and I'm glad we're all safe now."

Moore turned away and departed down the ladder into the submarine's control center. Watching from the top of the sail, at the moment the military police and security agents escorted the Monterey captain across the brow and away from his submarine, Caroline realized for the first time that she was crying. The tears were silent, an internal releasing of pain, streaming down her face in hot rivulets that crossed her neck and left dark marks on the top of her blue submarine uniform. During the past weeks of capture and hopelessness, during all the years now gone by since she had lost her mother, she had not really cried other than the tears of joy when she saw her father after being rescued by the SEALs. And now she was crying as she watched them take him away. Anger and ferocity had always been in her ready reserve, just below the surface, used with great effectiveness on many occasions, but not tears…they had never been needed.

Quietly climbing down the long ladder submarine's control room, she tried to breathe deeply as she brushed her hand across her burning eyes as they escorted her father away.

Detention and Confinement Facility, Pearl Harbor

The Navy car moved briskly across Pearl Harbor, leaving the submarine base and accelerating down the dark streets near the dry-docks and surface ship mooring docks, finally stopping in front of a small wooden house on the corner of Ticonderoga Street and Hale Alii Avenue. Moore looked out the car window to the porch of the house where Admiral Harris Zehner stopped pacing as he turned and waited for the delivery of his prisoner. This would be his home, he knew, while he awaited his hearing leading to the inevitable court-martial proceedings. Two military police and Agent Anderson escorted Moore up the stairs and into the living room as a glowering Zehner followed behind.

"Sit down," Zehner ordered crisply, pointing to a large red sofa spanning one of the walls. "Why isn't this prisoner cuffed?" he asked, turning to the NSA agent.

"Admiral Sullivan gave a direct order for the handcuffs to be removed…" Anderson began.

"Goddammit, Anderson, you're on a military base, why can't you follow the orders of a superior officer?" Zehner said curtly. "Get the tracker on him."

"Where have you taken my crew, admiral?" Captain Moore asked quietly.

"The men who colluded with you are in the brig at Ford Island, where they belong, and that bastard pirate you captured is being turned over to the Attorney General for a Goddamn public trial."

"The Attorney General? Isn't the prisoner an enemy combatant?"

"We haven't declared war on any island in the Philippines, Goddammit. Don't say a word about the chopper attack, Moore, which was a skirmish, a corrective action, not a war. The President has decided…."

“Okay, admiral,” Moore interrupted. “Why am I not with my crew?”

“You are not with the men who *used to be your crew* because you were the captain, the top of your submarine’s food chain, the *prima donna* who is now under arrest and being held accountable for giving the orders to those who followed your command.”

As one of the military police began to apply a large electronic monitor to Moore’s left ankle, Zehner began talking again, his voice assuming an official tone.

“Commander Moore, you have violated multiple provisions of the UCMJ, and I am advising you that you have the right, in fact *the responsibility* to not incriminate yourself, and…”

“Incriminate myself?” Moore interrupted, staring at the hardened face sitting on a chair across from him. “What are you talking about? I took the submarine, admiral. I took it, I stole it. Is that what you want to know?”

“Goddamit, Moore, stop talking. I *know* you took the submarine. *Nothing you say* incriminating yourself can be used at your court-martial, which sure as hell, is going to come your way after the hearing. I cannot order you to *not* incriminate yourself, but as you well know, I cannot pay any attention to your self-incrimination. Also, I don’t give a good Goddamn about anything else you have to say. Therefore, don’t bother incriminating yourself, don’t bother saying *anything*. Just listen.”

Moore settled back on the sofa while the MP finished securing the tracker on his ankle. A tiny red light began pulsating from the top of the device.

“Okay,” Zehner continued. “You took one of my submarines and you will be facing at least ten felony counts of conspiracy including the theft of government property, the killing of foreign citizens, the kidnapping of a civilian, one Ms. Amanda Peterson, the multiple violations of UNCLOS[49] with the sinking of a foreign ship and transiting submerged through territorial waters off the island of Palawan and the country of the Philippines, and finally, the murder of numerous foreign citizens using SEALs who followed your orders to kill these foreign citizens…”

“Foreign citizens?” Moore smiled. “Are you referring to the terrorists?”

Zehner stopped speaking, and for a moment, Moore watched the man's face turn a brilliant red with fury. The admiral glared at the captain again.

"Is this all some kind of funny to you?" he finally said. "I will continue. You have fired three Mark-48 torpedoes..."

"Four...."

"*What?*"

"Four, admiral, I fired four Mark-48 torpedoes. The bastards on the *Cho Ying Atlas* were firing at the hostages who were in the process of being rescued. I had to sink the ship to save the hostages. I determined that four torpedoes would do the job nicely." Moore smiled again.

"And, they did," he added.

Zehner stood tall, glanced at the ceiling, arched his back, sniffed the air twice, glared back at Moore and continued. "I am going to ignore your insubordinate attitude, commander. You refused direct orders from a superior officer, you evaded an Aegis Combat System submarine sweep that cost taxpayers millions of dollars, you have committed a flagrant dereliction of duty allowing the sail of a nuclear submarine to become severely damaged beyond repair, you have stolen two highly trained dolphins, each valued at more than one million dollars, and you will now be facing a UCMJ Article 32 investigation leading to a general court-martial." The admiral leaned forward, his face six inches away from Moore's. "Do you understand the charges?"

"Yes, sir," Moore said briskly, another smile beginning to form.

"I have just informed you about multiple felonies barreling down the track in your direction. You are smiling for *exactly what reason*?"

"Admiral, I brought the *Monterey* back to Pearl. I brought her back. She was damaged, that can happen in battle, but she was *already* heading for the end-of-service-time demolition yard. And, I brought the dolphins back. I got my daughter and her husband back, and I brought the other hostages to freedom in America. I think that was a good thing."

Zehner stepped back like he had been slapped, his face turning red again as he paced the floor in front of Moore. "Okay, that's fine, Commander, that's really fine. You did all those good things. You brought everybody back. You think that every time a submarine skipper's daughter or son gets into trouble, every time there's any distress from far away for anybody in *command authority*, it is acceptable to just go out and steal a submarine, or maybe a B-2 bomber, or perhaps a Goddamn guided missile cruiser?

"If you think that is a good thing, then you need some education to understand why your impending court-martial will send you away forever to the disciplinary barracks in Fort Leavenworth. The JAG lawyers and the United States Navy are going to make a prime example of you, Moore, so that this never happens again. In the meantime, you are under direct orders to remain in house arrest within this detention facility for the duration of pretrial confinement. You will have food brought to you, you will have a guard at the front and back doors 24-7, you will be monitored at all times, your only guests will be those cleared by the convening authority. Finally, your Corvette is permanently impounded, and there will be no conjugal visits."

"Conjugal visits? Admiral, my wife died twelve years ago, and I don't have any kind of…."

"Commander, do you understand what I am saying?"

"I do understand, yes, sir." He looked up at Tom Anderson. "Thank you, Agent Anderson. I would really like to get some sleep. Would you all mind leaving?"

Zehner stepped back a pace and crossed his arms across his chest. "One more thing before I go. You may have legal counsel appointed by the Navy free of charge."

"What's the point?"

"You may request a Navy counsel by name, or you may hire a civilian counsel. If you do none of these things, a military counsel officer will be appointed by the court."

Moore stood up and stared at the admiral. "Really admiral," he said, "what is the point? I did it, I told you I did it, you and your hearing will confirm that I did it. If God himself defended me, he would lose and you know it. My destiny may be to bake in hell, but if I had to do it all over again, I would do *exactly* the same thing. Now, please, all of you, leave my…home…or whatever you want to call this place."

Chris Krischer III was a refined man.

His Armani suit, his mirror-polished shoes, his perfectly manicured nails and his exquisitely groomed jet-black hair (with precisely the proper trace of white at the temples) left no doubt. When his gray Mercedes limousine pulled up in front of Commander Gary Moore's confinement house on the second day of the captain's detention, it was clear that a large amount of money was going to be spent on behalf of the *Monterey's* commanding officer. Krischer closed the limousine's back door, spoke some words to the driver, lifted his leather briefcase into his right hand and strode confidently towards Moore's front door. Moore looked out through the blinds at the street, noted his front-guard abruptly and respectfully stood to the side of the walkway upon seeing the arrival of this man of such obvious importance.

"Good morning, Commander Moore," Krischer said as Moore opened the door, his voice carrying a trace of a southern accent. "My name is Chris Krischer, and I'm here to represent you as the defendant in the Article 32 investigation next week. May I come in?"

Moore let the man into the living room, offered him a cup of coffee, and they both sat across from each other at the breakfast table.

"Where are you from, Mr. Krischer?" Moore asked, looking at the spotless blue tie and diamond-studded Rolex on the attorney's left wrist.

"I am the permanent in-house counsel," Krischer said, "employed by International Cyber Systems, Inc. in Seattle. You have saved our company a lot of money."

Moore raised his eyebrows. "What are you talking about?"

Krischer's brown eyes looked steadily at Moore. "You don't know?"

"Don't know *what*?" Moore replied, feeling himself becoming irritated.

"The ransom, commander. I am talking about the one hundred million dollars you saved the company by your hostage extraction."

"One hundred million for Peter Blackwell?"

"For Peter Blackwell *and* for your daughter. That was the negotiated hostage ransom, with a mandatory inclusion of your daughter per Mr. Randolph Blackwell, your daughter's father-in-law and the CEO of International Cyber Systems. Your SEALs interrupted the transfer of this money about two minutes before the payment was to be made, leaving the pirates with neither hostages, nor ransom, nor…I may add although I think it's classified… life itself."

"Holy Jesus…." Moore almost whispered.

"If I may make a personal comment, commander, nice work. Very nice work. By the way, Mr. Blackwell sends you his personal greetings and appreciation and has ordered me to save your beleaguered soul from a *very* motivated United States Navy, the Secretary of the Navy, the President of this whole fine country, and one COMPACFLT admiral named Stephen Kent. They collectively would like to expedite you straight to hell, or at the very least, to hard labor and a solitary confinement cell in the tundra of Alaska. They would like very much to make you an example to the Navy and the entire world.

"I expected that would be the case, but I did what I did, and I am ready to…"

"Be ready for nothing, Commander," Krischer interrupted. "Accept nothing they are bringing your way. You embarrassed the hell out of them for their inaction during a time of compelling need, you embarrassed the hell out of them because they couldn't find you until your reactor flaked out and you had to sputter back the final hundred miles on your diesel. As a result of this embarrassment, they are charging ahead for the hearing to lead to a full court-martial after which they want to lock you away, far away, forever. The COMPACFLT and COMSUBRON admirals consider your Article 32 investigation to be a slam-dunk guaranteed path to a court-martial, immediately followed by a long prison term at Leavenworth."

Krischer smiled. "And, I will tell you, commander, they are not going to win."

Moore shifted around in his chair, closely watching the attorney's face. "Okay," he said, "but I did do all those things…."

"Right, you did. We let them think they have a clear pathway, a greased skid to court-martial and prison, and then we surprise them. Of course, they have overwhelming evidence of your absconding with their submarine. We know the compelling reason you did this, we will have the grateful testimony from the hostages you freed, the thanks from the crew you assembled together, and we have the reluctance of the Navy to release secret evidence in an open hearing."

Moore took a quick sip of his coffee. "So, you think we have something on our side, then?"

Krischer smiled, revealing rows of perfect white teeth. "Nope, wrong. This is a court of law, not a court of sentiment. The judge, otherwise known as the investigating officer, will make his recommendation for or against court-martial on the basis of evidence, not on the basis of compelling moral grounds. However," he smiled bigger, "we do have one powerful ally on our side."

Moore tapped the table and scrutinized the attorney. "And that is?"

"The public and the media will be present at the investigation, which is usually the case with an Article 32 investigation. Admiral Zehner and a mean son-of-a-bitch JAG officer, Fred Dapper, honest-to-God that's his name, will act as the counsel representing the United States government, essentially acting as the prosecutor. The investigating officer conducting the hearing will be Carl Siegel, an older respected and veteran of thousands of hearings, no way to tell which way he will lean when he has all the evidence. Siegel, however, is a by-the-book judge in all elements of military law and will not likely be swayed by emotional testimony. Fortunately for you, you will have Admiral Sullivan and me on your side."

Moore looked surprised. "Admiral Sullivan is on my side?" he asked.

"You have friends in high places, commander, or at least you have one friend. By the way, his decision to support you is not exactly a career-advancing decision—he is, career-wise, going out on a limb for you. Word is that Admiral Kent is thoroughly pissed by Sullivan's decision."

"Pissed?" Moore said quietly. "I would guess that he has gone completely hermantile."

"Hermantile?"

"It's a Navy term, meaning…."

"Yeah, okay. So we start the hearing in three days." Krischer reached down to his briefcase and pulled out a stack of pages. "Read these, absorb these, let me have the names of everybody else you can think of who might be important to your defense, and I'll be back this afternoon to begin creating our battle plan." The lawyer closed his briefcase and stood up, looking happy, his smile bringing sunshine to all corners of the room.

Hearing Room, Pearl Harbor

The Article 32 Investigation into Commander Moore's activities during the previous two weeks began on schedule three days later, on Monday morning, in a Pearl Harbor conference room off Center Drive, located one block from his house of incarceration. Moore was dressed in his full dress-white officer's uniform that morning, one of the few items allowed him from his stateroom on the *Monterey*. His small home in Pearl City had been cordoned off by military police and was under continuous guard while investigators continued their thorough search of papers and computers, demolishing floors and walls, looking for everything short of Russian collusion.

A small cadre of four Marines stood at attention outside Moore's door as Chris Krischer and Admiral Samuel Sullivan rang the doorbell at exactly 0830 hours. Commander Moore exited the front door and, as the three men moved with the Marines up the street to the hearing room, nobody saying a word, the two officers marched in step to the cadence of one of the guards while Krischer followed closely behind.

The room, looking to Moore like a former storage facility, had been arranged to allow for the hearing. There were chairs filling almost two-thirds of the room and two benches set aside in front of a larger bench that belonged to a heavy-set man with puffy eyes, promptly identified as Captain Carl Siegel, the investigating officer. Moore, Sullivan, and Krischer sat in front at the desk on the left, and a beefy red-faced Captain Fred Dapper sat with Vice Admiral Harris Zehner at the desk on the right. The building was packed with spectators, all the chairs filled before the proceedings began with a line of reporters occupying the chairs on the side and the back wall of the assembly. Caroline and Peter Blackwell sat stiffly upright in the front row of spectators, quietly watching the proceedings. She quickly nodded a quick greeting to her father as he sat down behind the table.

At precisely 0900 hours, Captain Siegel slammed his gavel down and announced the beginning of the case against the defendant, one Commander Gary Moore, Commanding Officer of the Los Angeles class nuclear submarine USS *Monterey,* accused of multiple criminal activities violating the UCMJ and resulting in the deaths of an "indeterminate number" of foreign citizens.

"Would the JAG officer, Captain Dapper, begin?" he asked, directing his gaze to the prosecuting table.

Dapper's large frame rose and paced the floor as he began booming out the charges against the defendant, his voice itemizing each individual accusation. Moore noticed, with a trace of amusement, his red face with bulging veins was becoming a darker red. Each charge emerged from a seemingly unending list, presented as if Dapper was *personally* offended by the egregious behavior of the defendant. This went on for nearly an hour and was immediately followed by Chris Krischer who delivered an eloquent and refined statement of innocence by reason of compelling humanitarian need. After outlining the risks to innocent human life, he pointed out the threat to the hostages' fragile existence, including the pirates' wanton murder of almost everybody on the yacht, *The Sweet Caroline*. Speaking directly to Captain Siegel, and regularly turning to address the members of the press lining the walls, Krischer calmly noted the fact that these innocent victims, Caroline and Peter Blackwell and ten other hostages detained aboard the mother ship, had been imprisoned and threatened with death, and were desperately reliant on someone, *anyone*, brave enough to enter the pirate's haven to fulfill a mission of rescue and mercy.

While the rest of the world would stand idly by, Krischer said as he studied the face of each reporter one by one, there was only a single human being with the courage and the means, a man Krischer implied was nothing less than the Mother Theresa of the United States Navy, who would step forward in a desperate effort to achieve their salvation. In the meantime, the Seventh Fleet, with all of its firepower in the South China Sea, stood idly by out of harm's way, conducting its scheduled mundane exercises in distant stretches of ocean. This majestic Seventh Fleet was of no help to the captives until it was almost too late. *In contrast,* the captain of this one aging and battle-worn submarine, he pointed directly at Moore and paused for effect, this man with the help of ten other brave submariners, sailed directly into the heart of the enemy to rescue not one, not two, not three, but *all of the victims*!

Krischer glared at Siegel, pausing to gather his breath, then turned to face the audience as he boomed out the country's admiration for the integrity, and, yes, *the bravery*, of this one United States Naval officer, Captain Gary Moore, to save their lives and to bring them home.

As Krischer continued, he made frequent visual contact with Siegel, who alternatively stared back at the defense attorney and then looked at Dapper as if seeking a response to the rebuttal. Surprisingly for Moore, Krischer also spent most of his time making eye contact with the rows of reporters, several of whom seemed to nod as he spoke, as they listened to what he said, furiously writing and typing on an array of iPads and portable computers. He compared the International Cyber System's ransom demand to a kind of espionage against a solid American company supplying vital software to computers around the world. He amplified the threats to the American system, the way of life for thousands of employees at the company by the ransom requirement to sell a massive fortune in stock, threatening the very financial existence of the company.

The process of point and counter-point continued for the next five days between Dapper and Krischer, the two sides maneuvering back and forth, each side making the case and each side refuting the other, with questions and statements by Captain Siegel that gave no suggestion as to which way he was leaning in the deliberations. And everybody arguing before him knew it would be his decision, and his decision alone, as to what would happen to the captain. A long list of witnesses was called by the prosecution and by the defense, testimony was made, hostages were brought from their hotels with compelling stories of murder by pirates on the high seas and of their eventual rescue by the sailors of the USS *Monterey,* the Navy SEALs, and Commander Moore.

Admiral Sullivan struggled to remain expressionless as Captain Dapper called Commander Ralph Ginder, the captain of the USS *Stout*, for a fuming hostile recounting of how that *submariner* sitting "in that chair, right there," as he pointed at Moore, forced his guided missile cruiser to move in virtually ever-expanding circles while he and the entire crew searched unsuccessfully for the USS *Monterey.* Sullivan glanced at Moore quickly with just a trace of a smile as Ginder finished his testimony with, "And, before we knew it, *he was gone*!"

Krischer brought Caroline and Peter Blackwell to the witness stand to testify and tell their stories of capture, assault, molestation, airing their fears to all. Krischer called the other hostages and each testified about their near-death experiences and their subsequent salvation by the SEALs, Captain Moore and his submarine crew. Krischer finally called in the three SEALs who each described their activities, speaking carefully to avoid secret elements of methodology, summarizing with the assessment that they would follow Commander Moore "to the end of the earth," if necessary, to fulfill a mission of such urgent need.

It was at 1500 hours on Friday afternoon, that the final word was said from the final SEAL, and Captain Siegel hammered his gavel to the table. "Captain Dapper? Mr. Krischer?" he asked. "Have you finished presenting your case and do you have any more witnesses? If that is all, we will take a recess, and I will prepare to render my decision regarding the progression of this case for court-martial."

Captain Dapper and Admiral Zehner stood and firmly replied that their case against the defendant was complete and that they looked forward to Captain Siegel's "rendering of a decision."

As Chris Krischer stood, Admiral Sullivan and Commander Moore began to stand. Krischer quickly motioned the two men to be seated as he faced Captain Siegel and began to speak into his microphone.

"Captain, you have heard testimony from both sides, and I suspect you have enough information to make a determination for the defendant, be it court-martial or other disposition." The attorney began pacing in front of the defendant's table, his voice rising to an increasing level beyond that previously reached, his words frequently pausing as if to allow the information to sink in.

He abruptly stopped walking and turned to face the audience, watching in silence.

"The motivations of this man were underscored by the letters from his daughter, Caroline," he said, ignoring the startled look from Commander Moore as he walked to his briefcase and pulled out the plain white package secured with a golden string.

"No!" Moore hollered, beginning to stand.

"The defendant will remain in his chair!" Siegel hollered as Admiral Sullivan pushed down on Moore's shoulder.

"No, please," he demanded, his voice becoming emotional. "They are private, I cannot…."

“These letters,” Krischer said, turning away from Admiral Sullivan and Commander Moore, “will provide for the court the urgency in the commanding officer’s mind about why he had to rescue his daughter.” Krischer turned toward the audience. “They explain why this *had* to happen. Commander Moore really had no choice, the letters…”

The bang of Siegel’s gavel stopped Krischer in mid-sentence. “I will allow the letters, Mr. Krischer. Are you going to read them?”

“If it pleases this body, I will ask Caroline Blackwell to read them for the court. In that manner, there will be a complete understanding of what drives men to do the unusual, the extraordinary, and even the impossible.”

Gary Moore sank down in his chair, shaking his head as his daughter stood up and began walking to the microphone in the front of the room. He turned to her as she walked past, his face pleading with her as she took the letters from Krischer. She walked to the microphone, unwrapping the golden string, pulling the first letter from the stack.

As she opened the letter, Commander Moore suddenly stood up.

“I am firing my attorney!” he declared loudly as Siegel’s gavel slammed repeatedly against the block on his table and the room erupted in immediate chaos.

“There will be silence!” Siegel ordered. “This hearing will return to order, there will be silence!”

Several reporters stood up to rush out of the room as Siegel’s gavel hammered again and again against the block. He finally stood up and pulled his microphone close to his mouth. “Military police, bring order to this room!” he hollered. He glared at Captain Moore and said, “The defendant and his representatives will remand to my quarters, now.”

Captain Siegel’s quarters amounted to little more than a side room, recently cleared of boxes and crates, and with several metal chairs scattered about. After Caroline handed the packet of letters back to Krischer, the three men followed a fuming Siegel into the room where the investigating officer ordered them to sit down and be quiet as he pulled up a chair across from them.

“Moore,” he said angrily, “you cannot just fire your representation after days of competent legal efforts to plead your case.

You are free to *select* representation, as you have done, you are not free to *change* representation at will. Furthermore, you did not *hire* your representative, so you cannot *fire* him. Do you understand?"

"Yes, sir," Moore said. "I refuse to allow these letters…"

"What's the story on these letters?" Siegel asked, turning to Krischer.

"They are letters from his daughter, sir," he answered calmly. "They were part of the defendant's belongings removed from the *Monterey* after the submarine returned to port. They are compelling and they need to be introduced as evidence for the defense. They resoundingly establish *motive* for the defendant's actions. For this hearing to decide on guilt or innocence, there must be an understanding of motive."

"Gary," Sullivan said earnestly to Moore, "you need these to be read."

The room was silent for several seconds as everybody waited. Moore looked down and finally rubbed his forehead while shaking his head.

"Commander Moore," Siegel said. "I cannot compel you to have these letters introduced if…."

"*The final letter,*" Moore said, looking at his attorney. "I just do not want the final letter to be read."

"That is the most compelling letter," Krischer said, "it must be read…."

"It is *profoundly* private," Moore said, turning to look at the attorney. "It has dark secrets…." He looked down, quiet for a moment before continuing. "My daughter and I agreed that letter would forever be kept secret. It is simply too private to be read in an open hearing room."

Siegel stood up. "All right, gentlemen, I am going to make a ruling right now, and you will, by God, be bound by this ruling or I will hold you in contempt." He glared at Moore. "We are going to return to the hearing right now, and all the letters will be read. We will then adjourn until Monday morning when I will issue my ruling about the disposition of this Article 32 hearing."

He turned and left the room with the other three men slowly following.

Caroline was still seated in front of the microphone as Krischer handed her the packet and the other men returned to their seats. The room became silent as Captain Siegel leaned over to his microphone.

"The captain's daughter will read the letters, and this hearing will then be adjourned until 0900 hours Monday morning." He slammed his gavel again as all heads turned to watch Caroline.

She opened the letters, adjusted her position in the chair, straightened the first page and leaned over the microphone to begin reading slowly, her voice filled with emotion.

Chapter 18

Detention and Confinement Facility, Pearl Harbor

Caroline and Admiral Sullivan arrived at Commander Moore's detention house and walked up to the front door, nodding politely to the military policeman who gave a quick salute.

Caroline knocked gently on the door and an instant later, her father stood before them.

"Good to see you," Moore said as he gave his daughter a prolonged hug.

"I'm sorry, we should have called," Caroline said as they sat down on the sofa. "We didn't want you sitting around by yourself all weekend."

"No problem," Moore said. "I'm glad you came. I'm just sitting around thinking I need to learn some card games or start a long novel to pass the time."

"You may have a lot of time to pass, Gary. I think we have to be realistic," Sullivan said. "I think a general court-martial is very likely.

"What does Krischer think?"

"You know what Krischer thinks, Gary. Look, you tried to fire the man today, *publicly!* That hurts him, it hurts his credibility with the investigating officer, and it hurts you, no matter how compelling your case may be. And, Christ, your representation couldn't be more qualified…the man has even argued two cases before the Supreme Court. And won them both."

Sullivan stood up and tapped his chest. "I'm the only one at Pearl Harbor," he said, "and probably the only officer in the entire Navy, who has been pulling for you while you were trying to save this wonderful young lady. I'm the one who got Kent to launch the Seahawks against those bastards trying to destroy you. *Goddammit, you owe me, Gary!*"

"I owe you a great deal, Sully, not just with this but for many other things over a lot of years. But, with all due respect…"

"Goddammit, Gary!" Sullivan said, "The letters are *evidence.* They are evidence in your favor. Especially the final letter. Did you see the reaction of the reporters when she read them? When she read the final letter?"

"Sully," Moore said, "you know how much I appreciate your help, and everything you've done for me. The family has told me what happened in Seattle, how you figured out where we were off Palawan, and I know about your efforts to meet Randolph Blackwell. I'm sorry that didn't work out. But, I got it. I got the whole thing."

"Even if they send you up the river, forever?" Sullivan said. "The way things stand now, this case looks challenging. The legal evidence against you is overwhelming even though you have become an instant celebrity. Your face is now recognized by ninety-three per cent of the public. You've become a Goddamn hero to the entire world, the rescuer of hostages when nobody else was brave enough to do the job. People claiming to speak for you are on every talk show in the country and social media is going crazy. Christ, they're marching up and down Kalakaua Boulevard, carrying signs and hollering into loudspeakers on your behalf. They're blocking the entrances to Pearl Harbor, they're causing disruptions everywhere. This hearing is becoming like a national scandal!

"However, for now, while you may be famous and while you may be adored by everybody who knows what you did, we are talking about military law and as things look now, you are likely heading for Leavenworth. Remember, your entire life depends on what Captain Siegel's determination is on Monday morning."

"And so we wait…" Moore began.

"One bright light of salvation may be the President of the United States," Sullivan said. "He is the Commander-in-Chief. *The man is elected and the midterms are looking grim for his party.* It is not lost on him that virtually the entire country is screaming for your salvation. They are calling their elected representatives. They are calling the White House and they are calling the Pentagon. I am sure Captain Siegel is aware of this national uproar. With all this going on, I assure you that your hearing officer really does want to make the rank of admiral someday. And, on top of all that, the President has daughters….

"Would Captain Siegel follow the public sentiment?" Moore asked.

"No, he will follow the law. *However*, the law always has a margin of interpretation, and so we'll see. On the other hand, Dapper really wants to make an example of you."

Moore stood up and smiled. "Okay, so the more we think about it, the less we know, until, finally, as we keep thinking, we know nothing at all, great."

They walked to the door, they wished him good luck again, and they left the house of incarceration. Sullivan gave Moore a gripping handshake and a very worried Caroline gave her father a kiss on his cheek.

For the remainder of the weekend, Commander Gary Moore remained alone in his empty house, his mind tortured by the past, his heart aching for what his daughter wanted and needed, and his soul cursed by the future that was about to descend on him.

Pearl Harbor Hearing Room

Monday morning was a beautiful Pearl Harbor day. The sun struggled to climb above the clouds attached to the lush mountains surrounding the Pali Pass, the warm trade winds blew gently out of the northwest, rippling the deep blue waters of the harbor. The gathering of the reporters, the families, the Navy brass, and the former hostages assembled in the hearing room near the Navy dry-docks, nobody saying much. On the left side of the room, in an area cordoned off by a row of Marines, ten chairs became filled with the three SEALs, the three nuclear submariners, and with Doc Wheat, Petty Officer Wilson, Seaman Bodine, and Chief Berry.

Sullivan marched into the room with Moore, surrounded by their Marine detail, and following a quick and very cool nod from Krischer, the two men pulled up their chairs at the desk in front of the hearing officer. To their right, Vice Admiral Harris Zehner and Captain Fred Dapper sat in their chairs, stiffly alert and waiting for the investigating officer to arrive. At precisely 0900 hours, Captain Carl Siegel walked briskly into the room and sat alone at his large desk in front of the assembled gathering. His face looked exhausted, Moore noticed, but his manner was precise, intense, and official. He shuffled through a stack of notes on his desk, while everybody in the room shifted around anxiously in their chairs, waiting for the hearing officer's recommendation.

At 0903 hours, Captain Siegel adjusted a pair of enormous reading glasses onto his nose, peered down at the top page of his stack, picked up the paper and cleared his throat. His head lifted slowly as his eyes focused on Commander Moore.

"Does the defense have any further evidence to present in support of the defendant?" he asked, his voice sounding angry and almost harsh.

Chris Krischer immediately stood. "The defense rests, captain," he said softly.

"Very well," Siegel said, lifting the papers before his eyes again. "Regarding the matter of Commander Gary Moore versus the United States Government, the following determination in this Article 32 hearing under the guidelines within the current UCMJ has been made," he said into the microphone.

"One, Commander Moore is to be stripped of his rank as a United States Naval Commander, and will be reduced, effective immediately to the rank of Ensign, United States DoD paygrade designation O-1, NATO designation OF-1.

"Two, Commander Moore is to be stripped of his command over the United States submarine, USS *Monterey,* effective immediately.

"Three, Commander Moore will forfeit all future benefits including pay and time accrued retirement pay from the United States Government for the remainder of his natural life.

"Four, Commander Moore will receive a General Discharge from the United States Navy, effective immediately at the conclusion of this hearing.

"Five, because of Commander Moore's crew having been bound by his command authority and by the continuing ongoing directives of a superior officer for more than three weeks during the time of the removal of the USS *Monterey* from its rightful place in Pearl Harbor waters, those said members of this submarine crew shall be released from the brig without restriction and shall to be further assigned to future duty stations as deemed appropriate by the Department of Defense.

"Six, because of Commander Moore's persistent and repeated failure to follow orders, his stealing of government property, his destruction of government property including the loss of one submarine base brow, his directing special operatives to kill hostile enemy forces, his kidnapping of one civilian whose presence aboard the submarine was, by her existence, a violation of Naval regulations, his removal of valuable and highly-trained dolphins, his failure to prevent the extensive destruction of the sail of his submarine by hostile forces in the waters off Palawan Island, his prolonged delay of a scheduled demolition of one Los Angeles Class submarine by the shipyard at Bremerton, Washington, his being AWOL[50] for a prolonged time, and his directing of nuclear personnel to continue the operation of a nuclear reactor far beyond its useful lifespan; all of this *is balanced, mitigated, and nullified* by his remarkable bravery under fire during the humanitarian rescue of twelve hostages and the consequent saving of their lives. Commander Moore is therefore ordered to be released from custody, his ankle bracelet is to be removed, and said prisoner shall be released from his place of detention, with prejudice,[51] effective immediately.

Gary Moore," Siegel said, looking directly at the man, "you are free to go." He looked back down at his paper. "By this order of Captain Carl Siegel, Investigation Officer of Article 32 Investigation, this day of 14 October 2013, signed and sealed." He raised his arm holding the wooden gavel high and slammed it into the wooden block as his eyes raised again to look at Moore, with just the faintest trace of a smile.

The raucous roar of the cheering audience drowned out the pounding of Siegel's gavel. Caroline rushed up from her spectator's seat to embrace her father, as the two of them were immediately surrounded by a large number of men who had served with him before and during the *Monterey's* rescue mission. Several men in the original crew, who had not been a part of the mission, told the captain, almost in unison, "We would have gone too, if only you had asked us!" Moore smiled and thanked them as some of the men assured him that he would always be their captain and how they looked forward to many submarine reunions ahead.

The two prosecuting officers grabbed their briefcases and stormed out the side door as Sullivan and Krischer pushed through the throng to congratulate Moore. At the side of the room, the reporters activated their cell phones, calling the networks to announce the news.

During the final words of the investigating officer, Moore had felt, as much as heard, an internal roaring noise inside his mind, and he had sensed an almost numb feeling to the excitement pulsating around him during its aftermath. It was a crescendo of emotion, a release from the tension of the ordeal, and now even with a diminished financial future, the future would be his to create, a future outside the Navy, meager perhaps, and a future without further days at sea.

"You are free to go!" Krischer shouted over the noise. "They'll never come after you again!"

Moore tried to thank the man, but the words didn't come out right although his meaning was clear to the attorney. They shook hands warmly and then Moore turned to Sullivan.

"Sully," he said, "thank you for everything you have done for me, you are a great friend."

Sullivan looked closely at Moore and slowly broke into a smile. "It has been a helluva ride, Gary, but it has been my pleasure to help save the hindquarters of a Goddamn national hero. Also, it was a good way for me to finish my career.... May I presume we might have a beer from time to time, should the Navy decide to preemptively and prematurely retire me?"

Moore smiled and reached out to shake the admiral's hand. "The welcome mat will always be there for you, Sully, if you have the time to stop by."

Moore turned away to face Caroline and before he could say a word, she handed him the white envelope packet of letters with the gold string around it.

"You may have these back," she said, reaching up to give him a kiss.

"Thank you, honey," he said, smiling. "I will lock them up in a vault someplace."

He made a point of shaking the hand of each of the ten *Monterey* crewmen, and Amanda, looking into their eyes and expressing his appreciation for their sharing his risk for the hostage rescue. Amanda tugged on Moore's sleeve and said, "Captain, I'd like you to meet my father...he came here from Texas."

Moore turned to face a tall, lean, and weathered man who reached out to shake his hand. "I am happy you brought your daughter back, captain, but I wanted to thank you for bringing *my* daughter back as well."

"Mr. Peterson, from Texas..."

"Hank, and thank you again."

"She will be a great nurse someday," Moore smiled, "and we gave her some good practical experience, both with nursing and interrogation. Without her, we'd have never found my daughter."

"She told me everything that happened out there is hush, hush, top secret, but she did say that the injured SEAL she helped treat is doing fine. I'm not quite sure she would have *volunteered* for your rescue mission, but you took good care of her. Thank you again, sir. We are now, finally, going to go celebrate!"

"Have a drink for me, Hank," Moore said as the other men collectively asked the captain if he would like to join them in a successful mission party at O'Malley's, about to begin immediately. Chief Berry also informed him that Amanda had just been declared an honorary qualified submariner and her honorary dolphins would be pinned on her blouse by her fiancé at the celebration. Moore looked at his jubilant men and smiled.

"No captain on any ship of the Navy could do better than to have this crew on his boat, thank you for the invitation. The last time I was at O'Malley's, I got a telephone call from a lady named Caroline. I'm going to spend some time with her but thank you, I'll join you later—save a few cold ones for me."

The call from Admiral Kent came at that moment and as Moore saw the man's Chester A. Nimitz face on the cell phone ID, he hesitated and finally answered.

"Admiral Kent, it is over," Moore said into the device as he pressed it tightly against his ear, straining to hear.

"You're damn right it's over, Moore, and it was the right decision," Kent's voice blasted out of the phone. "It was the right decision for you to be held accountable, Goddammit, and it was the right decision to set you loose on the world. You stole my submarine but you brought all of them back. When I sent the choppers and the F-18 on those bastards, it was because I wanted you to get back here where I could kick your ass."

"Yes, sir, and now we move on."

"You're Goddamn right we do, Moore, and the only downside of it all is that I've lost the best submarine skipper I've ever seen in this man's Navy."

"I was heading for a desk job anyway, admiral, so it was all over no matter what."

"You're right, Moore, except that I won't have a captain, or an admiral-in-waiting I could trust back in DC, battling all those political sons-of-bitches. However, and this is off the Goddamn record, Moore, Admiral Sullivan is to be kicked up a notch, put up for vice-admiral, for helping save a bunch of civilian hostages… But, you need to know that if any word of this comes out before it happens, I will personally shoot your ass. Good luck, shipmate, don't fuck up again."

"Yes, sir, thank you for calling."

As Moore tucked his cell phone away and headed back to Caroline, he was stopped by Peter Blackwell.

"Thank you again, sir," Blackwell said, shaking Moore's hand, "for rescuing us and bringing us back, and congratulations on the outcome of the hearing and not going to jail ."

"You're welcome, Peter." Moore smiled. "For your next anniversary trip, I would like to suggest…"

"Yes, sir, this international travel concept has its limitations. Caroline and I will find a quiet little place on the beach, maybe in Maui, which should work out perfectly. I think your daughter and I need a little peace and quiet before we return to Seattle."

"Good plan," Moore said smiling. "I won't be visiting you on Maui, you'll be happy to know, but perhaps we could get together in Seattle some day?"

"On that subject, sir, my father would like to speak with you." He pointed to an elderly man with a shock of white hair and a full beard, standing off to the side of the crowd leaving the room.

Randolph Blackwell straightened up, his eyes fiery and alert as Moore approached. "You are the only Navy man I'll talk with," he said in a gravelly voice as he shook Moore's hand. "Nobody else gave a damn about Peter or Caroline, until you arrived on the scene, so to speak. Thank you, Captain Moore."

"I'm no longer a Navy man, sir," Moore said.

"Bullshit, captain, you will always be a Navy man, and I am going to address you as captain for the rest of my life."

"Thank you, Mr. Blackwell…"

"Randolph, call me Randolph."

"Yes, sir…Randolph…I understand from Mr. Krischer, there was a ransom for your son," Moore said.

"A helluva ransom, the bastards, and thank you for not getting there ten minutes later. At least now I know what the boy is worth. I actually had a front row seat on the SEAL attack, that is, and I did hear your mines going off at Boayan. The computer display screen at ICSI was lit up for several seconds with flashes and gunfire before the heist of my treasure came to a halt. At that instant, when the first flash went off, everything went dead. I thought it was over, that…my son and your daughter…." He hesitated, cleared his throat, and looked away for a moment.

"I know," Moore said. "Caroline told me. I'm just happy that they didn't kill her on the yacht in the beginning. Somehow, she was included in the ransom demand."

"Somehow, they just wanted to include her in the ransom deal," Blackwell said, shrugging and smiling. "Also, I have offered that Mombo chef character a position in our home…we could use some culinary excellence around our kitchen in Seattle. Regarding money and your future…"

"Oh, no problem," Moore said, raising his hand to wave off the consideration. "I will just miss the Navy, it has been..."

"Bullshit again, captain. I have come to learn money has an effect on life, and if you do the right things with it, money can have a very positive effect on life. They have just cut you off from what would have certainly been a paltry and disgraceful retirement fund. I have taken preemptive action with Mr. Dominic Mathews, the Chairman of the Board of International Cyber Systems, and he has enthusiastically carried my request to the Board. The emergency vote, conducted five minutes ago, was unanimous. Our company would like to offer you…."

"Thank you, sir, for your efforts. However, I have saved some money over the years…"

"You're not going to decline this, captain. This is a position on the Board, and as that investigating officer, Captain Siegel, likes to say, effective immediately. I might add, the position is *extremely well-compensated*, commensurate with your United States Navy experience. Also, since you're a Goddamn national hero, I probably don't need to tell you that having a Goddamn national hero on our Board does great things for our stock position. Would you be willing to think this over? As a Board member, it would be helpful for you to reside in the Seattle area, maybe in a place like Medina…ever heard of it?"

Moore smiled broadly. "Thank you for your consideration, sir, that is very kind."

"'Kind,' hell, it is *appropriate*."

"Yes, sir, and I assure you that I will give your offer a highly favorable consideration. Also, I will no longer be staying in Hawaii. After these past couple of weeks, and after the decades of submarine life, the years under the ocean with thousands of men, I will be moving to a very quiet little place I know about in Gig Harbor, where I will seek some element of peacefulness."

"Gig Harbor! Hell, that's just a half hour away from our Board meetings and from where Caroline and my son live."

"Yes, sir, I thought we might have a visit from time to time."

"Okay, captain, thank you. In the meantime, I am sending you the best literary agent in the country. The people out there need to know the details, *all* the details…."

Randolph Blackwell shook hands with the captain and disappeared out the side door to his waiting limousine. Gary Moore took his daughter's hand, and with Peter Blackwell walking at their side, they avoided the reporters and departed through the back door of the Hearing Room to another sleek and shiny black limousine. They stopped by the Detention House where Moore picked up his bags and tossed them in the back of the vehicle. As he climbed in and settled back on the plush seat with Caroline and Peter, he smiled and said, "Pearl City?"

"Pearl City," Blackwell called out to the driver who accelerated them out the Makalapa Gate, past a green signal, and past an enthusiastic crowd of noisy demonstrators on Kamehameha Highway holding signs supporting Captain Moore. Twenty minutes later, they pulled up in front of Moore's small rental on Annanue Street in Pearl City at the base of Oahu's National Forest. A glance at the garage confirmed that his glistening red Corvette had been returned and was waiting for him…Sullivan had arranged that, he was sure. He kissed his daughter goodbye again and thanked Peter Blackwell for the ride.

Moore unlocked the front door, dropped his bags on the floor, took a deep breath and sat down as he absorbed the silence of his home. He ignored for a moment the damage to the walls and the floors, he rubbed his tired eyes as he ran a hand through his hair, and he finally looked around his living room again. The framed pictures were all in the correct location but many of them were not level and his computers were gone. He looked at the furniture—everything was in its place, but off just a foot or two from before.

Moore walked over to the bigger of the two bags stuffed with his belongings and slowly unzipped the top. He pulled out a white pouch enclosed by a gold string. He placed the packet on the sofa, walked over to the refrigerator, pulled a bottle of Firestone 805 Golden Ale from the shelf and popped open the top. Returning to the sofa, he sat back, took a long sip of the ice cold beer before carefully untying the string around the letters from Caroline. He pulled out the final letter, the one on expensive embossed stationery that reflected Caroline's increased attention to such details and protocol since leaving college.

Moore slowly took another very long sip of the chilled beer before settling back to read the letter one last and final time.

Dear Daddy,

This letter will probably shock you when you return from your current mission, but God knows we've had our share of shocks over the years. I'll just say it right out, right at the beginning, and get it over with. A gentleman named Peter Blackwell has just asked me to marry him and I have accepted.

There! Now, if you haven't just had a heart attack, you need to understand some things that are very important. First of all, it is not Peter's fault, nor is it yours, that you were out to sea when he wanted to call you to ask permission. He wanted to ask you but there was just no way he could; instead of waiting another month or two for your return, he went ahead and asked me "the big question" during a very romantic walk on a beautiful day in Washington Park, near where he works in Seattle. He is a wonderful man, and he will make a great husband and father—he wants about four kids but I may draw the line at three! He works very hard at a large company that makes software for most of the world, including...you'll be happy to know...for the United States Navy.

Second, you are not losing your daughter with this marriage. I know it is still burning in your heart, the memories of little

Alexander, and what happened on that terrible day when Mom was giving him a bath. I know you were gone off to sea, again, and I know you have forgiven her for the wine before that telephone call. It was only a little bit of wine and they said it had nothing to do with his death in the bathwater.... And then, your moving us all away from that neighborhood, moving us to the other side of Oahu and keeping the tragedy undisclosed from everyone after the police determined it was an accident, was probably the best thing for us all as we tried to forget, as we tried to forgive, and as we tried to move on.

However, you not only lost a son, but then you lost your wife five years later. I understand. I know that when a man loses his son, and then his wife, the last thing he wants to hear is that he is also going to lose his daughter. Especially to some guy who will take her away to a new destiny that would be hard to understand or appreciate. I know you love me, as I love you and will forever, but remember that I not only lost my brother, and then my mother, but for most of the years of my life I have regularly lost my father to the Navy and to the string of submarines that have taken him away so often. While you were gone so far away, my only communication has been with letters such as this. I'm not blaming you for that, I know it's not your fault; I just needed to mention it because it is so important. You really need to know that I'm not marrying Peter because of any of those reasons, or because I am lonely. I am marrying him because I have come to love him as much as I love you.

This letter, therefore, is to let you know that you are not about to lose a daughter, but you are about to gain a son. The son you will gain is a fine man, the kind of son (okay—call him a son-in-law, if you must) who will make you proud, who will make your only daughter very happy, who will provide very well for me, and most importantly, who will bring me children and bring you grandchildren. For this is our collective future, Daddy, your daughter, your new son, and hopefully someday not too far away, your grandchildren.

I want you to call me as soon as you return from your patrol, wherever you are, for I miss you, and I look forward to when we may be together again.

I love you,

Caroline

THE END

What Did You Think of Rogue Captain?

First of all, thank you for purchasing my book. I know you could have picked any number of books to read, but you picked "Rogue Captain" and for that I am extremely grateful. I hope that it added some reading pleasure to your everyday life. If so, it would be really nice if you could share this book with your friends and family by posting to Facebook and Twitter. Also, if you enjoyed this book and found some benefit in reading this, I'd like to hear from you and hope that you could take some time to post a review on Amazon. Your feedback and support will help me to greatly improve my writing craft for future projects and make this book even better.

You can go directly to my Web link (https://rogercdunham.com) to navigate to the Amazon page with the stars, or you could go directly to Amazon's star review page:

https://www.amazon.com/review/create-review/

To leave a review, all you have to do (after signing in) is click on the review link for "Rogue Captain" and away you go.

Thank you again for purchasing Rogue Captain and thank you for your help.

Dedication

This book is dedicated to Clarence E. Moore (Captain, USN, retired), commanding officer of the nuclear submarine USS *Halibut* during the 1960's, whose leadership, competence, and perseverance led to remarkable success under difficult circumstances while conducting covert operations under the Pacific Ocean. This book is further dedicated to the officers and men who served as *Halibut* submariners, bravely serving the United States of America during her Regulus missile deterrent patrols and during a series of extraordinarily dangerous classified special operations between 1959 and 1976 during the Cold War.

Presidential Unit Citation[52] (1968):

For exceptional meritorious service in support of National Research and Development efforts while serving as a unit in the Submarine Force, U.S. Pacific Fleet. Conducting highly technical submarine operations, over an extended period of time, USS HALIBUT (SSN-587) successfully concluded several missions of significant scientific value to the Government of the United States. The professional, military, and technical competence, and inspiring devotion to duty of HALIBUT's officers and men, reflect great credit upon themselves and the United States Naval Service.

Presidential Unit Citation (1972):

For extraordinary heroism and outstanding performance of duty as a unit in the Submarine Force, United States Pacific Fleet during 1972, USS HALIBUT successfully accomplished two highly productive and complex submarine operations of immeasurable value to the Government of the United States. The superb professional competence, extremely effective teamwork and exemplary devotion to duty displayed by the officers and men of USS HALIBUT reflect great credit upon themselves, the Submarine Force and the United States Naval Service.

Acknowledgements

It has been my good fortune to have the association of many accomplished, intelligent, and experienced people during the development of this fictional manuscript. Some of these people are patients in my medical practice, some have served honorably and bravely in the Armed Forces, some are relatives, and several are people with unique knowledge that has helped the progression of this story. In this regard, I have benefited from the advice and encouragement of Alfred Shuman, Kelsey Martin, Bernard Girod, Stephen Dunham, Adam and Rochelle Karr, Sandy Munroe, Clarence E. Moore, William Esrey, Daniel Brown, Dan Peterson, Sam and Ruth Dover, Michelle L. Meredith, Jeffery Maurer, John and Hazel Blankenship, and Norm and Jane Habermann. Three unnamed U.S. Navy SEALs also provided valuable assistance. The generous providing of professional and precise editorial skills by Ms. Laura Long will forever be appreciated. Without their input, many areas of this story could not have been developed to the fullest extent. Finally, and most importantly, I am forever indebted to my wife, Keiko, for her superb and diligent editing skills, and for her encouragement and enthusiasm in the creation and development of this work. Without her, this story would not have been possible.

[1] Anti-Submarine Warfare

[2] closed-circuit television

[3] Light Enhancement System

[4] U.S. Navy slang for crazy

[5] "critical" refers to the level of reactor power operation that becomes continuous and self-sustaining

[6] Commander of Submarine Forces, Pacific

[7] Antisubmarine Warfare

[8] Commander of the Pacific Fleet

[9] A hearing for individuals accused of committing a minor violation of the UCMJ (Uniform Code of Military Justice).

[10] When the screws "cavitate" at high speed, small bubbles are formed that then collapse, creating a loud underwater hissing noise that can be detected by searching sonar systems.

[11] Water temperature changes under the ocean create different thermal layers or "thermoclines." A thermocline tends to reflect searching sonar signals, creating a sonar shield below which deep-diving submarines may hide.

[12] SECNAV is the United States Secretary of the Navy

[13] CJCS is the Chairman of the Joint Chiefs of Staff

[14] FISA is the Federal Intelligence Surveillance Act

[15] SSXBBT--Submarine Launched Expendable Bathythermograph

[16] LEO refers to the altitude of satellites in a Low Earth Orbit.

[17] The citadel is a safe room with armor protection allowing retreat of the crew and simultaneously allowing the crew to remotely disable the ship's engines and electronic systems. It is usually located in a concealed location to reduce the ability of pirates to locate the crew before help arrives.

[18] Variable Depth Sonar

[19] Dry Deck Shelter—an HY-80 steel chamber on the outside deck of the *Monterey*, holding a minisubmarine and a full suite of weapons, connected to the submarine's hatch behind the sail. It can remain at one atmosphere of pressure all the way down to the submarine's crush depth. It has three interconnecting compartments, including a decompression chamber in the front, a transfer trunk in the middle to allow the SEALs to enter from the *Monterey*, and an elliptical hangar compartment holding a minisubmarine ("SDV") that may depart and return through a hangar door facing the stern of the boat.

[20] Judge Advocate General's Corps, also known as JAG or JAG Corps, the

legal branch or specialty in the military concerned with military justice and military law. Officers serving in a JAG Corps are typically called Judge Advocates. They also serve as prosecutors for the military in a court-martial.

[21] A kilometer, about .6 miles. Two klicks would be about 1.2 miles.

[22] SEAL Delivery Vehicle, a wet minisub used to deliver SEALs into target areas and also to attack enemy ships and facilities.

[23] The TAILS system is a titanium grappling hook attached to a Kevlar line, fired by a nearly silent pneumatic gun to quietly deliver a rope or a rope ladder as high as 100 feet to allow the boarding of a ship.

[24] 13-20 foot waves

[25] Ship's Inertial Navigation System, an extremely precise system for navigation on the open seas.

[26] National Oceanic and Atmospheric Administration, the government agency that provides weather reports and forecasts.

[27] Estimated Time of Departure

[28] Shore Patrol, the military police in the Navy

[29] The "conn" is a nautical term referring to the position commanding the helm and directing the course and speed of the ship through the ocean.

[30] The master is the commanding officer of a ship that carries commercial products.

[31] Vertical Launching System

[32] A device that pulls in submarine air and "scrubs" away the excess carbon dioxide, using a chemical monoethanolamine (MEA) that absorbs and removes the CO2.

[33] A Q-Route refers to the pathway the dolphins can clear through a minefield to allow the SEALs to pass safely through to shore.

[34] The banana, also called a "YB," is a C-4 plastic charge, looking like an oversized banana, to be attached to a collar on each dolphin, allowing the delivery of the charge to the cable of a mine.

[35] the stimulant amphetamine, producing heightened attention and energy, excessive talking, euphoria, and decreased fatigue

[36] LED refers Light Emitting Diodes, small emitters of extremely bright white light.

[37] A "bone phone" is a communications device attached to the tissue over the jaw bone, used by SEALs to allow conversations and transmissions in high-noise environments, using a bone vibration sensing capability to send and receive voice transmissions.

[38] Littoral refers to action on or near a shoreline

[39] The Seahawk is almost identical to the Sikorsky Blackhawk helicopter of Osama bin Laden fame used by the Army, except for a hinged tail assembly to reduce its footprint aboard ships.

[40] The submarine has been identified by the pilots.

[41] "Winchester" references that the pilot has expended all his

ammunition.

[42] The "F/A-18" refers to the F/A-18 Hornet, a twin-engine supersonic, all-weather carrier-capable multirole fighter jet, designed to dogfight and attack ground targets (F/A designation for Fighter/Attack).

[43] "bent laser" refers to an unworkable laser.

[44] "Holster check" calls for all pilots to check for battle damage at the end of the engagement.

[45] FARM-E refers to Fuel, Ammo, Rockets, Missiles, and Expendables remaining at the end of the engagement.

[46] SIX is a general term referring to the SSIXS, a component of the Navy's Ultra High Frequency Satellite Communications System (UHF SATCOM)

[47] UCMJ refers to the Uniform Code of Military Justice. This set of rules was enacted by Congress in 1950 to establish a set of procedural and substantive criminal laws for all the U.S. military services. The UCMJ changed Military Law in many ways, especially by providing safeguards for an accused, including the right to be represented by counsel, to be informed of the nature of the accusation, to remain silent, and to be told of these rights.

[48] Antisubmarine Warfare

[49] UNCLOS—United Nations Convention on the Law of the Sea, also called the Law of the Sea treaty, an international agreement allowing the right of passage through territorial waters that would not be prejudicial to the peace, good order, or the security of the coastal state. Under UNCLOS, submarines and other underwater vehicles are required to navigate on the surface and to show their flag.

[50] Away Without Leave, absent from one's post but without intent to desert.

[51] "with prejudice" refers to the directive that the case has been settled may not be retried in the future.

[52] The Presidential Unit Citation (PUC), originally called the Distinguished Unit Citation, is awarded to units of the United States Armed Forces for extraordinary heroism in action against an armed enemy. The unit must display such gallantry, determination, and *esprit de corps* in accomplishing its mission under extremely difficult and hazardous conditions so as to set it apart from and above other units participating in the same campaign.

Made in the USA
Monee, IL
04 November 2026

67383854R00157